To Rachel

ANIMAL LAW

by

Julian Palmer

LL.M., Solicitor

THIRD EDITION

Shaw & Sons

Published by
Shaw & Sons Limited
Shaway House
21 Bourne Park
Bourne Road
Crayford
Kent DA1 4BZ

www.shaws.co.uk

© Shaw & Sons Limited 2001

First published – April 1978
Second Edition – March 1984
Third Edition – November 2001

ISBN 0 7219 0802 0

A CIP catalogue record for this book is available from
the British Library

Printed and bound in Great Britain by
Creative Print and Design (Wales), Ebbw Vale

CONTENTS

PREFACE

This third edition has continued the ethos of Godfrey Sandys-Winch in presenting in a reasonably compact and comprehensive form the many facets of the law affecting those who have any sort of dealing with animals, whether their own or other people's.

The references to cases and legislation in the footnotes of this edition have increased in volume to assist the legal practitioner, local government officers, police, non-government organisations and others who may wish to refer to case law, Acts of Parliament, Statutory Instruments and departmental guidance. Similarly, where appropriate, in the age of the World Wide Web, Internet sites have been included to assist readers to obtain further information.

Since the second edition in 1984, there have been important legislative changes, especially directives and regulations generated from Britain's membership of the European Union. When the first edition of this book was published in 1978, the author commented that "there are roughly 1,000 pages of statute and regulations on diseases of animals alone". Over the last seventeen years, a huge body of secondary legislation has been made to implement legislation emanating from Brussels, which far outstrips that relating to diseases of animals. To continue the philosophy behind the first and second editions, I have restricted the coverage but wherever possible directed the reader to further sources of information.

Some of the most significant changes have involved the transportation of agricultural animals, both within the United Kingdom and between Member States. This has necessitated a move away from an epidemiological analysis of transport legislation to a more general statement of the principle requirements effecting the movement of animals. Likewise, European legislation has introduced additional restrictions on the licensing and movement of endangered species, in addition to the prohibition laid down in CITES.

As for domestic animals, the Dangerous Dogs Act 1991 introduced a penal system for dealing with the ownership of certain types of dogs; the Dogs (Fouling of Land) Act 1996 allows local authorities to designate land on which dog fouling may be controlled; whilst the Environmental Protection Act 1990 gives powers to local authorities to deal with those keeping any animals in such a position or in such circumstances as to cause a substantial discomfort or annoyance to the public in general. For the traveller wishing to take his pet abroad, or bring his pet into this country, the most significant change has been the relaxation of the quarantine laws. Domestic cats and dogs may be freely transported to Britain from certain countries under the Pet Travel Scheme, which is dealt with comprehensively in Chapter 3.

The legislation concerning diseases has been modified to reflect the further integration of the European Union. Despite the fact that foot and mouth disease has been in the headlines since February of this year, I have not dwelt on the statutory instruments that have been generated almost on a daily basis, mainly because they have been relatively minor modifications to the Animal Health Act 1981, but more significantly because they have, on the whole, been concerned with preventing the movement of animals within certain areas of the country and do not add significantly to the underlying principles laid down in the Act.

There is no longer a specific chapter on farm animals, although there are references throughout the book to relevant law. My reasoning has been that there is an enormous amount of guidance, advice and links to legislation on the DEFRA website and a book of this size could not accommodate a detailed overview of the current law. Likewise, there is no longer a chapter on byelaws relating to animals because many such byelaws either are geographically localised or have been superseded by secondary legislation.

New chapters have been introduced on horses and animal experimentation. The remaining chapters have been rewritten to take into account the many statutory instruments that have been passed, modifying primary legislation.

In June of this year, the overarching Department for Environment, Food and Rural Affairs (DEFRA) was created. The effect has been that matters previously dealt with by the Home Office (such as animal experimentation) and by the Department for Environment, Transport and the Regions (such as wildlife conservation), and the Ministry for Agriculture, Fisheries and Foods are now dealt with by DEFRA. Whilst much of the legislation necessary for the transfer of powers has not yet been passed, this book has pre-empted such transfer and responsibilities; for example with respect to agriculture, where references are made to DEFRA but, technically, the current Minister responsible for the Department is also the Minister for Agriculture during this transitional period.

With the advent of devolution, where appropriate I have highlighted in the footnotes those powers that have been transferred to the National Assembly of Wales.

I would like to thank those persons who have helped me in the preparation of this book, namely Wendy Coombey for scanning the second edition into an electronic format, Crispin Williams of Shaw & Sons for his unstinting patience in receiving the final draft, and to Rachel for putting up with me and a cottage that I promised would be renovated last year, but has yet to be.

Finally, should the reader have any comments or observations, please submit them to the publishers or via my email address.

The law is stated as at 1st August 2001.

Julian Palmer
jpp@whitteybrook.com

THE AUTHOR

Julian Palmer is a solicitor specialising in animal law. He previously practised in Herefordshire and is now a Senior Lecturer in Agricultural Law and Animal Law, both at University and through a number of professional training agencies. He is also involved with a number of national and international agricultural companies and is a director of the British Deer Society, a national charity promoting welfare and research into deer.

TABLE OF STATUTES

TABLE OF STATUTORY INSTRUMENTS

TABLE OF CASES

Chapter 1

OWNERSHIP, THEFT AND OWNERS' RESPONSIBILITIES

A. OWNERSHIP

In law the term "animals" includes all creatures not belonging to the human race. They are then broadly divided into two groups: domestic and wild. Domestic animals include all those domestic or tame animals as by habit or training live in association with man.[1] Wild animals include not only those which are savage by nature but also those of a more mild or timid nature which cannot be classed as domestic or tame. But a domestic animal which reverts to a wild state is no longer domestic but wild.[2]

Domestic animals are owned in the same way as personalty, such as cars and furniture. Ownership is retained when the animal is lost or strays, and the owner has the same legal rights against anyone detaining it as he would have for his own goods;[3] keeping and feeding another person's animal does not of itself permit retention of the animal until its keep is paid.[4] Generally, the young of domestic animals are owned by the mother's owner,[5] but in the case of a lease of livestock the young belong to the lessee in the absence of a clear indication to the contrary.[6]

The position about ownership of wild animals is more complicated. Unlike domestic animals, no one can have complete ownership of living wild animals, and so they cannot be regarded as personalty, but in three cases there can be a qualified ownership. First, a person who lawfully takes, tames or reclaims a wild animal may claim it as his property until it regains its natural liberty,[7] and may take

---

[1]   *Halsbury's Laws of England,* 4th Ed., Vol. 2 (Reissue), para 201.
[2]   *Falkland Islands Co v R* (1864) 2 Moo PCC NS 266.
[3]   E.g. an action in court for detention or trover. See *Putt v Roster* (1682) 2 Mod Rep 318.
[4]   *Binstead v Buck* (1777) 2 Wm Bl 1117.
[5]   *Halsbury's Laws of England,* 4th Ed., Vol. 2 (Reissue), para 203.
[6]   *Tucker v Farm & General Trust Limited* [1966] 2 All ER 508.
[7]   *Sutton v Moody* (1697) 1 Ld Raym 250.

1

legal remedies against another who takes it from him.[8] This right applies, for example, to hares, pheasants or partridges kept in a warren or enclosure.[9]

Secondly, the owner of land has a right to the young of wild animals born on his land until they can run (or fly) away, and may take legal action against a person taking them.[10] Thirdly, a landowner also has the right[11] to hunt, take and kill wild animals as long as they are on his land.[12] This right may be transferred by a letting of the sporting rights; the terms of the letting will determine whether the right extends to all wild animals or, as is often the case, only to game.[13] The grant of an incorporeal hereditament is an interest in realty and amounts to a profit à prendre which may be granted by deed[14] or acquired by prescription.[15]

The proprietary rights in animals are greatly increased once the animal is dead, as such different rules operate for dead wild animals. These are fully owned by the owner or occupier[16] of the land where they lie or by the tenant of the sporting rights if these are let.[17] Exceptions arise where a landowner kills an animal from his land on that of another, or where a trespasser chases the animal from one person's land to that of another and kills it there; in both cases the carcase belongs to the killer.[18]

B. THEFT

Although for a long time most kinds of domestic and tame animals were the subject of larceny, quite illogically a few kinds could not

---

8   *Grymes v Shack* (1610) Cro Jac 262.
9   *Mallock v Eastly* (1685) 3 Lev 227.
10   *Case of Swans* (1592) 7 Co Rep 15b at 17b; *Blades v Higgs* (1865) 11 HL Cas 621.
11   Concurrently with the right of an occupier to take hares and rabbits; see pp. 125-126.
12   *Blades v Higgs* (1865) 11 HL Cas 621.
13   See, further p. 124 *et seq.*
14   Law of Property Act 1925, s. 52.
15   For example, piscary, the right to take fish in another person's lakes, streams or rivers. See *Harris v Chesterfield* (1911) AC 623.
16   I.e. the occupying owner or the tenant of the land if let.
17   *Fitzgerald v Firbank* [1897] 2 Ch 96.
18   *Churchward v Studdy* (1811) 14 East 249; *Sutton v Moody* (1697) 1 Ld Raym 250; *Blades v Higgs* (1865) 11 HL Cas 621.

be stolen,[19] and it was not until the Theft Act was passed in 1968 that the law was rationalised. The position now is that all domestic animals, and wild animals which are tamed or ordinarily kept in captivity,[20] can be the subject of theft if the person from whom they were taken had possession or control of them, or had a proprietary right or interest[21] in them.[22] A wild animal not within this description (or its carcase) can only be stolen if:

a. it has been reduced into possession[23] by or on behalf of another person and possession of it has not since been lost or abandoned; or

b. another person is in course of reducing it into possession.[24]

When, within these limits, animals can be stolen, it follows that they may also be the subjects of the offences of obtaining property by deception and receiving stolen goods.[25]

To advertise publicly a reward for the return of any animal stolen or lost, using any words to the effect that no questions will be asked, or that the person producing the animal will be safe from apprehension or inquiry, or that any money paid for its purchase or advanced by way of loan on it will be repaid, is an offence for which the advertiser, printer and publisher can be liable[26] on summary conviction to a fine.[27]

---

19 These were dogs, cats and "animals of a base nature". *Halsbury's Laws of England,* 4th Ed, Vol 2 (Reissue), para 229.

20 The pre-Theft Act 1968 cases may still be useful as to what is or is not treated as "tame or ordinarily kept in captivity". See *Halsbury's Laws of England,* 4th Ed., Vol. 2 (Reissue), para 230, note 1.

21 But not an equitable interest, which is an interest arising only from an agreement to transfer or grant an interest (Theft Act 1968, s. 5(1)).

22 Theft Act 1968, ss. 1(3), 4(1), 5(1).

23 No statutory definition is given of the phrase "reduce into possession". It is suggested that this means the doing of some act by the other person to assert his ownership, e.g. caging or possibly trapping the animal, or putting the carcase in a game bag or car, or hiding it.

24 Theft Act 1968, s. 4(4).

25 Theft Act 1968, ss. 15(1), 22(1), 34(2)(b).

26 This is an offence of strict liability, viz. not involving *mens rea.* See *Denham v Scott* [1983] Crim LR 558.

27 Theft Act 1968, s. 23.

C. OWNERS' RESPONSIBILITIES

The owner of an animal will in many different circumstances be liable for injuries it causes to people and other animals and for damage to property. This responsibility often attaches, not only to the owner, but to the person who at the time has possession of the animal and, sometimes, to a person whose household includes a youngster who owns or possesses the animal. These are mainly matters of civil law with the sanction of an action in court, usually for damages for the injury or damage done.

Over the centuries a body of case law on the subject was created with sometimes complicated and unsatisfactory results. The Animals Act of 1971 was an attempt to rationalise this law, though not to change it except about animals escaping on to roads. Much of the law still rests on the precedents of legal cases. (A large body of law deals specially with dogs and this is contained in Chapter 4.)

A study of the subject, which can be quite involved, falls fairly conveniently into a number of sub-headings which will now be dealt with in turn.

Strict Liability

"Strict liability" is a legal term meaning that there is liability without proof that the person claimed against was negligent; if he was responsible for the animal and the animal caused the injury or damage, then, without more, that person is responsible for that injury or damage. Nevertheless, since liability is based on negligence, recoverable damage would seem to depend on direct causation and not reasonable foreseeability.[28] This is a part of the law codified by the Animals Act 1971 and itself falls into two parts: animals[29] belonging to a dangerous species, and those which do not. Therefore the Act preserves the common law action known as *scienter* – that being based on the keeper's knowledge of the animal's dangerous propensities. Although it should be noted that the keeper's knowledge is irrelevant if the animal is one belonging

---

[28] *Behrens v Bertram Mills Circus* [1957] 2 QB 1 at 17 *per* Devlin J.
[29] The Animals Act 1971 does not define "an animal" but it has been suggested to include birds, reptiles and insects, but not bacteria (North, *The Modern Law of Animals* (1972)).

to a dangerous species. Whilst much of the earlier common law remains relevant, the wording of the Act prevails.

A dangerous species is a species[30] which is not commonly domesticated in the British Islands;[31] and whose fully grown animals normally have such characteristics that they are likely, unless restrained, to cause severe damage[32] or that any damage they may cause is likely to be severe.[33] Where any damage is caused by such an animal, any person who is a keeper[34] of the animal is liable for the damage except in the following cases:[35]

1. Where the damage was due wholly to the fault of the person suffering it;[36] or

2. If the person injured voluntarily accepted[37] the risk of injury;[38] or

3. If the damage was caused by an animal kept on any premises or structure to a trespasser[39] there if it is proved:

   i. either that the animal was not kept there for the protection of persons or property; or

   ii. if the animal was kept there for that purpose, that the keeping for the purpose was not unreasonable.[40]

---

[30] The word species includes sub-species and variety (Animals Act 1971, s. 11).

[31] I.e. the United Kingdom, the Channel Islands, the Isle of Man, and the Republic of Ireland (Interpretation Act 1978 ss. 5, 22(1), Sch. 1, Sch. 2, para. 4(2)).

[32] "Damage" includes the death of, or injury to, any person (including any disease and any impairment of physical or mental condition) (Animals Act 1971, s. 11). Similarly it appears to include damage to property (see the definition – Animals Act 1971, s. 11, and the substantive – Animals Act 1971, s. 2(1)).

[33] Animals Act 1971, s. 6(2).

[34] For the meaning of "keeper", see p. 68. Importantly, one keeper may sue another keeper of the same animal under the Animals Act 1971, s. 2 (*Flack v Hudson* (2000), *The Times*, 22 November 2000).

[35] Animals Act 1971, s. 2(1).

[36] Animals Act 1971, s. 5(1).

[37] A servant of a keeper of an animal who incurs a risk incidental to his employment is not to be treated as accepting that risk voluntarily (Animals Act 1971, s. 6(5)). See *Canterbury City Council v Howletts and Port Lympne* [1997] ICR 925 in which the employer encouraged the keepers to "bond" with the tigers, involving the keepers to enter the cages regularly.

[38] Animals Act 1971, s. 5(2).

[39] Briefly, a trespasser is a person on premises without the occupier's permission.

[40] Animals Act 1971, s. 5(3).

It follows from i. that a trespasser in a properly fenced field who is gored by a savage bull has no remedy.[41] What is reasonable in case ii. will depend upon the circumstances; the keeping of a fierce dog in the access to a house which injures innocent visitors on lawful business would not be excusable;[42] but the keeping of an untamed Alsatian dog at loose at night in a scrapyard in East London to protect property is not unreasonable, although the court conceded that this decision might have been otherwise if section 1 of the Guard Dogs Act 1975 (see pages 89 to 91) had been in force at the time.[43]

Since damage caused by a dangerous species attracts strict liability, provided that there is a causal link, there would seem to be no requirement that the damage must be of a kind connected with the classification of the species as dangerous.[44]

In the case of an animal not belonging to a dangerous species as defined, its keeper[45] is strictly liable, but with the same defences as have just been enumerated, for the damage[46] it causes if:

a. the damage is of a kind which the animal, unless restrained, was likely to cause or which, if caused by the animal, was likely to be severe;[47] and

b. the likelihood of the damage or of its being severe was due to characteristics of the animal not normally found in animals of the same species[48] or not normally so found except at particular times or in particular circumstances;[49] and

---

41 For legislation about bulls in fields, see pp. 20-21.
42 *Sarah v Blackburn* (1830) 4 C & P 297 at 300.
43 *Cummings v Grainger* [1977] 1 All ER 104.
44 *Clarke and Lindsell on Tort* (1995) p. 997 n 17.
45 For the meaning of "keeper", see p. 68.
46 For the meaning of "damage", see note 32 above.
47 Animals Act 1971, s. 2(2)(a).
48 The word "species" includes sub-species and variety (Animals Act 1971, s. 11).
49 Animals Act 1971, s. 2(2)(b). The unpredictable nature of a horse is not to be regarded as a normal characteristic of horses (*Wallace v Newton* [1982] 2 All ER 106) nor is the propensity of a dog to attack people carrying bags to be regarded as a normal characteristic of dogs (*Kite v Napp, The Times,* 1 June 1982). The words "characteristics…not normally found in animals of the same species" are to be given their ordinary meaning (*Wallace v Newton* [1982] 2 All ER 106; *Smith v Ainger, The Times,* 5 June 1990; cf *Halsbury's Laws of England,* 4th Ed., Vol. 2 (Reissue), para. 468, note 7). Likewise, it follows that characteristics which are

c. those characteristics were known to the animal's keeper or were at any time known to a person who at that time had charge of the animal as the keeper's servant or, where the keeper is the head of a household, were known to another keeper of the animal who is a member of that household and under the age of 16.[50]

It follows that the plaintiff must show:

1. That the keeper had knowledge[51] or must be taken to have known[52] of the precise characteristic displayed by the animal being one which is abnormally dangerous;[53] and

2. That damage "if caused by the animal" was likely[54] to be severe;[55] and

3. If relying on section 2(2)(b), that there was a causal link between the relevant characteristic of the specific animal[56] and the injury the subject of the complaint.[57]

---

normally found in animals of the same species but only at "particular times or in particular circumstances" will be regarded as abnormal – M A Jones, *Textbook on Torts*, 5th Ed, Blackstones, London, 1997, 321; cf *Curtis v Betts* [1990] 1 All ER 769. It has been held that there is no liability where an animal acts in accordance with its training in the characteristic way of other animals so trained: *Gloster v Chief Constable of Greater Manchester* [2000] PIQR p114.

50 Animals Act 1971, s. 2(2)(c).

51 See *Glanville v Sutton & Co Ltd* [1928] 1 KB 571; *Brock v Richards* [1951] 1 KB 529.

52 Knowledge may be acquired not simply by past occurrences but by the apparent propensity of the animal to cause the harm in fact caused – Clerk & Linsell on Torts (1995) p. 998 (*Kane v McKenna,* unreported, 30 November 1990; cf *Smith v Ainger, The Times,* 5 June 1990).

53 *Whitehead v Alexander* [1999] unreported, 4 August 1999; cf *Osborne v Choqueel* [1896] 2 QB 109; *Glanville v Sutton & Co Ltd* [1928] 1 KB 571; *Worth v Gilling* (1866) LR 2 CP 1; *Jones v Perry Harvey* [1911] 2 KB 725; *Judge v Cox* (1816) 1 Stark 285; *Hartley v Harriman* (1818) 1 B & Ald 620; *Hudson v Roberts* (1851) 6 Exch 697; *Beck v Dyson* (1815) 4 Camp 198; *Thomas v Morgan* (1835) 2 Cr M & R 496; *Sanders v Teape and Swan* (1884) 51 LT 263.

54 The Court of Appeal held that the words "was likely" in s. 2(2)(a) means "such as might well happen" or "where there is a material risk that it will happen" and not "more probable than not" (*Smith v Ainger, The Times,* 5 June 1990).

55 It is not necessary to establish that the severity of that damage ensued from the normal characteristics of that animal (*Curtis v Betts* [1990] 1 W L T 459; *Wallace v Newton* [1982] 1 WLR 459).

56 The animal must be capable of being identified (*Draper v Hodder* [1972] 2 All ER 210).

57 *Jaundrill v Gillett, The Times,* 30 January 1996.

The special provisions about guard dogs are discussed on pages 89 to 91.

Negligence

In addition to the strict liability cases just mentioned, the owner of a domestic and normally harmless animal, and the person having charge of it at the time, can be liable for injury or damage which it causes through his negligence.[58] The word "negligence" has more than its ordinary meaning here; to succeed in a case of negligence the plaintiff must prove to the satisfaction of the court that the defendant had a duty to him to take care, that he failed in that duty and that the injury or damage resulted from that failure. Whether there is a duty in any particular case will depend mainly on case law. So far as animals are concerned, it is established that a person who brings an animal on to a highway has a duty to use all reasonable care to prevent it doing damage to other persons there. If he is driving animals along the highway he must have them under sufficient control.[59] These are admittedly imprecise tests; they cannot be otherwise. Each case depends on its own facts and on the precedents of case law.[60]

Diseased Animals[61]

The owner or possessor of animals having an infectious or contagious disease is liable for the damage caused by their disease in the following cases:

---

58   An action for negligence would be more appropriate where the keeper did not have actual or imputed knowledge of the animal's characteristics, but ought to have known of such characteristics since the keeper will not be liable under s. 2(2).

59   *Halsbury's Laws of England*, 4th Ed., Vol. 2 (Reissue), para. 470.

60   E.g. *Draper v Hodder* [1972] 2 All ER 210; *Jones v Owen* (1871) 24 LT 587; *Fardon v Harcourt-Rivington* (1932) 146 LT 391; *Seymour v Ley* (1932) 147 LT 342; *Pitcher v Martin* [1937] 3 All ER 918; *Deen v Davies* [1935] 2 KB 282; *Gomberg v Smith* [1962] 1 All ER 725; *Turner v Coates* [1917] 1 KB 670; *Harpers v Great North of Scotland Railway Co* (1886) 13 R 1139; *Pinn v Rew* (1916) 32 TLR 451; *Turnbull v Wieland* (1916) 33 TLR 143; *Rose v G H Collier Ltd* [1939] WN 19; *Lathall v A Joyce & Son* [1939] 3 All ER 854; *Aldham v United Dairies (London) Ltd* [1940] 4 All ER 522; *Wright v Callwood* [1950] 2 KB 515; *Bativala v West* [1970] 1 All ER 332; *Walker v Crabb* (1916) 33 TLR 119; *Catchpole v Minster* (1913) 109 LT 953; *Galer and Pope Ltd v B Davies & Son Ltd* [1924] 2 KB 75.

61   For the rules enacted by Parliament and the Department for Environment, Food and Rural Affairs about animal diseases, see Chapter 9. See also the section on nuisances on pp. 18-20.

1. If, knowing them to be diseased, he allows them to mingle with the animals of another person;[62]

2. If, knowing them to be diseased and infectious to persons handling them, he employs a person to handle their carcases who is ignorant of their state, and that person becomes infected;[63]

3. If, knowing of their diseased state, he bails[64] the animals, knowing that the person to whom they are bailed probably will or may place them with other animals which are healthy, without warning that person of their diseased state;[65]

4. If he sells them with a warranty[66] that they are free from disease, whether he knows of their diseased state or not;

5. If he is guilty of fraud or actual concealment about the disease in the sale;

6. If, knowing them to be diseased and that they may be put in with healthy animals, he sells them at a public market or fair, or at a public auction; and possibly even if he sells them privately.[67]

Trespass by Animals Generally

In broad terms, an animal is said to trespass in the same way as a human trespasses, namely when it is on land where it has no right to be or, more precisely, where its owner has no right to put it; this includes an animal straying on to a highway as well as those straying from a highway on to private land.[68]

For trespass to take place, it is enough if any part of the animal crosses the boundary of the properties in question, e.g. the stretching of its neck over the boundary. But what is called trespass to the

---

[62] *Cooke v Waring* (1836) 2 H&C 332, but see *Weller v Foot and Mouth Disease Research Institute* [1966] 1 QB 569.

[63] *Davies v England & Curtis* (1864) 33 LJQB 321.

[64] "Bail" is a legal word meaning in this context, briefly, to deliver goods to another person for an agreed purpose, e.g. to keep them safely or to do work on them.

[65] *Penton v Mudruck* (1870) 22 LT 371.

[66] A warranty is an agreement collateral to the sale. See also pp. 26-28.

[67] *Halsbury's Laws of England*, 4th Ed., Vol. 2 (Reissue), para. 471.

[68] *League Against Cruel Sports v Scott* [1986] QB 240. Trespass is committed by the owner where his animals stray from the owner's land by intention or negligence of the owner.

person or to goods (including horses or cattle), that is the touching of them by the animal, does not generally render the owner liable where there is no trespass to land.[69]

The rules of the law on the subject are concerned mainly with trespass of livestock. A cat[70] holds a unique position in that its owner is not responsible for the consequences of its trespasses. Owners' liabilities for the trespasses of their dogs are governed by the particular rules which are examined on pages 67 to 70. Owners and keepers of cats and dogs which cause damage or injury when not trespassing may be liable under the strict liability rules or the law of negligence which have been considered on pages 4 to 8. Responsibilities for wild animals are dealt with in a concluding section on this topic. There remains some doubt about the position of a trespassing animal which is neither wild nor a dog, cat or livestock.[71] It appears that for animals in this residual category their owners will be liable for damage caused when they trespass which is in their nature ordinarily to commit.[72]

Trespass by Livestock on Private Land

Where livestock belonging[73] to any person strays[74] on to land in the ownership or occupation of another person, the first person is strictly liable[75] for the following damage and expenses unless he can establish any of the defences later considered:

1. Damage done by the livestock to the land or to any property on it[76] which is in the ownership or possession of that other person;

---

[69] *Halsbury's Laws of England*, 4th Ed., Vol. 2 (Reissue), para. 472.
[70] I.e. the domestic cat.
[71] For this purpose "livestock" means cattle, horses, mules, hinnies (offspring of she-asses by stallions), sheep, pigs, goats and poultry, and deer not in a wild state (Animals Act 1971, s. 11).
[72] *Halsbury's Laws of England*, 4th Ed., Vol. 2 (Reissue), para. 472, note 4.
[73] For this purpose livestock belongs to the person in whose possession it is (Animals Act 1971, s. 4(2)). For the meaning of "possession", see note 23 on p. 3.
[74] As to what constitutes straying see *Wiseman v Booker* (1878) 3 CPD 184.
[75] For the meaning of strict liability, see p. 4.
[76] The words here used are wide enough, it is suggested, to cover the land itself and anything in, on or above it, and so embracing all growing things, buildings and objects placed, however temporarily, on the land, provided these are owned or possessed as described. The earlier definition of "damage" (in note 32 on p. 5) will not apply but s. 4 of the Animals Act 1971 makes it clear that damage to land and property is included within the statutory definition of damage.

2. Expenses which are reasonably incurred by that other person[77] in keeping the livestock while it cannot be restored to the person to whom it belongs or while the occupier of the land is exercising his right to detain it,[78] and the expenses of finding out to whom the livestock belongs.[79]

There is no responsibility for straying livestock if:

a. the damage is due wholly to the fault of the person suffering it,[80] but he is not to be treated as at fault solely because he could have prevented the damage by fencing;[81] or

b. it is proved that the straying would not have occurred but for a breach of a duty to fence[82] imposed on another person who has an interest in the land in question. (This has the effect, for example, of a tenant being unable to claim for damage and expenses if his landlord had failed to honour the landlord's agreement with another person to fence as a result of which the animals had strayed on to the tenant's land); or

c. the livestock strayed from the highway and its presence there was a lawful use of the highway.[83] The highway need not adjoin the land; the stock may have wandered from the highway through other land. The only lawful use of the highway for livestock is to pass and re-pass on it.[84]

In addition to his right to claim for damage and expenses, the occupier of land on to which livestock strays without being under the control of any person has the right to detain it unless ordered by

---

[77] Where that person is a local authority, it is proper for it to have reasonable standard charges if it would be impossible to keep exact and detailed records of each animal; an itemised bill in such circumstances is unnecessary (*Morris v Blaenau Gwent District Council, The Times*, 6 July 1982).

[78] For the right of detention, see below.

[79] Animals Act 1971, s. 4(1).

[80] Animals Act 1971, s. 5(1).

[81] "Fencing" includes the construction of any obstacle designed to prevent animals from straying (Animals Act 1971, s. 11).

[82] A duty to fence against common land may arise by custom (*Egerton v Harding and Another* [1974] 3 All ER 689).

[83] Animals Act 1971, s. 5(1), (5), (6).

[84] Grazing verges does not amount to lawful user (*Mathews v Wilks, The Times*, 25 May 1987).

a court to return it.[85] This right ceases:

1. At the end of 48 hours unless beforehand the occupier gives notice of the detention to the officer in charge of a police station and to the person to whom the livestock belongs if the occupier knows who that person is; or

2. If the person claiming the livestock offers to the occupier money sufficient to cover his proper claim for damage and expenses;[86] or

3. If the occupier has no such claim, when the livestock is claimed by someone entitled to its possession.[87]

When the occupier has detained the livestock for at least 14 days he may sell it at market or public auction, unless court proceedings are then pending for the return of the livestock or for his claim for damage or expenses.[88] The occupier is entitled to the net proceeds[89] of sale. Any excess over his claim is to be paid to the person who would be entitled to possession of the livestock but for the sale.[90] If there is a shortfall, presumably, though the Act does not say so, the occupier may pursue his claim for that.

The occupier is liable for any damage caused to livestock detained by him by failure to treat it with reasonable care and supply it with adequate food and water.[91]

References in these matters to the occupier's claim do not include a claim arising before the particular straying as a result of which the stock was detained.[92]

---

[85]   A court may so order on payment into court of a sum of money against the claim for which the stock is held.

[86]   I.e. a claim within the limitations described on pp. 10-11.

[87]   Animals Act 1971, s. 7(2), (3).

[88]   Animals Act 1971, s. 7(4).

[89]   I.e. after deducting sale costs and other costs "incurred in connection with" the sale.

[90]   Animals Act 1971, s. 7(5).

[91]   Animals Act 1971, s. 7(6). It is an offence under the Protection of Animals Act 1911, s. 7 to fail to feed and water any impounded stock.

[92]   Animal Act 1971, s. 7(7).

Trespass from the Highway

As we have seen,[93] there is no claim under strict liability for damage or expenses by a landowner or occupier for livestock straying on to his land, directly or indirectly, following their lawful presence on a highway. To succeed in a claim in these circumstances the person suffering loss must prove negligence by the person having charge of the livestock; in brief, he must show that reasonable control over the animals was not being exercised while they were being driven along the road. The law takes the view that it is a risk which a man takes who has property adjoining a road and, in the absence of negligence by the drover, the loss falls upon him if he does not take precautions by fencing or otherwise protecting his property. Though there is no legal decision on the point, it is suggested that an unreasonable delay in removing an animal that has strayed on to land from a road, though otherwise driven quite properly along it, could justify a claim for damage caused by the delay.[94]

Straying on the Highway

Until 1971,[95] unless there were special circumstances, owners of animals were not responsible for any injury or damage they caused by straying on to a highway. Now, owners of animals and those having control of them have a duty to take reasonable care to see that such injury or damage is not caused.[96] This does not by itself oblige all owners to fence[97] but, for example, failure to fence where animals are kept near a busy road is likely to be treated as a breach of the duty.[98] However, no breach is caused when a person, having the right to do so,[99] places animals on unfenced land which is

---

[93] Page 11, item c.

[94] *Halsbury's Laws of England,* 4th Ed., Vol. 2 (Reissue), para. 476.

[95] 1 October 1971 when the Animals Act came into force.

[96] Effectively the common law rules of negligence apply (*Pike v Wallis, The Times,* 6 November 1981).

[97] References to fencing in the Act include references to other obstacles designed to prevent animals from straying (Animals Act 1971, s. 11.)

[98] If a fence, though not 100% secure, is reasonably adequate to prevent the animal in question from escaping, it appears that the duty of care is fulfilled (*Smith v Sudron and Coulson* Court of Appeal Transcripts 140, 10 April 1981; *Hoskin v Rogers, The Times,* 6 November 1981).

[99] Persons having the right to put animals on the land described will include a person licensed to do so by another person having that right, provided the number of animals permitted for that other person is not exceeded (*Davies v Davies* [1974] 3 All ER 817).

common land,[100] or a town or village green,[101] or is in an area where fencing is not customary.[102]

The position is different, as has been shown on page 8, when animals are deliberately brought on to a highway.

If any horse,[103] or any cattle, sheep, goats or swine are found straying,[104] or lying[105] on or at the side of any highway[106] (except such part of it as passes over any common or waste or unenclosed ground), the keeper[107] of the animals is liable to be prosecuted and fined. He may also be charged with the reasonable expenses of removing the animals to his premises or the common pound or other place provided, and with the proper charges of the pound-keeper.[108] Any person lawfully using the highway may remove the animals to a pound but if so must feed and water them.[109]

---

[100] "Common land" means land subject to rights of common (which includes cattlegates or beastgates and rights of sole or several vesture or herbage or of sole or several pasture but not rights held for a term of years or from year to year) whether those rights are exercisable at all times or only during limited periods, and waste lands of a manor not subject to rights of common but does not include a town or village green or any land forming part of a highway (Animals Act 1971, s. 11; Commons Registration Act 1965, s. 22(1)).

[101] "Town or village green" means land which has been allotted by or under any Act for the exercise or recreation of the inhabitants of any locality or of which such inhabitants have a customary right to indulge in lawful sports or pastimes or on which they have indulged in such sports and pastimes as of right for not less than 20 years (Animals Act 1971, s. 11; Commons Registration Act 1965, s. 22(1)).

[102] Animals Act 1971, s. 8.

[103] "Horse" includes pony, ass and mule (Highways Act 1980, s. 329(1)).

[104] Animals are not "straying" if they are under the control of an attendant (*Lawrence v King* (1868) 18 LT 356).

[105] The presence of a keeper by itself is not an excuse for "lying", but apparently animals on a journey may be allowed to rest for a reasonable time (*Lawrence v King* (1868) 18 LT 356; *Horwood v Goodall* (1872) 36 JP 486).

[106] "Highway" means the whole or part of a highway other than a ferry or waterway, and includes a bridge over or a tunnel through which the highway passes (Highways Act 1980, s. 328 (1), (2)). Within this definition, a highway is, briefly, any road or other way over which the public has the right to pass to and fro.

[107] "Keeper" means the person in whose possession the animals are and not necessarily the owner, although they may be one and the same (Highways Act 1980, s. 155 (1)). As to "possession", see p. 68.

[108] Highways Act 1980, s. 155(3).

[109] Protection of Animals Act 1911, s. 7(1). He may be fined if he fails to do so. Food and water may be given to them by anyone if the animals are without them for 6 hours. In either case, the cost of food and water is chargeable to the animal's owner (Protection of Animals Act 1911, s. 11).

Presumably,[110] such person might also remove them to their owner's premises.

These provisions do not apply in the case of a person having a right to pasture his animals on the side of a highway[111] but a keeper exercising this right must keep his animals from straying, except temporarily, or lying on the actual road.[112]

Except in the Greater London area, cattle[113] found at large in streets[114] without any person having charge of them may be impounded by any constable or resident in any common pound within the district or in such other place as the local authority may appoint for the purpose. They may be detained until the owner pays the authority a penalty and the reasonable expenses of impounding and keeping them. The cattle may be sold if the money is not paid in three days, but seven days' notice of the sale must first be given to the owner of the cattle or, if he is not known, by newspaper advertisement.[115]

Trespass by Wild Animals

A landowner is not liable for damage caused by wild animals from his land "trespassing" on and causing damage to another's land, unless he brings on to his land a greater quantity of wild animals than can reasonably and properly be kept on it. Mere failure to keep the existing stock of wild animals within reasonable limits is another matter, and there would, for example, be no liability for a natural increase of rabbits on one person's land which caused damage to his neighbour's.[116]

If a man reclaims wild animals and puts them on his land, he is liable, if they trespass, for any damage caused by them which it is

---

[110] The law does not appear to cover the point.

[111] Highways Act 1980, s. 155(5).

[112] *Halsbury's Laws of England,* 4th Ed., Vol. 2 (Reissue), para. 474.

[113] "Cattle" includes horses, asses, mules, sheep, goats and swine (Town Police Clauses Act 1847, s. 3).

[114] A "street" means any street, road, square, court, alley, thoroughfare or public passage (Town Police Clauses Act 1847, ss. 2, 3).

[115] Town Police Clauses Act 1847, ss. 24–27; Public Health Act 1875, s. 171; Local Government Act 1972, s. 180(2), Sch. 14, Part II paras. 23, 26(a).

[116] *Halsbury's Laws of England,* 4th Ed., Vol. 2 (Reissue), para. 477. As to control of rabbits generally, see pp. 226-229.

in their ordinary nature to commit. A question still open is for how long the owner of a reclaimed animal is liable after its escape; this may depend on whether, at the time of damage, the animal has fully reverted to its wild state.[117]

Animals and Vehicles on Roads

When a collision occurs on a public road between an animal and a vehicle and damage, injury or death is caused, the principles discussed on pages 8, 13 and 14 will be relevant in deciding where responsibility should lie. Breach of one of the duties there described will make the person in breach responsible. That is not to say that the driver of the vehicle involved has no duty of care in driving. Careless driving causing death or injury to an animal whose presence or behaviour on the road was blameless will make the driver liable. Often a measure of blame attaches to both sides in which case damages claimed will be reduced or apportioned.

The circumstances in which accidents of this kind may happen vary widely; the principles mentioned have to be applied to the facts of each case. A conclusion which emerges from what is said earlier on pages 13 to 16 is that a driver passing by unfenced land on which animals may be should be especially careful.

As a matter of criminal law,[118] if owing to the presence of a mechanically propelled vehicle[119] on a road[120] an accident occurs whereby personal injury is caused to an animal[121] (other than an

---

[117] *Halsbury's Laws of England*, 4th Ed., Vol. 2 (Reissue), para. 473.

[118] Road Traffic Act 1988, s. 170.

[119] A mechanically propelled vehicle is not defined, but would include a motor car, motor cycle, motor tractor and motor vehicle as defined by the Road Traffic Act 1988, s. 185(1), but would not include an implement for cutting grass which is controlled by a pedestrian and is not capable of being used or adapted for any other purpose, nor any vehicle controlled by a pedestrian which may be specified by regulations made by the Secretary of State for the purposes of section 189 and section 140 of the Road Traffic Regulation Act 1984, nor an electrically assisted pedal cycle of such a class as may be prescribed by regulations (i.e. The Electrically Assisted Pedal Cycle Regulations 1983, SI 1983/1163); Road Traffic Act 1988, s. 189(1).

[120] "Road" means any highway and any other road to which the public has access, and includes bridges over which a road passes (Road Traffic Act 1988, s. 192). As to "highway", see the brief non-statutory meaning in note 106 on p. 14.

[121] "Animal" means any horse, cattle, ass, mule, sheep, pig, goat or dog (Road Traffic Act 1988, s. 170, amended by the Road Traffic Act 1991, Sch. 4).

animal in or on that motor vehicle or a trailer[122] drawn by it), the driver of the vehicle must stop.[123] If required to do so by any person having reasonable grounds for so requiring, the driver must give his name and address, the name and address of the vehicle's owner and the identification marks, i.e. the registration number, of the vehicle.[124] If he does not give his name and address,[125] he must report the accident at a police station or to a police constable as soon as reasonably practicable, and in any case within 24 hours of the accident.[126] Failure to comply with any of these requirements is an offence.[127]

The person in charge of any animal[128] which is carried by a vehicle[129] using a motorway shall, so far as practicable secure that:

a. the animal shall not be removed from or permitted to leave the vehicle while the vehicle is on the motorway, and

b. if it escapes from, or it is necessary for it to be removed from, or permitted to leave, the vehicle:

   i. it shall not go or remain on any part of the motorway other than a hard shoulder,[130] and

   ii. it shall whilst it is not on or in the vehicle be held on a lead or otherwise kept under proper control.[131]

---

[122] "Trailer" means a vehicle drawn by a motor vehicle (Road Traffic Act 1988, s. 185(1)).

[123] A driver is obliged to stop immediately the accident occurs and he will fail to comply with the requirements of Road Traffic Act 1988, s. 170(2) if he does not do so as soon as he can safely and conveniently stop (*Hallinan v DPP* [1998] Crim LR 754). A driver should stop for such time as in the circumstances will enable any person entitled to do so to require the information from the driver personally (*Lee* v *Knapp* [1966] 3 All ER 961; *Ward v Rawson* [1978] RTR 498).

[124] Road Traffic Act 1988, s. 170(2).

[125] This includes the case where nobody requires this information from the driver (*Peek v Towle* [1945] 2 All ER 611).

[126] Road Traffic Act 1988, s. 170(3).

[127] Road Traffic Act 1988, s. 170(4). No offence is committed by a driver who does not stop, being unaware that an accident has happened (*Harding* v *Price* [1948] 1 All ER 283).

[128] The word "animal" is not defined.

[129] The word "vehicle" is not defined but will include a trailer.

[130] "Hard shoulder" means any part of the motorway which is adjacent to and situated on the left hand or near side of the carriageway when facing in the direction in which vehicles may be driven and which is designed to take the weight of the vehicle (Motorway Traffic (England and Wales) Regulations 1982, SI 1982/1163).

[131] Motorway Traffic (England and Wales) Regulations 1982, Art. 14.

But the person in charge of the animal need not comply with these requirements if so directed by the police or if such is indicated by a traffic sign.[132] Similarly the person will be exempt from the regulations where it is necessary for him to avoid or prevent an accident or to obtain or give help required as the result of an accident or emergency, and he does so in such a manner as to cause as little danger or inconvenience as possible to other traffic on a motorway.[133]

There still remains on the statute book a sizeable body of law regulating animal traffic on public roads and in other public places which has been inherited from the pre-motor age when horses were used for transport and farm animals were more commonly to be found on roads than they are now. It is not proposed here to deal in detail with these matters, which have only slight relevance in modern times, but rather to indicate those aspects on which legislation impinges so as to warn the reader of their existence.

Such aspects are: the driving, leading or riding of animals on footpaths at the sides of roads or their tethering which allows them to go on roads is generally not allowed; the turning loose, selling, cleaning, dressing, shoeing, bleeding, treating, exercising, breaking or slaughtering of animals on public roads or in other public places is forbidden; regulations exist about the marking, loading, construction and driving of horse-drawn vehicles, and about the leading or driving of animals through streets and their hiring there.

Nuisances

The keeping of any animals in such a position or in such circumstances as to cause a substantial discomfort or annoyance to the public in general or to a particular person constitutes, in law, the civil wrong of nuisance for which action may be taken in the courts. Examples from law cases include instances of a large number of pigs in premises adjoining a village street,[134] and cockerels crowing in the early morning.[135] The remedy is the award of damages or the granting of an injunction.[136]

---

[132] Motorway Traffic (England and Wales) Regulations 1982, Art. 16(1)(a).
[133] Motorway Traffic (England and Wales) Regulations 1982, Art. 16(1)(c).
[134] *Attorney General v Squire* (1906) 5 LGR 99.
[135] *Leeman v Montagu* [1936] 2 All ER 1677.
[136] An injunction is an order of the court forbidding the committing of a further nuisance, the penalty for non-compliance usually being imprisonment.

The local authority,[137] if they are satisfied that a statutory nuisance[138] exists, or is likely to occur or recur, may serve an abatement notice on the person requiring the abatement of the nuisance by prohibiting or restricting its occurrence or recurrence[139] within a specified time. The person on whom the abatement notice is served has 21 days from the date on which he was served to appeal[140] against the notice to the magistrates. If the notice is not complied with, without reasonable excuse,[141] the person served with it may be summoned before a magistrates' court and, if it is proved that the nuisance exists, will be liable to a fine on conviction for contravening an abatement notice and for each day of contravention of an order after conviction.[142] Where the person commits the offence on industrial, trade or business premises a fine not exceeding £20,000 may be imposed. In this latter case it is a defence that the best practical means[143] were used to prevent, or to counteract, the

---

[137] This is the district council outside Greater London; in London it is the borough council, the Common Council of the City of London, or the Sub-Treasurer or Under-Treasurer in the Temples, but, in relation to Wales, means the council or county or county borough (Environmental Protection Act 1990, s. 79(7)).

[138] A statutory nuisance occurs when any animal is kept in such a place or manner as to be prejudicial to health or a nuisance (Environmental Protection Act 1990, s. 79(i)(f)). "Prejudicial to health" means injurious, or likely to cause injury, to health: Environmental Protection Act 1990, s. 79(7).

[139] An abatement notice or a nuisance order may also require works to be done if necessary for the abatement.

[140] See Environmental Protection Act 1990, s. 81 and Sch. 3 and the Statutory Nuisance (Appeals) Regulations 1990 for further provisions.

[141] Failure to challenge the validity of the notice within the provisions of Environmental Protection Act 1990, s. 170(3) will not be a reasonable excuse unless there has been some special reason (A Lambert Flat Management Ltd v Lomas [1981] 2 All ER 280). Once raised by the defendant, the burden is on the prosecution to disprove reasonable excuse (Polychronakis v Richards and Jarrom [1998] JPL B35).

[142] Environmental Protection Act 1990, s. 170(5).

[143] "Best practical means" is to be interpreted by reference to the following provisions:
   (a) "practicable" means reasonably practicable having regard among other things to local conditions and circumstances, to the state of technical knowledge and financial implications;
   (b) and means to be employed include the design, installation, maintenance and manner and periods of operation of plant and machinery, and the design, construction and maintenance of buildings and structures;
   (c) the test applies only so far as compatible with any duty imposed by law;
   (d) the test applies only so far as compatible with safety and safe working conditions and with the exigencies of any emergency or unforeseeable circumstances: Environmental Protection Act 1990, s. 79(9).

effects of the nuisance.[144] Where the local authority consider that the foregoing penalties would afford an inadequate remedy they may take proceedings in the High Court for the purpose of securing abatement, prohibition or restriction of the nuisance and the proceedings will be maintainable notwithstanding that the local authority has not suffered any damage from the nuisance.[145] Non-compliance with a nuisance order entitles the local authority to abate the nuisance themselves[146] and to recover their reasonable expenses from the person on whom the order was made. They may also recover their expenses incurred in court proceedings.[147]

Bulls on Public Paths

It is an offence, punishable by a fine, for the occupier of a field or enclosure which is crossed by a public path to permit a bull to be at large in it.[148] But this is not to apply to any bull:

1. Whose age does not exceed ten months; or

2. Which is not of a recognised dairy breed[149] and is at large in any field or enclosure in which cows or heifers are also at large.[150]

The public paths to which this provision applies are ways over which the public have the following rights of way:

1. On foot only, exclusive of a footpath at the side of a public road;

2. Only on foot and a right of way on horseback[151] or leading a horse, with or without the right to drive animals along the way;

3. For vehicular and all other kinds of traffic, but which are used

---

[144] Environmental Protection Act 1990, s. 8(a).
[145] Environmental Protection Act 1990, s. 81(5).
[146] Environmental Protection Act 1990, s. 81(3).
[147] Environmental Protection Act 1990, s. 81(4).
[148] Wildlife and Countryside Act 1981, s. 59(1).
[149] "A recognised dairy breed" means one of the following breeds: Ayrshire, British Friesian, British Holstein, Dairy Shorthorn, Guernsey, Jersey and Kerry: Wildlife and Countryside Act 1981, s. 59(4). The Secretary of State may by order add any breed to, or remove any breed from this list: Wildlife and Countryside Act 1981, s. 59(5).
[150] Wildlife and Countryside Act 1981, s. 59(2).
[151] "Horse" includes a pony, ass and mule, and "horseback" is to be interpreted accordingly: Wildlife and Countryside Act 1981, s. 66(1).

by the public mainly as in 1. or 2. above.[152]

Formerly, in many areas, district council byelaws were in force which prohibited bulls from being at large in fields crossed by public paths. Such byelaws are now superseded by the new provisions.[153]

---

[152] Wildlife and Countryside Act 1981, ss. 59(1), 66(1). Public paths have been surveyed and the different categories are marked on maps which have been deposited at one or more places in each local authority area for free inspection at all reasonable hours: Wildlife and Countryside Act 1981, s. 57(5). These maps are to a major extent conclusive as to the status and particulars of the paths contained in them: Wildlife and Countryside Act 1981, s. 56.

[153] Wildlife and Countryside Act 1981, s. 59(3).

Chapter 2

SALE AND AGISTMENT

A. SALE

Generally

In law, domestic animals are treated as goods and chattels for sale purposes, and the ordinary law about sale of goods applies to them. Since there can be no absolute ownership of wild animals whilst alive,[1] they cannot be bought and sold.

The buying of an animal can be hazardous for no prudence can guard against all latent defects.[2] A buyer can gain protection in law through requiring a condition or warranty of quality as part of the sale. Otherwise, the legal tag *"caveat emptor"* applies, that is, "let the buyer beware", and he must accept the animal as he finds it then and later and have no redress.

However, Acts of Parliament since 1893 have intervened to give buyers of goods (and therefore of domestic animals) some protection when there is no expressed condition or warranty on a sale. The position is complicated, and for a full understanding of this protection the legislation itself must be studied.

The principal legislation is the Sale of Goods Act 1979. The starting point in any issue concerning the sale of animals is to establish how the Act would treat them. The Act subdivides goods: one is existing and future goods,[3] the other specific[4] and

---

[1] See p. 1.
[2] Cf *Jones v Bright* (1829) 5 Bing 533 at 544 per Best CJ.
[3] Sale of Goods Act 1979, s. 5(1) states that: "The goods which form the subject of the sale may be either existing goods, owned or possessed by the seller, or goods to be manufactured or acquired by him after the making of the contract of sale, in this Act called future goods". "Future" goods are also defined as "goods to be manufactured or acquired by the seller after the making of the contract of sale". "Manufactured" is not defined but may be given its ordinary meaning. In the case of animals, future goods would be those which have yet to be acquired by the seller at the time of the contract, although animals which are genetically modified could be construed as being manufactured: See GD McLeish, *Hello Dolly*, NLJ 1997, 682.
[4] "Specific goods" are those that are "identified and agreed on at the time a contract is made and includes an undivided share, specified as a fraction or percentage, of the goods identified and agreed on": Sale of Goods Act 1979, s. 61(1).

unascertained.[5] Clearly, animals that are in existence may be future goods, for example where the seller has agreed to sell goods that at the time of the contract are owned by someone else. Thus, for instance, where a seller agrees to sell poults to the buyer but he has yet to purchase them from his supplier. Likewise, existing and future goods may be specific goods or unascertained.

The buyer is entitled to rely on certain implied conditions, and these are that:

a. the seller in the case of a sale has the right to sell the goods and in the case of an agreement to sell that he will have such a right at the time when the property in those goods is to pass;[6]

b. if the animal is described (for instance in an advertisement) then the goods must correspond with that description.[7] What is covered by this condition depends upon the type of animal being sold. Thus, a sale of future or unascertained goods will be by description, as where goods are ordered from a catalogue. Equally, provided that the buyer relies on the description, despite his careful inspection of the animal, there may still be a sale by description. This is important since issues of quality do not cover private sales;

c. where the seller sells goods in the course of a business, there is an implied term that the goods supplied under the contract are of satisfactory quality.[8] Goods are of satisfactory quality if they meet the standard that a reasonable person would regard as satisfactory, taking into account any description of the goods, the price (if relevant) and all the relevant circumstances.[9] The Act goes on to list aspects of quality:

---

[5] "Unascertained goods" are not defined by the Act but it is clear that goods that are not specific are unascertained. There appear to be three categories into which unascertained goods fall: goods to be acquired (or manufactured) by the seller; purely generic goods (e.g. 500 poults); and an unidentified part of a specific whole (e.g. 500 poults of a particular stock of, say, 1,000).

[6] Sale of Goods Act 1979, s. 12(1). This is to a technical condition: Sale of Goods Act 1979, s. 12(5A).

[7] Sale of Goods Act 1979, s. 13.

[8] Sale of Goods Act 1979, s. 14(2) as substituted by Sale and Supply of Goods Act 1994, s. 1.

[9] Sale of Goods Act 1979, s. 14(2B).

i. fitness for all purposes for which goods of the kind in question are commonly supplied;

ii. appearance and finish;

iii. freedom from minor defects;

iv. safety;

v. durability.

The redefined requirement of quality does not extend to any matter making the quality unsatisfactory:

i. which is specifically drawn to the buyer's attention before the contract is made;

ii. where the buyer examines the goods before the contract is made, which the examination ought to reveal; or

iii. in the case of a contract for sale by sample, which would have been apparent on a reasonable examination of the sample;

d. where the seller sells goods in the course of a business[10] and the buyer, expressly or by implication, makes known to the seller any particular purpose for which the goods are being bought, there is an implied term that the goods supplied under the contract are reasonably fit for that purpose, whether or not that is a purpose for which such goods are commonly supplied, except where the circumstances show that the buyer does not rely, or that it is unreasonable for him to rely, on the skill or judgment of the seller.[11]

Whilst some elements of the foregoing, such as durability or finish, may be difficult to apply to animals rather than inanimate objects, nevertheless the underlying principles remain important in all

---

[10] The seller will be treated as selling goods in the course of business even though the goods being sold are not integral to the business. Accordingly, s. 14(2) distinguishes between a sale made in the course of a seller's business and a purely private sale of goods outside the confines of the business carried on by the seller (*Stevenson and Another v Rogers* [1999] 1 All ER 613).

[11] Sale of Goods Act 1979, s. 14(3).

transactions and what will be reasonable will depend upon the nature of the animal. Thus, dangerous goods have been held to be in breach of section 14(2B)(d),[12] but a tiger *(panthera tigris)* is regarded elsewhere in law as *de facto* dangerous, and it would be difficult for a buyer to claim that the subject matter of the transaction breaches the implied terms as to safety unless it had particularly aggressive characteristics.

Since 1st February 1978, sellers' rights to exclude or restrict their liabilities on sales of goods by means of exemption clauses and guarantees have been limited.[13]

Notwithstanding these provisions, it is wise and usual for a buyer to protect himself by requiring an express warranty to cover any quality or virtue which he needs in the animal. He may equally well do this by making the matter in question a condition[14] of his purchase. The difference is that if a condition is broken the buyer may repudiate the contract which means that he may return the animal and be entitled to have his money back; but a warranty is collateral to the main purpose of a sale and breach of it only entitles the buyer to sue the seller for the loss thereby suffered.[15]

A buyer should therefore carefully consider, not only what protection he needs, but also whether he wants it in the terms of a warranty or a condition. Obviously, either should be in writing and signed by the seller. In law both are effective if given orally, but then dispute may follow as to what was actually said and whether it was a warranty or a condition.

A statement by the seller that an animal is sound will on the face of it amount only to a warranty, but if he also undertakes to take back the animal if it proves not to be as stated, the warranty becomes a condition.[16] Any statement of fact made by the seller of

---

[12] *Grant v Australian Knitting Mills* [1936] AC 85.

[13] See Unfair Contract Terms Act 1977 and the Unfair Terms in Consumer Contracts Regulations 1999, SI 1999/2083.

[14] The Sale of Goods Act 1979 does not define "condition" but states that "a stipulation in a contract of sale is a condition, the breach of which may give rise to a right to treat the contract as repudiated, ... and a stipulation may be a condition, though called a warranty in the contract": Sale of Goods Act 1979, s. 11(3).

[15] Sale of Goods Act 1979, s. 61(1).

[16] *Harling v Eddy* [1951] 2 All ER 215.

the animal may give rise to a right to repudiate the contract for misrepresentation,[17] and this right would survive the subsequent conversion of the statement as a term of the contract, unless the court declares that the warranty forms a term of the contract and awards damages in lieu of rescission.[18]

Warranties[19]

A warranty is not intended to guard against a defect which is obvious to the senses. This implies the use of ordinary care in examination of the animal by the buyer if he inspects it beforehand. However, the buyer is not treated as an expert for the purposes of such examination.[20] If he does not inspect it, a warranty will cover patent defects.[21] Likewise, if the seller warrants the animal with the intention of preventing the buyer from examining it and discovering a patent defect, or if the seller uses any other artifice to conceal such a defect.[22] A person buying a horse, knowing it to be blind, cannot sue the seller on a general warranty of soundness.[23]

A person authorised by the owner as his agent to sell an animal is not necessarily authorised to give a warranty. It appears that, certainly in cases of selling horses,[24] a warranty given by an employee or agent of a horse-dealer will be effective against the horse-dealer, even though he expressly forbade the giving of a warranty or even if it was shown that it was not customary for

---

[17] Misrepresentation Act 1967, s. 1(a).
[18] Misrepresentation Act 1967, s. 2(2). cf G H Treital, *The Law of Contract*, 9th Ed., Sweet and Maxwell, London, 1995, 719.
[19] A warranty here is generally used, as in the cases cited, in the sense of guarantee, promise or representation, and not to denote a contractual term distinct from a condition. Consequently, a warranty may be treated, depending on all the circumstances, as becoming a term of the contract, and breach of such a term may give rise to damages or rescission of the contract.
[20] *Holliday v Morgan* (1858) 28 LJQB 9.
[21] *Drew v E* (1412) YB 13 Hen 4, fol 1B. From the wording of the Sale of Goods Act 1979, s. 14(2C)(b) the test appears to be subjective rather than objective. As such it is what the actual examination would reveal rather than what a reasonable examination would reveal.
[22] *Dorrington v Edwards* (1621) 2 Roll Rep 188, although the seller may be subject to a claim under the Misrepresentation Act 1967, s. 1(a) if the seller has made any statement of fitness.
[23] *Margetson v Wright* (1831) Bing at 603.
[24] Though the principle stated is based upon cases concerning the selling of horses, it is suggested that it would be equally applicable to the sale of other animals.

horse-dealers to give warranties. But a dealer will not be bound by an unauthorised warranty given by his employee outside the negotiation of the sale; for example, by something said by the employee when delivering the animal after sale. On the other hand, in the case of a private sale, a warranty given by his employee or agent without authority will not bind the seller unless the sale is at a fair or other public market.

A buyer sending an employee with instructions to accept a horse with a warranty has been held not to be bound if the employee accepts it without warranty, and the buyer could return the horse.

No particular form of words is necessary to make a warranty; the word "warranty" need not be used. A warranty covers the defects warranted against, whether known to the warrantor or not, unless special words are used to limit it to defects within the seller's knowledge.[25] To be effective the warranty must be given at the time of bargaining and sale and before the sale is completed.

If the word "warranty" is used, the warranty extends only to so much wording as is governed by the word. If the word is used alone without referring to any particular quality of the animal, it is taken to relate to its soundness only. The warranty may be limited in any way by the words used, and any quality may be warranted.

The fact that the price is a good or fair price for a sound animal is not a warranty of soundness. Statements of fact in an auctioneer's catalogue conferring additional value on the animal sold amount to warranties. Unless a warranty is worded as to extend to the future, it relates only to facts as they are at the time of the sale.

If at the time of sale an animal has any disease or defect which actually diminishes, or in its ordinary progress will diminish, its natural usefulness, it is not sound. The slightness of a disease, or the ease with which it is cured, may affect the amount which can be claimed for breach of warranty but does not affect the principle, unless so trifling as not to amount to unsoundness at all. A cough and temporary lameness have thus both been decided to be unsoundness.

---

[25] *Wood v Smith* (1829) 5 Man & Ry KB 124.

A breach of warranty does not affect the sale of the animal; ownership passes to the buyer notwithstanding. His remedy is to claim from, and if necessary sue in the courts, the seller for the amount of loss caused by the breach. The buyer should give notice to the seller of alleged breach of warranty as soon as possible, though this is not absolutely necessary.

Return of Animal on Breach of Condition

The Sale of Goods Act 1979 relating to acceptance has been modified by the Sale and Supply of Goods Act 1994 in relation to acceptance. This is significant because a buyer who has accepted an animal may not return the animal but may only claim damages. There are two situations in which the buyer will be deemed to have accepted the animal, namely, when the buyer intimates to the seller that he has accepted it, or when the animal has been delivered to the buyer and he does any act in relation to it which is inconsistent with the ownership of the seller.[26] Section 35(1) is subject a number of provisos, namely:

1. When the seller tends delivery of the animal to the buyer, he is bound on request to afford the buyer a reasonable opportunity of examining the animal for the purpose of ascertaining whether it is in conformity with the contract;[27]

2. Where the animal has been delivered to the buyer, and he has not previously examined it, he is deemed not to have accepted it until he has had a reasonable opportunity of examining it for the purpose:

    i.   of ascertaining whether it is in conformity with the contract, and

    ii. in the case of a contract for sale by sample, of comparing the bulk with the sample;[28]

3. Importantly for the consumer (i.e. a buyer not making a contract in the course of a business), the buyer cannot lose his right in 2.

---

[26] Sale of Goods Act 1979, s. 35(1).
[27] Sale of Goods Act 1979, s. 34.
[28] Sale of Goods Act 1979, s. 35(2).

above by agreement, waiver or otherwise.[29]

If a buyer has reserved a right to return the animal within a specified time, he may return it at any time within that period and is not bound to do so the moment he discovers the defect; so that if any injury happens to the animal while in his possession and without his fault, he is not liable for it and may still return the animal within the period.[30] If the animal under these circumstances becomes injured so that it cannot be returned within the specified time, the non-return by the buyer within that time will not bar a claim for breach of warranty.[31]

If an animal is sold with a condition that it may be returned within a specified period in case of unsuitability or for any other reason, and it dies in that period without the buyer's fault, the loss falls on the seller.[32]

An animal will be deemed to be accepted after the lapse of a reasonable time, during which the animal is retained by the buyer without him intimating that he has rejected it.[33] However, the Sale of Goods Act 1979 envisages a reasonable opportunity to have examined the animal and it would appear that if, say, a consumer purchases a trained Teckel, then the reasonable period of examination may extend into the open season for deer, if purchased during the close season, and it's tracking ability could not be reasonably assessed.[34]

Selling Diseased Animals

In a sale of diseased animals without any warranty or condition being given by the seller the maxim *"caveat emptor"* applies, unless the seller was guilty of fraudulent misrepresentation. The fact that the buyer suffers loss arising from a breach of statutory duty does not impute liability on the seller.[35]

---

[29] Sale of Goods Act 1979, s. 35(3).
[30] *Weston v Downes* (1778) 1 Doug KB 23; Cf *Head v Tattersall* (1871) LR7 Ed 7; *Hinchcliffe v Barwick* (1880) 5 Ex D 177
[31] *Chapman v Withers* (1888) 20 QBD 824; as for death of an animal before return see *Elphick v Barnes* (1880) 5 CPD 321.
[32] *Halsbury's Laws of England,* 4th Ed., Vol. 2 (Reissue), para. 226.
[33] Sale of Goods Act 1979, s. 35(4).
[34] Sale of Goods Act 1979, s. 35(2).
[35] *Halsbury's Laws of England,* 4th Ed., Vol. 2 (Reissue), para. 219.

B. AGISTMENT

A contract of agistment is a contract under which one man, the agister, takes another man's cattle, horses or other animals to graze on his land for reward, usually at a certain rate per week. It is implied that he will redeliver the animals to their owner on demand. Given that it does not confer an interest in land, the contract need not be in writing.

The agister is not an insurer[36] of the beasts taken by him, but he must take reasonable and proper care of them and is liable for injury caused to them by negligence[37] or neglect of such care.[38] However, if the animals' owner is aware of the dangerous state of a field in which the animals are to be pastured, the agister will not be liable for injury thereby caused. If the animals are stolen, even without the agister's fault, he is expected to use reasonable diligence to recover them; otherwise he may be liable for their loss.[39]

In the absence of special agreement, the agister has no right to keep the animals until paid (in law called "a lien"); his remedy is to sue their owner for the price of the grazing.[40] He has, however, sufficient property in the animals to entitle him to take legal action against others who improperly take or interfere with the animals.[41]

---

36 *Broadwater v Blot* (1817) Holt NP 547.
37 *Turner v Stallibrass* [1898] 1QB 56.
38 *Smith v Cook* (1875) 1 QBD 79. See *Halsbury's Laws of England,* 4th Ed., Vol. 2 (Reissue), para. 215 note 1.
39 *Coldman v Hill* [1919] 1 KB 443.
40 *Chapman v Allen* (1631) 79 ER 836; *Jackson v Cummins* (1839) 151 ER 145.
41 *Sutton v Buck* (1810) 127 ER 1094 (an agister may bring trover). Cf *Rooth v Wilson* (1817) 106 ER 22 (an agister might, as gratuitous bailee, maintain an action for negligence against a third party).

Chapter 3

MOVEMENT, IMPORT AND EXPORT OF ANIMALS

Introduction

Since the second edition, there has been a significant body of secondary legislation implementing European Community Directives, some relating to the harmonisation of trading within the Community, others relating to intra-Community transportation standards and others concerned with the prevention of diseases. The second edition dealt with the provisions of the Animal Health Act 1981 and the orders arising in an epidemiological manner. This chapter takes a more general approach highlighting the main Statutory Instruments that affect the movement of animals, whether within Great Britain or through trade with another country. Such legislation is difficult to compartmentalise into the chapter sub-headings, because of overlap in application. So, for instance, The Welfare of Animals (Transport) Order has been dealt with under the heading of Movement (Section A) because the Order applies to domestic transportation as much as it does with the movement of imported or exported animals. Given that much of the remaining legislation is applicable both to the importation and exportation of animals, these provisions have been grouped together and dealt with under Section B.

A. MOVEMENT OF ANIMALS

Generally

The movement of animals is regulated by the Animal Health Act 1981 and by many ministerial regulations made under powers given in that Act and its predecessors. The Act itself only deals directly with the obligation of railways to provide food and water to animals travelling on them whereas the regulations broadly fall into two groups. The first of the regulations is aimed at securing decent conditions, the supply of food and water and protection from unnecessary suffering whilst animals are travelling by road,

31

rail, sea or air. The second concerns the prevention of diseases of animals, either when disease is suspected or has occurred, of which instances are given on pages 203 to 206 and 208, through cleansing and disinfection of transport.

Welfare of Animals during Movement

This section will concentrate on the provisions of the Welfare of Animals (Transport) Order 1997 which came into force on 1st July 1997. The Order revokes and re-enacts with modifications the Welfare of Animals During Transport Order 1994, as amended, and other animal welfare legislation which, together with that Order, implemented Council Directive 91/628/EEC on the protection of animals during transport.[1]

The Order applies to the transportation[2] of:

a. cattle, sheep, pigs, goats and horses;[3]

b. poultry, domestic birds[4] and rabbits;

c. domestic dogs and cats;

d. all other mammals[5] and birds;

e. other vertebrate animals and cold blooded animals.[6]

Whilst there is a general prohibition against the transportation of

---

[1]   The Welfare of Animals (Transport) Order 1997, SI 1997/1480, explanatory note, as amended.

[2]   "Transport" means any movement of animals (including birds), effected by a means of transport, and includes loading and unloading the animals; whilst a "means of transport" means those parts (including detachable parts) of road vehicles, rail wagons, vessels and aircraft used for loading and carrying animals.

[3]   "Cattle" means all domestic animals of the bovine species; "sheep" means any domestic animal of the ovine species; "pigs" means all domestic animals of the porcine species; "goats" means all domestic animals of the carpine species; "horse" means a horse, pony, ass, hinny or mule: The Welfare of Animals (Transport) Order 1997, Art. 3(1).

[4]   "Poultry and domestic birds" means (a) domestic fowl; (b) domestic breeds of turkey, guinea-fowl, ducks, geese and quails; and (c) pheasants and partridges: The Welfare of Animals (Transport) Order 1997, Art. 3(1).

[5]   With the exception of man.

[6]   The Welfare of Animals (Transport) Order 1997, Art. 2(1). The definitions in footnotes 3 and 4 above extend the definition of animals and poultry in the Animal Health Act 1981, s. 87.

any animal in a way which causes or is likely to cause injury or unnecessary suffering to the animal,[7] the Order does not apply to transport of a non-commercial nature; nor the transportation of any individual animal accompanied by a natural person[8] who has responsibility for the animal during transport; nor to the transportation of pet animals accompanying their owner on a private journey.

There are detailed provisions relating to the competency of the transporter:[9] such person must be a fit person, namely one who has not committed an offence involving animal welfare, nor contravened any provision of the Order or any other order,[10] nor have been responsible for anything which would cause the Minister to revoke or suspend an authorisation made under the Order.[11] The transporter may not need authorisation for certain journeys, or may be authorised under a general authorisation (for which he need not apply) or he may be required to obtain a specific authorisation.[12] Which authorisation is appropriate is dependent upon the type of animals being transported and the length of the journey. Thus, for instance, from the 1st October 1997, specific authorisation from the Minister is required for the transportation of cattle, sheep, pigs, goats and horses where journey times exceed eight hours. Such authorisation may be granted to the transporter named in the application. From

---

[7] The Welfare of Animals (Transport) Order 1997, Art. 4(1).
[8] Presumably the term "natural person" is used to distinguish transportation by bodies corporate.
[9] "Transporter" means any natural or legal person transporting animals on his own account; or for the account of a third party; or by providing a third party with a means of transport of animals, where such transport is of a commercial nature and carried on in the course of a trade or business.
[10] I.e. under the Animal Health Act 1981, ss. 37, 38, 39.
[11] The Welfare of Animals (Transport) Order 1997, Sch. 9(2). The corollary is that any person deemed to be "unfit" could not be involved in the transportation of animals; either by engaging or being engaged by another authorised transporter.
[12] The distinction between the two types of authorisation is that the general authorisation does not name individual transporters, whilst the specific authorisation must be obtained by the transporter, upon application in the prescribed format. The general authorisation may be amended or revoked by publication in such manner as the Minister considers fit. Individual transporters may be excluded from the provisions of the general authorisation or further impositions may be added to the provisions of the general authorisation. The Minister must serve such modifications in writing on the transporter. The Minister may revoke or suspend the specific authorisation, either temporarily or permanently in the event of certain infringements: see further The Welfare of Animals (Transport) Order 1997, Sch. 9.

1st July 1998, the applicant must have obtained a qualification approved by the Minister or through an assessment of practical experience. Upon being issued with a specific authorisation, the transporter will no longer be permitted to carry out the transportation of animals under the general authorisation save for those covered by the specific authorisation. Indeed, if the specific authorisation is revoked or modified the transporter cannot revert to transporting animals under the general authorisation.[13] Where a specific authorisation is not granted, revoked or suspended the Minister is obliged to provide the transporter with written reasons, who in turn may make written representations to the Minister. The Minister may then nominate an appointed person who is specifically qualified to consider the reasons given by the Minister and any representations made by either the Minister or the transporter.[14]

Where the journey is less than 50 km, no authorisation is required. However, if the transporter is established in Great Britain, and the journey distance is greater than 50 km, then it will be dependent upon the type of animal being transported as to whether or not the general authorisation applies or whether the transporter must obtain a specific authorisation. Thus, for instance, if the consignment comprises cattle, sheep, pigs, goats or horses, but is less than eight hours travel by road then the general authorisation is applicable. If, however, the journey is greater than eight hours by road (or involves sea or air transport) specific authorisation is required. Likewise, if the transporter operates from outside of the European Union, specific authorisation is required from an appropriate authority of the Member State at which he first intends to transport vertebrate animals. If the transporter is established in another Member State, then the transporter must be authorised according to that Member State's[15] provisions.[16] In every case, the animals should be entrusted to a person who has had specific training or equivalent practical experience in moving animals of the relevant nature.

---

[13] See further The Welfare of Animals (Transport) Order 1997, Sch. 9(1).
[14] The Welfare of Animals (Transport) Order 1997, Sch. 9, 4–5.
[15] Of course, similar provisions to the Order should be implemented in all Member States, and if not then the Council Directive will have direct effect.
[16] The Welfare of Animals (Transport) Order 1997, Arts. 10, 11.

The transporter and those responsible for the welfare of animals during the journey[17] must have a prescribed framework of competency relating to the movement of animals, in addition to which he should also be able to identify and minimise stress in the animal the subject of his care. Similarly, when an animal becomes injured or unnecessarily suffers, the person responsible for welfare should know how to mitigate such injury or suffering; and when it is appropriate to transport such animals for veterinary treatment or slaughter.[18]

The Order recognises that animals should be fit[19] to travel and that suitable provisions should made for the care of the animals during the journey and on arrival at the place of destination.[20] Mammals may not be transported if they are likely to give birth during transport; or have given birth during the preceding 48 hours; or are new-born animals in which the navel has not completely healed.[21] Similarly, infant mammals and infant birds, within d. on page 32, which are not accompanied by their mother are not considered fit for their intended journey if they are incapable of feeding themselves.[22] It is clear from the foregoing that not only must the consignee consider the welfare of the animal at the commencement of the journey,[23] but he must also have regard to the type of journey being undertaken and the facilities for debarkation, rest, food and water at the animal's destination.

Despite these provisions certain animals may be transported

---

17 In the case of specialist transportation such as sea-going vessels and aircraft, the master, ship operator, or air carrier is also required to reach the prescribed competency.

18 See further The Welfare of Animals (Transport) Order 1997, Sch. 8.

19 Without limitation, an animal is not considered fit for its intended journey if it is ill, injured, infirm or fatigued, unless it is only slightly injured, ill, infirm or fatigued and the intended journey is not likely to cause it unnecessary suffering: The Welfare of Animals (Transport) Order 1997, Art. 6(2).

20 The Welfare of Animals (Transport) Order 1997, Art. 6(1). These provisions do not apply to animals transported while undergoing regulated procedures authorised under the Animals (Scientific Procedures) Act 1986 provided that they are not likely to be caused injury or unnecessary suffering by the intended journey: The Welfare of Animals (Transport) Order 1997, Art. 6(5).

21 The Welfare of Animals (Transport) Order 1997, Art. 6(2).

22 The Welfare of Animals (Transport) Order 1997, Art. 6(3).

23 Including the availability of liquid and foods at the commencement of the journey in appropriate accommodation for the animal: The Welfare of Animals (Transport) Order 1997, Art. 8(1).

provided that the animal is not subjected to injury or unnecessary suffering during transport;[24] for example unfit cattle, sheep, pigs, goats or horses requiring veterinary treatment or diagnosis, or slaughter, may be transported.[25] Similarly, if the animal falls ill or is injured during transport, the person in charge[26] of the animals is obliged to administer first aid to the animal, seek veterinary treatment and, if necessary, have the animal slaughtered in a humane manner.[27]

The provisions relating to journey times exceeding eight hours are shown in a tabular format in Appendix A and relate to the feeding, watering and resting of animals. Additionally, certain types of welfare transportation documentation must accompany the animals. Thus, a Route Plan[28] in prescribed form must accompany the animals if:

a. the journey is over 50 km; and

b. the animals being transported comprise cattle, sheep, pigs, goats or unregistered horses;[29] and

c. the journey is over eight hours in duration; and

d. the destination is to another Member State or third country.

---

[24] See footnote 2 on p. 32 for the meaning of "transport".

[25] The Welfare of Animals (Transport) Order 1997, Art. 6(6). Where the animal is likely to be dragged, pushed or mechanically lifted during transportation, a veterinary surgeon must supervise and arrange the transportation.

    Deer in velvet may not travel more than 50 km and special precautions must be taken to prevent them from injury or unnecessary suffering: The Welfare of Animals (Transport) Order 1997, Art. 6(7).

[26] Where the animal is transported by sea or air the master of the vessel or the commander of the aircraft; he is obliged to slaughter the animal in such a way as does not involve unnecessary suffering, having first regard to the availability of appropriate veterinary treatment or of landing the animal: The Welfare of Animals (Transport) Order 1997, Art. 7(2). This provision does not apply to horses and reference should be made to the Animal Health Act 1981, s. 46: The Welfare of Animals (Transport) Order 1997, Art. 7(3).

[27] The Welfare of Animals (Transport) Order 1997, Art. 7(1).

[28] Form ERA 20, available at the Department for Environment, Food and Rural Affairs website www.defra.gov.uk, or from the Animal Health Divisional Offices.

[29] DEFRA advise that all horses (including registered horses) require Route Plans to accompany them if being transported to or through Germany. There is a pilot scheme in place to test modes of electronic submission of Route Plans: Welfare of Animals (Transport) (Electronic Route Plans Pilot Scheme) (England) Order 2000, SI 2000/646.

An Animal Transport Certificate[30] (ATC) will be required to accompany the animals rather than a Route Plan if b. is not satisfied. Likewise, an ATC will be required if a. and b. are satisfied but not c. An ATC is not required if:

a. the journey is less than 50 km; and

b. the animals comprise:

    i. 50 or fewer poultry or domestic birds; or

    ii. any number of poultry or domestic birds on land occupied by their owner; or

    iii. animals other than cattle, sheep, pigs, goats, horses, poultry, or domestic birds; or

    iv. cattle, sheep, pigs, goats or horses to, from or within agricultural land in a vehicle owned by the occupier and with an internal length of up to 3.7 metres available to carry such animals.

If the consignment does not fall within the foregoing no documentation is required.

The Order further prescribes the means of transport or the receptacles used,[31] and, where the journey[32] is over 50 km, details the amount

---

[30] An ATC (available from local Animal Health Offices) is not prescribed, but sufficient information must be carried in order that an enforcement officer can readily identify: the name and address of the transporter; the name and address of the owner of the animals; the place that the animals were loaded and their final destination; the date and time that the first animal was loaded; the date and time of departure; the time and place for rest periods for domestic journeys over eight hours; other information that may be requested by the enforcement officer, such as the species and whether adult or unweaned, the number of animals and status (slaughter, breeding etc.), the date and time of unloading, the registration number of the vehicle: DEFRA Guidance, p. 24.

[31] The Welfare of Animals (Transport) Order 1997, Art. 4, Schs. 1–6.

[32] "Journey" means transport from the place of departure to place of destination. Whilst "place of departure" means, subject to certain exceptions (see The Welfare of Animals (Transport) Order 1997, Art. 3(2), (3) – relating to markets and approved assembly centres) the place at which the animal is first loaded on to a means of transport, or any place where animals are rested in the course of a journey; and "place of destination" means the place at which an animal is finally unloaded from a means of transport (see note 2 on p. 32), but excluding any transfer point or place where animals are rested in the course of a journey: The Welfare of Animals (Transport) Order 1997, Art. 3(1).

of space available to each animal in order to avoid unnecessary suffering or injury.[33] These provisions are lengthy and cannot be accommodated in a text such as this. The reader is referred to the Department for Environment, Food and Rural Affairs website for further guidance on the specifications for, amongst others, ramps, pen lengths, partition heights, transport containers and vehicles and stocking densities.[34]

At the end of the journey, for which see Appendix A, animals must be unloaded, fed and watered and rested for at least 24 hours.[35] Unless such rest is taken at the place of destination, then such rest must be taken at a staging post approved under Council Direction (EC) No 1255/97.[36]

Cleansing and Disinfection

To avoid the transmission of disease, the transporter of animals (or such person responsible for cleaning the means of transport)[37] is obliged to cleanse and disinfect the means of transport and associated equipment. Where hoofed animals, racing pigeons, and domestic fowls, turkeys, geese, ducks, guinea-fowls, quails, pigeons,

---

[33] Consideration must be given to the animal's weight, size and physical condition, the means of transport, weather conditions and the likely journey time: The Welfare of Animals (Transport) Order 1997, Art. 5, cf Chapter VI of Council Directive 91/628/EEC.

[34] See www.defra.gov.uk/animalh/welfare/transport. The material is also available from DEFRA Publications, ADMAIL 6000, London, SW1A 2XX.

[35] The Welfare of Animals (Transport) Order 1997, Sch. 7, Part 1, para. 4.

[36] The Welfare of Animals (Transport) Order 1997, Sch. 7, Part 1, para. 4A (added by The Welfare of Animals (Staging Points) Order 1998, SI 1998/2537). The 1998 order makes provision for the administration, execution and enforcement of Council Regulation (EC) No 1255/97 concerning Community criteria for staging points and amending route plans referred to in the Annex to Directive 91/628/ EEC. The principal provisions of the Order are (a) designate the appropriate Minister to be the competent authority for the purpose of approving staging points, and withdrawing, suspending and restoring such approvals, as necessary, in accordance with the Council Regulation (Art. 3); (b) confer a power on a veterinary inspector enabling him to serve a notice to protect the welfare of animals that are resting at a staging point in respect of which a notice has been served suspending or withdrawing its approval (Art. 4); create offences in respect of non-compliance of the Council Regulation for bodies corporate and incorporate (Arts. 5 and 6); and provide for the enforcement of the Order by local authorities (Art. 7).

[37] "Means of Transport" includes its fittings, its detachable parts and any containers (whether detachable or not) used with it: Transport of Animals (Cleansing and Disinfection) (England) (No 2) Order 2000, SI 2000/1618, Art. 2(1).

pheasants, partridges, and ratites reared or kept in captivity for breeding, the production of meat or eggs for consumption or for restoring supplies of game[38] are transported, the means of transport must be cleansed and disinfected in the prescribed manner.[39] Thus, at the commencement of the journey, or before the continuance of the journey, the means of transport must be cleansed and disinfected in accordance with Schedule 1 of the Order[40] where the means of transport has been soiled since last cleansed and disinfected or, if not cleansed and disinfected, would give rise to a risk of transmission of disease.[41] As soon as possible, and not less than 24 hours, after the journey is completed the means of transport and its equipment must be cleansed and disinfected in accordance with Schedule 1 of the Order or (in the case of containers) destroyed.[42] Additionally, any dead animals, soiled bedding and excreta must be removed as soon as possible along with any other material of animal origin and feedstuffs to which the animals had access. This material must be destroyed, or treated so as to remove the risk of transmission of disease, or disposed of so that animals do not have access to it, as applicable.[43]

The foregoing obligations do not apply to journeys made within a single farming enterprise in one ownership, horses used for recreational or sporting purposes, nor horses kept at stables licenced by the Jockey Club.[44] Similarly, animals transported between the same two points are exempt.[45] In these cases, and for all other

---

[38] Transport of Animals (Cleansing and Disinfection) (England) (No 2) Order 2000, Art. 3(1).

[39] For which see Transport of Animals (Cleansing and Disinfection) (England) (No 2) Order 2000, Sch. 1.

[40] I.e. Transport of Animals (Cleansing and Disinfection) (England) (No 2) Order 2000.

[41] Transport of Animals (Cleansing and Disinfection) (England) (No 2) Order 2000, Arts. 3(3), (4).

[42] Transport of Animals (Cleansing and Disinfection) (England) (No 2) Order 2000, Art. 3(2).

[43] Transport of Animals (Cleansing and Disinfection) (England) (No 2) Order 2000, Arts. 3(5), 5.

[44] Transport of Animals (Cleansing and Disinfection) (England) (No 2) Order 2000, Sch. 2, paras. 2, 3.

[45] Transport of Animals (Cleansing and Disinfection) (England) (No 2) Order 2000, Art. 4. But there is an obligation to cleanse and disinfect the means of transport within 24 hours of the last journey on which an animal is transported during that day (Art. 4(1)).

animals and birds not mentioned above, the person transporting or causing or permitting the transport of such animals must ensure that they are loaded on to a means of transport which has been cleansed, and where necessary disinfected, in accordance with Schedule 1 of the Order, and that dead animals, soiled litter and excreta are removed as soon as possible.[46]

The local authority undertakes the enforcement of these provisions.[47] Where an inspector considers that the provisions of this Order have not been complied with he may serve a notice on the persons appearing to him to be in charge of the means of transport compelling him so to do within a prescribed period and prohibit the use of means of transport until the requirements of the notice have been satisfied.[48] Where the provisions of the notice have not been fulfilled within the prescribed period, the inspector may arrange for the provisions of the notice to be complied with at the expense of the person on whom the notice was served.[49]

This Order does not apply in the case of:

a. non-commercial transport;

b. an individual animal accompanied by a person having responsibility for the animal during transport;

c. the transport of pet animals accompanying their owner on a private journey.[50]

B. INTRODUCTION TO IMPORTATION AND EXPORTATION OF ANIMALS

In addition to the welfare considerations necessary for the movement of animals within, through or between Member States, there has

---

[46] Transport of Animals (Cleansing and Disinfection) (England) (No 2) Order 2000, Art. 4(2).

[47] Transport of Animals (Cleansing and Disinfection) (England) (No 2) Order 2000, Art. 7.

[48] Transport of Animals (Cleansing and Disinfection) (England) (No 2) Order 2000, Art. 6.

[49] Transport of Animals (Cleansing and Disinfection) (England) (No 2) Order 2000, Art. 6(5).

[50] Transport of Animals (Cleansing and Disinfection) (England) (No 2) Order 2000, Art. 4(1).

been harmonisation of European veterinary inspection procedure. As a result of major changes to the provisions relating to the movement of animals within the European Community, it has been necessary to move away from checks at the point of entry or post import controls. The requirement for animals to be routinely checked at ports or airports has been replaced with an obligation for export animals to be checked and certificated free from disease before movement. Such harmonisation means that only those animals complying with Council Directives are transported from one Member State to another; whilst those entering from outside the EC must have originated from such countries as are approved by the European Community.

General Controls

The Animals and Animal Products (Import and Export) (England and Wales) Regulations 2000[51] implement (a) the procedure for Intra-Community and Third Country movement of such animals subject to EC Directives; and (b) some 95 Council and Commission Decisions and Directives dealing with, amongst others, veterinary checks on imports from third countries, species restrictions and conditions, slaughter of horses, temporary admission of registered horses, etc. and it is to these provisions that this section now turns. A person[52] contravening the Regulations or any notice served on him is guilty of an offence and liable on summary conviction to a fine, imprisonment not exceeding three months, or both; or on conviction on indictment, to a fine or to imprisonment not exceeding two years or both.[53]

The Regulations do not apply to veterinary checks on movements of pets (other than equidae) accompanied by and under the responsibility of a natural person, where such movements are not the subject of a commercial transaction.[54] All other animals and animal products are subject to the provisions of the Regulations,

---

[51] The Animals and Animal Products (Import and Export) (England and Wales) Regulations 2000, SI 2000/1673 as amended by SI 2000/2524 and SI 2000/2900.

[52] A person include a body corporate, its director, manager, secretary or other similar officer of the body corporate: SI 2000/1673, Reg. 32.

[53] SI 2000/1673, Reg. 33.

[54] SI 2000/1673, Reg. 2.

which are enforced by the local authority[55] or, where the Minister[56] directs, in particular cases, discharged by the Minister. Whilst the Regulations deal with animal products, the emphasis below is on the exportation, movement and importation of live animals.

Exports

Animals[57] which are subject to EC Directives or measures referred to in Part I of Schedule 3[58] may not be exported nor consigned for export to another Member State unless they comply with the relevant Directive. If the animal was acquired through an assembly centre, the Minister must have approved the centre. If prescribed by the Directive relevant to the animal, the animal may be required to be accompanied by an export health certificate signed by a veterinary inspector (or where specified in a Directive or other measure, signed by a veterinary surgeon nominated by the exporter) or be accompanied by details of any notification of a disease on an appropriate holding form.[59] Where an inspector has cause to suspect that a person in charge of the animals intends to export them in contravention of the Regulations he may, by notice served on the consignor, his representative or person in charge of the animals, prohibit the exportation or require that the animals are taken to such place as prescribed in the notice and dealt with in such manner as specified.[60] An inspector may seize the animals where the person on whom the notice was served fails to comply with the terms of notice.[61]

---

[55] "Local authority" means each London Borough (except in relation to live imports when "local authority" means the Common Council), unitary authority, metropolitan district or non-metropolitan county, the council of that borough, unitary authority, district or county, and in Wales, the council of each county or county borough: SI 2000/1673, Reg. 1.

[56] "The Minister" means the Minister for the Department for Environment, Food and Rural Affairs or in the case of Wales, the National Assembly for Wales: SI 2000/1673, Reg. 1.

[57] The animals described in the Schedule are bovine and swine, sheep, goats, horses, poultry and hatching eggs, fish and other animals subject to the Directives set out in SI 2000/1673, Sch. 3, para. 10.

[58] Sch. 3 Part 1, para. 1 has been amended by SI 2000/2524 and SI 2000/2900. Sch. 3 Part 1 is reproduced in Appendix B at the end of this book.

[59] SI 2000/1673, Reg. 5(1). See also Art. 5(4) which prohibits the export to another member State of any animal subject to the provisions of Articles 7, 9 and 10 of Council Directive 92/65/EEC, unless the animal originates from a registered holding and the owner or person in charge of the holding gives an undertaking in accordance with Article 4 of 92/65/EEC.

[60] SI 2000/1673, Reg. 5(2).

[61] SI 2000/1673, Reg. 5(3).

Imports

As with the exportation of animals, no animal in free circulation within the European Community may be imported from another Member State, unless it complies with the Directive, measure or any additional measure specified in Part I of Schedule 3.

Where an animal has originated from outside the European Community it must be accompanied by the certificate of examination and the authenticated copy of the original health certificate issued at the point of importation into the European Community.[62] Animals imported directly into England and Wales from outside the European Community must enter into the country through the prescribed border inspection posts.[63] Additionally, the person importing the animals must give one working day's notice in writing to the official veterinarian of the border inspection post of his intention to so do, specifying the number, nature and estimated time of arrival of the animals.[64] The importer or his agent will be directed to convey the animals to an examination area or, if applicable,[65] quarantine centre. The animals may not be moved until:

a. such times as all necessary veterinary checks have been carried out by the official veterinarian; and

b. he has issued a certificate in prescribed format;[66] and

c. an officer of Customs and Excise has authorised the removal of the animals; and[67]

---

[62] SI 2000/1673, Regs. 24, 25. The purpose of such certification is to ensure that all checks required under Council Directive 91/496/EEC have been carried out in another Member State.

[63] SI 2000/1673, Reg. 17(1). If animals are imported at any place other than shown in the table, an inspector may give notice to the person in charge of the consignment to detain and isolate the animals. Following inspection by a veterinary inspector the animals may be released from restriction or be required to be destroyed (Reg. 17(2),(3)).

[64] SI 2000/1673, Reg. 18(1).

[65] By a Directive or other measure in SI 2000/1673, Sch. 5 or the animal health conditions applicable for such animals.

[66] I.e. a certificate in the form required under Council Directive 91/496/EEC.

[67] The officer must be presented with the certificate previously mentioned before authorising the release of the animals: SI 2000/1673, Reg. 18(4).

d. and the official veterinarian is satisfied that all chargeable veterinary checks have been paid for, and where relevant appropriate deposits have been lodged.[68]

Table of Border Inspection Posts[69]

Border inspection post	Animals which may be imported
East Midlands Airport	Tropical fish only
Bristol Port (Royal Porthbury Dock)*	Ungulates** other than registered equidae as defined in Council Directive 90/426/EEC (as amended) on health conditions governing the movement of equidae and their import from third countries.
Heathrow Airport	All animals
Immingham Port *	Registered equidae as defined in Council Directive 90/426/EEC (as amended) on health conditions governing the movement of equidae and their import from third countries
Luton Airport*	Ungulates**
Manchester Airport	Cats, dogs, rodents, lagomorphs, live fish, reptiles and birds other than ratites
Stansted Airport	Ungulates**
Tilbury Port*	Zoo animals and ungulates**

* Not border inspection posts for any species of animals specified in the Rabies (Importation of Dogs, Cats and Other Mammals) Order 1974.

**Ungulates include registered equidae as defined in Council Directive 90/426/EEC, as amended.

It will be appreciated from the foregoing that, for intra-community import, provided the animals are appropriately certified free from disease they are relatively unencumbered in their movement,

---

68   SI 2000/1673, Reg. 19. For fees see the Animals (Third Country Imports) Charges Regulations 1997, SI 1997/639.
69   SI 2000/1673, Sch. 2.

whereas animals from outside the European Community are isolated before certification at border inspection posts or quarantine centres. Accordingly, the treatment of illegal consignments is treated differently dependent upon whether the animal has been imported from another Member State or from outside the European Community. The principal distinction[70] is that, in the former case, where a veterinary inspector knows of or suspects the presence of agents responsible for a scheduled disease,[71] or of a zoonosis, or any other hazardous disease, whether to humans or animals, he may by giving notice to the person appearing to him to be in charge of the animals require that they are immediately detained at such place as the inspector may nominate, or without delay have the animals slaughtered and destroyed in accordance with the notice; whereas in the latter case, the veterinary inspector may, upon serving notice to the person in charge of the animals, require that the animals are appropriately sheltered, watered and fed, placed in isolation or quarantine, or re-despatched outside the territory of the European Community.[72]

The provisions relating to the import of animals from outside the European Community extend beyond the border inspection post. Accordingly, where a veterinary inspector knows or suspects that import conditions have not been complied with or there is doubt as to the identity of an animal, he may carry out such checks as he deems necessary. If those checks confirm that import conditions have not been complied with then the provisions just mentioned may be imposed.[73] As for those animals which may have been

---

[70] Where there are residue levels which do not comply with the Animals and Animal Products (Examination for Residues and Maximum Residue Limits) Regulations 1997, the animals may be detained for observation, slaughter or return to the Member State of despatch: SI 2000/1673, Reg. 13(2). Where there is an irregularity in the documentation the consignor, agent or person in charge of the animals has seven days, from the date of notice being served by an inspector, in which to rectify the matter: SI 2000/1673, Reg. 13(3).

[71] The diseases are: foot and mouth, classical swine fever, African swine fever, swine vesicular disease, Newcastle disease, rinderpest, peste des petits ruminants, vesicular stomatitis, blue tongue, African horse sickness, viral equine encephalomyelitis, Teschen disease, avian influenza, sheep and goat pox, lumpy skin disease, Rift valley fever, contagious bovine pleuropneumonia, bovine spongiform encephalopathy, infectious haematopoietic necrosis: SI 2000/1673, Sch. 4.

[72] SI 2000/1673, Reg. 22.

[73] SI 2000/1673, Reg. 23.

imported into England and Wales from another Member State, a veterinary inspector may inspect such animals to ensure that the relevant provisions of the Directive or other measures have been complied with.[74]

In both cases, an animal imported for slaughter must be slaughtered without undue delay or, where there has been delay, within the prescribed period of a notice served by an inspector.[75]

Remaining Provisions – Intra-Community Trade

If required to do so by notice served on him by the Minister, a dealer[76] must register as such with the Minister and is required to give undertakings to comply with the Regulations. Additionally, he is required to keep a record[77] of all deliveries of animals and, where a consignment is divided up or subsequently marketed, of the subsequent destination of the animals.[78] Where the dealer trades in cattle and pigs, he must keep more detailed records and ensure that he only imports and exports animals that are identified and come from herds[79] that are officially free of tuberculosis, brucellosis and leucosis. Such a dealer will be allocated a registration number, as will the premises from which he operates.[80]

Consignees are under a duty not to accept a consignment of animals, other than registered horses accompanied by an appropriate identification document,[81] unless the importer or consignee has notified to an authorised inspector in writing, at least 24 hours in advance, the nature of the consignment, its anticipated date of arrival and the place of destination. The consignee must retain the certificates accompanying animals for 12 months from the date of arrival.[82]

---

[74] SI 2000/1673, Reg. 10.
[75] SI 2000/1673, Reg. 6(1), (2) in respect of intra-Community trade and Reg. 16(4) in respect of third countries. An inspector may seize animals which have not been slaughtered within the prescribed notice period: Regs. 6(3), 16(5) respectively.
[76] "Dealer" means any person who buys and sells animals commercially either directly or indirectly, who has a regular turnover of these animals and who within 30 days of purchasing animals resells or relocates them from the first premises to other premises not within his ownership: SI 2000/1673, Reg. 1.
[77] The records must be kept for 12 months from the arrival of the consignment.
[78] SI 2000/1673, Reg. 8.
[79] "Herd" means an animal or group of animals kept as an epidemiological unit.
[80] SI 2000/1673, Reg. 8(4), Sch. 3.
[81] The document is in prescribed format: Council Directive 90/427/EEC.
[82] SI 2000/1673, Reg. 11.

Destructive Animals

Under the Destructive Imported Animals Act 1932 the Minister may make orders prohibiting, either absolutely or except under licence, the import into and the keeping within Great Britain[83] of musk-rats (*fiber zibethicus*) or musquash (*ondetra zibethica*).[84] The Minister may make orders of the same effect applying to any animals of any non-indigenous mammalian species[85] if he is satisfied that by reason of their destructive habits it is desirable to prohibit or control their import or keeping in this country and to destroy any which may be at large.[86]

The Minister may at his discretion grant licences authorising the importing and keeping of these kinds of animals[87] in accordance with the terms of the licences and regulations which he may make. Licences are renewable but may be revoked on failure to comply with those terms or if the holder is convicted of an offence under the 1932 Act.[88]

A person wishing to keep these kinds of animals for exhibition, scientific research or other exceptional purposes may apply to the Minister to grant him a special licence (revocable at any time) authorising him to import and keep a limited number of the animals in the manner and upon the conditions described in the licence.[89]

A person commits an offence if:

a. He imports, or attempts to import, these kinds of animals at a time when their import is absolutely prohibited by order;

b. He imports, or attempts to import, such animals without a

---

[83] "Great Britain" means England, Wales and Scotland and excludes the Channel Islands and the Isle of Man.

[84] Destructive Imported Animals Act 1932, s. 1(1).

[85] "Non-indigenous mammalian species" means a mammalian species which on 17th March 1932 was not established in a wild state in Great Britain or had only become so established during the preceding 50 years; but any species commonly kept in Great Britain on that date in a domesticated state is excluded from the definition: (Destructive Imported Animals Act 1932, s. 10(2)).

[86] Destructive Imported Animals Act 1932, s. 10(1).

[87] I.e. any kind of animal in respect of which an order has been made as described above.

[88] Destructive Imported Animals Act 1932, s. 3.

[89] Destructive Imported Animals Act 1932, s. 8(1).

covering licence at a time when their import is prohibited except under licence;

c. Being the holder of a licence, he acts in contravention of any term of it or of the Minister's regulations;

d. He obstructs an officer of, or a person authorised by or employed by or on behalf of, the Minister's department in the execution of his duties[90] under the 1932 Act.[91]

On conviction of an offence described at a., b. or c. above, the court may order the animals concerned to be forfeited and destroyed.[92] A police officer and any person authorised by the Minister may seize animals when they have reason to believe that an offence under a. or b. above has been committed with respect to them. They may detain them until prosecution of the offence is completed or it is decided that a prosecution is unlikely.[93]

Under the order-making powers described on page 47, the import and keeping of musk-rats or musquash,[94] grey squirrels (*sciurus carolinensis*)[95] and rabbits other than the European rabbit (*oryctolagus cuniculus*)[96] are absolutely prohibited; i.e. no licence can be granted. The import of mink and coypu, which was previously controlled by general licences issued by the Minister, is now governed by the Rabies (Importation, etc.) Order 1974.[97]

The provisions described above relate principally to the import of destructive animals. Other provisions (mainly about their keeping) will be found on pages 233 to 237.

---

[90] Such duties will presumably include the seizure of animals described later in the text above.

[91] Destructive Imported Animals Act 1932, s. 6(1).

[92] Destructive Imported Animals Act 1932, s. 6(1).

[93] Destructive Imported Animals Act 1932, s. 6(2).

[94] Musk-Rats (Prohibition of Importation and Keeping) Order 1933 (S.R. & O. 1933/106).

[95] Grey Squirrels (Prohibition of Importation and Keeping) Order 1937 (S.R. & O. 1937/478).

[96] Non-indigenous Rabbits (Prohibition of Importation and Keeping) Order 1954 (SI 1954/927).

[97] For the provisions of this Order, see pp. 55-58 and 271-273. Coypus are included in the list on p. 272 because they belong to the Order *"Rodenila"*.

Endangered Species

Great Britain is signatory to the international treaty concluded at the Convention on International Trade in Endangered Species of Wild Fauna and Flora (CITES) in Washington in 1973. CITES is protectionist and regulates international trade in species of wild animals and plants, including parts of those species and, subject to certain exceptions, further prohibits trade in those species that are threatened with extinction. The Treaty is also an international trade agreement, in that it controls the trade of those species which are not as yet threatened by extinction by the use of a permit system. Additionally, there is a mechanism for individual countries to introduce legislation regulating the export of species not covered by the Treaty.

The animals covered by the Treaty are divided into three categories. Appendix I prohibits the trade of "all species threatened with extinction" and requires an export licence and an import licence from the respective States. The Berne criteria have since amended the prohibition to those species which are "currently threatened with extinction", or where the identification of a particular genus is difficult, or where one genus is either seriously declining in number or threatened with extinction. Export permits may be obtained only where the species has been lawfully obtained, where trade will not be detrimental to the species and there are appropriate transport facilities. An import licence can only be granted if it is not detrimental to the species, there is appropriate housing, and the trade should not be primarily for commercial purposes.[98]

Appendix II does not require the trader to apply for an import licence, an export licence will suffice – which has to be presented to the importing authorities for prior approval.[99] Those species listed in Appendix III are those which individual States are prepared to have regulated and require co-operation from fellow signatories for protection.

In addition to the administration of export and import permits, the Treaty requires that detailed public records are kept on all trade authorised under CITES and for those records to be regularly submitted to the Secretariat based in Geneva.

---

98 CITES, Art 3.
99 CITES, Art 4.

Article XIV(1) states that the provisions of CITES do not affect the right of the State to introduce stricter measures than are required by the convention. Thus, Great Britain prohibits the import of species listed in Appendix II without an import permit, even though CITES only requires a permit from the State of export. EC Regulations 338/1997 and 939/1997 give the provisions of CITES legal effect throughout the EC. The combined consequence of the EC Regulations is to identify species requiring protection including those listed in the appendices to CITES, together with requirements relating the standardisation of forms, certificates, and labels used for all imports and exports both within the EC and worldwide; and the restrictions of the movements and trade in such animals with the EC and worldwide. The Regulations have four annexes which have extended the CITES species. Thus, Annex A includes all Appendix I species, together with almost 200 Appendix II and III species, and some non-CITES species. Annex B includes the remaining species not in Annex A, but subject to individual/country bans, together with over 50 Appendix III and non-CITES species. Annex C includes approximately 200 Appendix III species, while Appendix D contains non-CITES specimens imported into the European Community in such numbers as to warrant monitoring by a simple notification procedure.[100]

At a domestic level, the Endangered Species (Import and Export) Act 1976[101] initially gave effect to the CITES provisions, but much of this has been superseded by EC law.[102] The Endangered Species (Import and Export) Act 1976 (Amendment) Order 1996[103] resulted in the removal of import and export controls of non-CITES species, whilst the Endangered Species (Import and Export) Act 1976 (Amendment) Regulations 1996[104] removed the import and

---

[100] Michael Bradley Taylor (Ed.) *Wildlife Crime, A Guide to Wildlife Law Enforcement in the United Kingdom* 1996, London, The Stationery Office, p. 116. See also http://europa.eu.int/en/comm/dg11/cites/citeshome.htm and www.ukcites.gov.uk for detailed guidance on European Community wildlife trade regulations.

[101] As amended by the Wildlife and Countryside Act 1981; Customs and Excise Management Act 1979; Criminal Justice Act 1982; SI 2677/1996 and SI 2684/1996.

[102] Initially by Council Regulations (EEC) 3626/82 (as amended by (EEC) No 558/95) and 3418/83 and more recently, by EC 338/97 and 939/97.

[103] SI 1996/2677.

[104] SI 1996/2684.

export controls of species under CITES which are now implemented by EC Wildlife Trade Regulation 338/1997. The EC Regulations require Member States to introduce enforcement controls; in the United Kingdom these controls are contained in the Control of Trade in Endangered Species (Enforcement) Regulations 1997 and it is to these Regulations that this section now turns.

Where any specimen[105] is being imported or exported or has been imported or brought to any place for the purpose of being exported, which is subject to the permit or notification requirements of EC Regulation 338/97, a person commissioned by the Commissioners of Customs and Excise, or a person authorised by them, may require any person possessing or having control of that specimen to furnish proof that its importation or exportation is or was not unlawful by virtue of the said regulation or, as the case may be, EC Regulation 939/97. Until such proof is furnished the specimen may be detained under the Customs and Excise Management Act 1979 and, if such proof is not furnished to the satisfaction of the Commissioners, the specimen may be forfeited.[106]

A person is guilty of an offence if he knowingly or recklessly:

a. makes a statement or representation which is false in a material particular;[107]

---

[105] "Specimen" means any plant or animal, whether alive or dead, of the species listed of Annexes A to D, or any part derived thereof, whether or not contained in other goods, as well as any other goods which appear from an accompanying document, the packaging or mark or label, or from any other circumstances, to be or to contain parts or derivatives of animals or plants of these species, unless such parts or derivatives are specifically exempted from the provisions of EC Regulation 338/97 or from the provisions relating to the Annex in which the species concerned is listed by means of an indication to the effect in the Annex concerned.

A specimen will be considered to be a specimen of a species listed in Annexes A to D if it is, or is part of or derived from, an animal or plant at least one of whose "parents" is of a species so listed. In cases where the "parents" of such animal or plant are of species listed in different Annexes, or of species only one of which is listed, the provisions of the more restrictive Annex shall apply.

"Species" means a species, sub-species or population thereof, and "population" means a biologically or geographically distinct total number of individuals: EC Regulation 338/97, Art. 2.

[106] The Control of Trade in Endangered Species (Enforcement) Regulations 1997, SI 1997/1372, Reg. 5.

[107] The Control of Trade in Endangered Species (Enforcement) Regulations 1997, SI 1997/1372, Reg. 3(1)(a).

b. furnishes a document or information which is false in a material manner;[108]

c. uses or furnishes a false, falsified or invalid permit or certificate or one altered without authorisation for any purpose in connection with EC Regulation 338/97 or 939/97;[109]

d. makes an import notification whish is false in a material particular;[110]

A person is guilty of an offence if he knowingly:

a. falsifies or alters any permit or certificate;[111]

b. uses a permit, certificate or import notification for any specimen other than for which it was issued;[112]

c. uses a specimen of a species listed in Annex A of EC Regulation 338/97 otherwise than in accordance with the authorisation given at the time of issue of the import permit, or subsequently;[113]

d. contravenes any condition or requirement of a permit or certificate issued in accordance with EC Regulation 338/97 or 939/97.[114]

Each of the foregoing offences carry on summary conviction a fine or imprisonment not exceeding three months, or both; and on indictment a fine, or imprisonment for not more than two years or both.

Where an import permit or any certificate issued in accordance

---

[108] The Control of Trade in Endangered Species (Enforcement) Regulations 1997, SI 1997/1372, Reg. 3(1)(b).

[109] The Control of Trade in Endangered Species (Enforcement) Regulations 1997, SI 1997/1372, Reg. 3(1)(c).

[110] The Control of Trade in Endangered Species (Enforcement) Regulations 1997, SI 1997/1372, Reg. 3(2).

[111] The Control of Trade in Endangered Species (Enforcement) Regulations 1997, SI 1997/1372, Reg. 4(1).

[112] The Control of Trade in Endangered Species (Enforcement) Regulations 1997, SI 1997/1372, Reg. 4(2).

[113] The Control of Trade in Endangered Species (Enforcement) Regulations 1997, SI 1997/1372, Reg. 4(3).

[114] The Control of Trade in Endangered Species (Enforcement) Regulations 1997, SI 1997/1372, Reg. 6(1).

with EC Regulation 338/97 in respect of a live specimen of a species listed in Annex A specifies an address at which the specimen must be kept, he shall be guilty of an offence under these Regulations, and Article 9 of EC Regulation 338/97, if he causes or permits the specimen to be transferred from that address without prior written authorisation from the Secretary of State.[115]

If a person transports any specimen for sale[116] listed in Annex A, not within the terms of any certificate or general derogation granted pursuant to Article 8 of EC Regulation 338/97,[117] he shall be guilty of an offence,[118] unless he proves to the satisfaction of the court that at the time the alleged offence was committed he had no reason to believe that the specimen was a specimen so listed.[119]

If a person transports any specimen for sale[120] listed in Annex B which has been imported or acquired unlawfully[121] he shall be guilty of an offence,[122] unless he proves to the satisfaction of the court that:

a. at the time the alleged offence was committed he had no reason to believe that the specimen was a specimen so listed; or[123]

b. at the time when the specimen first came into his possession he

---

[115] The Control of Trade in Endangered Species (Enforcement) Regulations 1997, SI 1997/1372, Reg. 7(b). He will similarly be guilty of an offence if he keeps that specimen at premises other than the specified address or location without the prior written authorisation from the Secretary of State: Reg. 7(b). Note that, at the time of publication, the functions of the Secretary of State were being transferred to the Minister for the Department for Environment, Food and Rural Affairs.

[116] Or purchases, offers to purchase, acquires for commercial purposes, displays to the public for commercial purposes, uses for commercial gain, sells, keeps for sale, or offers for sale any such specimen.

[117] The Control of Trade in Endangered Species (Enforcement) Regulations 1997, SI 1997/1372, Reg. 8(3).

[118] The Control of Trade in Endangered Species (Enforcement) Regulations 1997, SI 1997/1372, Reg. 8(1).

[119] The Control of Trade in Endangered Species (Enforcement) Regulations 1997, SI 1997/1372, Reg. 8(4).

[120] Or purchases, offers to purchase, acquires for commercial purposes, displays to the public for commercial purposes, uses for commercial gain, sells, keeps for sale, or offers for sale any such specimen.

[121] The Control of Trade in Endangered Species (Enforcement) Regulations 1997, SI 1997/1372, Reg. 8(3).

[122] The Control of Trade in Endangered Species (Enforcement) Regulations 1997, SI 1997/1372, Reg. 8(2).

[123] The Control of Trade in Endangered Species (Enforcement) Regulations 1997, SI 1997/1372, Reg. 8(4).

made such enquiries as in the circumstances were reasonable in order to ascertain whether it was imported carefully; and

c. at the time the alleged offence was committed, he had no reason to believe that the specimen was imported or acquired unlawfully.[124]

The Regulations grant powers of entry to a constable, upon application to a justice of the peace, for the purposes of searching property and/or attaining blood samples from any specimen in order to determine the species identity or ancestry, along with powers of seizure.[125] There is a general authority for an authorised person to enter and inspect premises for verifying information, ascertaining whether any live specimens are at the specified address and for ensuring that any conditions of a permit or certificate are being complied with.[126]

Where a person[127] is convicted of an offence under these Regulations the court must order the forfeiture of any specimen or other thing in respect of which the offence was committed and may order the forfeiture of any vehicle, including aircraft, hovercraft or boats, equipment or other things which were used to commit the offence.[128]

To assist in discovering the illegal import of animals, the Secretary of State may make orders[129] prohibiting and regulating the import of live animals by certain means.

As a result of amendments to the Endangered Species (Import and Export) Act 1976, by the Statutory Instruments referred to in the footnotes above,[130] it was necessary for the Secretary of State to

---

[124] The Control of Trade in Endangered Species (Enforcement) Regulations 1997, SI 1997/1372, Reg. 8(5). Reg. 8(6) gives guidance as to what the court will construe as appropriate enquiries.

[125] The Control of Trade in Endangered Species (Enforcement) Regulations 1997, SI 1997/1372, Reg. 9(1), (2), (3), 10.

[126] The Control of Trade in Endangered Species (Enforcement) Regulations 1997, SI 1997/1372, Reg. 9(4), (5).

[127] Which includes a body corporate.

[128] The Control of Trade in Endangered Species (Enforcement) Regulations 1997, SI 1997/1372, Reg. 11.

[129] The Control of Trade in Endangered Species (Designation of Ports of Entry) Regulations 1985.

[130] See notes 103 and 104 on p. 50.

implement the Import of Seal Skins Regulations 1996[131] to give effect to the EC Seals Directive. The effect is to prohibit the commercial importation of raw, tanned or dressed furskins[132] of certain species of seal[133] and articles made wholly or partly of furskins of such seals, save for products resulting from traditional hunting by the Inuit people.[134]

Restrictions to Prevent the Introduction of Rabies

For the purpose of preventing the introduction of rabies into Great Britain[135] the Minister made an order in 1974[136] which controls the landing[137] in this country of any animal belonging to the ten orders of mammals which are listed in Parts I and II of Appendix C at the end of this book.

All animals[138] which are subject to the Council Directives and other measures contained in Schedule 3 Part I and Schedule 5 of the Animals and Animal Products (Import and Export) (England and Wales) Regulations 2000 which are imported by way of trade and can be shown to have been born on the holding of origin and kept in captivity since birth are exempt from the provisions of this

---

[131] SI 1996/2686.

[132] Including furskins of such seals assembled in plates, crosses or similar forms: Import of Seal Regulations 1996, SI 1996/2686, Reg. 2(1)(a).

[133] Namely, whitecoat pups of the species Phoca (Pagaphilus) groenlandica (harp seal) or pups of the species Cystophora cristata (hooded seal): Import of Seal Regulations 1996, SI 1996/2686, Art. 2

[134] Import of Seal Regulations 1996, SI 1996/2686, Arts. 1, 3.

[135] For meaning of "Great Britain", see note 83 on p. 47.

[136] The Rabies (Importation of Dogs, Cats and Other Mammals) Order 1974, SI 1974/2211. There is a maximum fine of £1,000 for contravention of the order (Animal Health Act 1981, s. 75(2)(3)).

[137] An animal is deemed to have been landed immediately it is unloaded or taken out of, or in other manner leaves or escapes from, a vessel, vehicle or aircraft, or immediately it crosses the frontier through the Channel Tunnel: Rabies (Importation of Dogs, Cats and Other Mammals) Order 1974, Art. 2 as amended by the Channel Tunnel (Amendment of Agriculture, Fisheries and Food Import Legislation) Order 1990, SI 1990/2371 and, in relation to the Channel Tunnel, the animal is deemed to have landed immediately it is brought into a control zone in France or Belgium: Art. 2(2) amended by SI 1993/1813, SI 1994/1405. References to "vessel" include hovercraft: Animal Health Act 1981, s. 90 and the Hovercraft (Application of Enactments) Order 1972, SI 1972/971.

[138] Animals, here, excludes all carnivores, primates and bats: the Animals and Animal Products (Import and Export) (England and Wales) Regulations 2000, SI 2000/1673, Reg. 34, Sch. 6. (as amended by SI 2000/2524 and SI 2000/2900).

Order.[139] Likewise, the Order does not apply in relation to pet cats and dogs brought into England in accordance with the provisions of the Pet Travel Scheme (Pilot Arrangements) (England) Order 1999.[140]

In all other circumstances, the Order prohibits the landing of those animals in Great Britain except under the authority of, and in accordance with the conditions of, a licence previously granted by the Minister.[141] However, licences are not needed for animals coming from Northern Ireland, the Irish Republic, the Channel Islands and the Isle of Man if they have not been outside the British Isles in the preceding six months. Nor is a licence necessary for an animal that is landed at a British port or airport for the purpose of re-export from the same port or airport within 48 hours, although in this case the animal is subjected to stringent controls on its movement, detention and isolation.

Other than in exceptional circumstances,[142] animals may only be licensed to be landed at the following points of entry:

Airports	*Ports*	*Channel Tunnel*
Birmingham	Dover, Eastern Docks	Cheriton
Edinburgh	Harwich, Parkeston Quay	
Gatwick	Hull	
Glasgow	Portsmouth	
Heathrow	Southampton	
Leeds		
Manchester		
Norwich		
Prestwick		

---

[139] The Animals and Animal Products (Import and Export) (England and Wales) Regulations 2000, SI 2000/1673, Reg. 34, Sch. 6 (as amended by SI 2000/2524 and SI 2000/2900).

[140] SI 1999/3443, as amended by SIs 2000/1641, 2001/6 extending the provisions of Art. 4 and inserting Arts. 4A and 4B in the Rabies (Importation of Dogs, Cats and Other Mammals) Order 1974, SI 1974/2211.

[141] Rabies (Importation of Dogs, Cats and Other Mammals) Order 1974, Art. 4(3), SI 1974/2211.

[142] In exceptional circumstances the Minister may license an animal to be landed at another port or airport. In addition, if the ship or aircraft is diverted in the interest of safety, or in other exceptional circumstances, the animal may be landed at a port or airport different from that for which it is licensed if the prior written authority of a Ministry inspector is given.

The animals must be moved as soon as practicable after landing to authorised quarantine premises.[143] All kinds of animals, except vampire bats, are quarantined for six months. Offspring born in quarantine may be released 15 days after they have been weaned if both the dam and the offspring are certified to be healthy. Vampire bats and their progeny born here are quarantined for life. The expenses of maintaining animals in quarantine must be borne by their owners.[144]

Any domestic cat or dog which is brought into England on or after 17th January 2000, and which is taken into quarantine, whether or not the animal failed some or all of the conditions prescribed by the Pet Travel Scheme (Pilot Arrangements) (England) Order 1999, may by Ministerial order be released provided that he is satisfied that:

a. it has been microchipped, vaccinated and blood tested in accordance with the 1999 Order; and

b. a veterinary surgeon has treated it against *echinoccus multiloculais*[145] and ticks[146] at least 24 hours before the animal is released; and

c. the animal has not been out of the British Isles, the Republic of Ireland or the countries and territories listed in Schedule 2 of the 1999 Order; or

d. in the case of an animal from countries or territories listed in Schedule 6 of the 1999 Order, it arrived in a sealed container, with its seal intact.[147]

---

[143] I.e. premises approved under licence from the Minister.

[144] An authorised carrying agent, being in charge of an animal on landing, may also be liable for their expenses (*City of London Corporation v British Caledonian Airways* (1980)).

[145] The active ingredient in treating *echinococcus multilocularis* must be praziquantel.

[146] If the animal has been in Cyprus, Malta or one of the countries or territories in Schedule 6 of the 1999 Order the treatment against ticks must contain fipronil as the active ingredient.

[147] Rabies (Importation of Dogs, Cats and Other Mammals) Order 1974, Art. 5A, as substituted by The Pet Travel Scheme (Pilot Arrangements) (England) (Amendment) Order 2001, SI 2001/6.

During quarantine every dog and cat,[148] the subject of this Order, must at its owner's expense be vaccinated against rabies. But if the Minister is satisfied that it has been brought to Great Britain for scientific research and vaccination might interfere with that, he may excuse vaccination.

The Order contains detailed provisions for the movement of animals during quarantine, the licensing of carrying agents[149] and of quarantine premises, and the control of animals that are on board a vessel in a British port. The Minister also has power to deal with certain animals[150] that come into contact with animals from abroad.

If an animal is landed illegally, or if there is a breach of the terms of a licence, a Ministry or local authority inspector may destroy the animal and the expenses of so doing recovered from its owner.[151] Alternatively, the inspector may require the animal to be re-exported or detained in quarantine, also at the owner's expense. In addition, any person[152] contravening the Order may be prosecuted.[153]

Pet Travel Scheme

From 28th February 2000 a person may bring a pet cat or pet dog[154] into England without complying with the foregoing quarantine

---

148 These are domestic dogs and cats only, the import of which has breached, or not satisfied, the Pet Travel Scheme (Pilot Arrangements) (England) Order 1999 (as amended): Rabies (Importation of Dogs, Cats and Other Mammals) Order 1974, Art. 6(1).

149 The movement of an animal from quarantine for urgent veterinary treatment which is not available there can only be done by a carrying agent approved by the Minister.

150 These animals are all those animals that are listed at Appendix C at the end of this book.

151 Rabies (Importation of Dogs, Cats and Other Mammals) Order 1974, Art. 14.

152 Note that liability to prosecution is not restricted to owners of the animals and includes agents and carriers whether bodies corporate or incorporate.

153 Rabies (Importation of Dogs, Cats and Other Mammals) Order 1974, Arts. 16, 17.

154 "Cat" means a domestic cat (*Felis catus*); "dog" means a domestic dog (*Canis familiaris*); and "pet cats" and "pet dogs" means cats and dogs which are not traded commercially under the provisions of Article 4A of the Rabies (Importation of Dogs, Cats and Other Mammals) Order 1974, SI 1974/2211, as amended: The Pet Travel Scheme (Pilot Arrangements) (England) Order 1999, SI 1999/3443, Art. 2.

restrictions provided that the conditions relating to the importation of the animal are complied with.[155]

The animal must be brought into England using an approved carrier, travelling directly from one of the permitted countries or territories,[156] without leaving the vessel, aircraft or train in which it is travelling between arrival and departure. In the event of an aircraft being diverted from its scheduled destination, the carrier must, at its own expense, transport the animal to the scheduled destination.[157]

The animal must be identified by means of a microchip[158] implanted into its body.[159] If the carrier does not have a reader capable of reading the microchip, the person bringing the animal into England must provide a reader for the microchip at the time the carrier checks the identity of the animal.[160]

After it has been microchipped, the animal must (a) have been vaccinated against rabies in a specified country or in the British Islands or the Republic of Ireland after the age of three months by injection of an inactivated vaccine approved by the competent authority of the country in which the vaccination takes place; and (b) have had any necessary booster injections in a specified country or in the British Islands or the Republic of Ireland at intervals specified by the manufacturer of the vaccine.[161] After it

---

[155] Namely, The Pet Travel Scheme (Pilot Arrangements) (England) Order 1999, SI 1999/3443, as amended by SI 2000/1641, 2001/6, The Pet Travel Scheme (Pilot Arrangements) (England) Order 1999, Art. 3. The pet travel scheme, is, except where otherwise provided, executed and enforced by the local authority: Art. 14.

[156] Namely, animals from countries and territories listed in Part 1 of Schedule 2 or Schedule 6: The Pet Travel Scheme (Pilot Arrangements) (England) Order 1999, Art. 2A as inserted by SI 2001/6, Art. 2(2). Hereafter a "specified country" means one listed in Part 1 of Schedule 2 and "specified island" means one listed in Schedule 6.

[157] The Pet Travel Scheme (Pilot Arrangements) (England) Order 1999, Art. 4, as substituted by SI 2001/6, Art. 2(3).

[158] "Microchip" means an electronic transponder: The Pet Travel Scheme (Pilot Arrangements) (England) Order 1999, SI 1999/3443, Art. 2.

[159] The Pet Travel Scheme (Pilot Arrangements) (England) Order 1999, SI 1999/3443, Art. 5(1).

[160] The Pet Travel Scheme (Pilot Arrangements) (England) Order 1999, SI 1999/3443, Art. 5(2).

[161] The Pet Travel Scheme (Pilot Arrangements) (England) Order 1999, SI 1999/3443, Art. 6(1) as substituted by SI 2001/6, Art. 2(4).

has been vaccinated against rabies, and at least six months[162] before it is brought into England, a blood sample must have been taken from the animal and tested for rabies antibodies using a virus neutralisation test at a recognised laboratory, with the result of that test demonstrating a protective antibody titre of at least 0.5 international units per millimetre.[163] The requirement for a six month delay between taking the blood sample for testing and the animal being brought into England does not apply in the case of an animal which was microchipped, vaccinated and blood sampled before 28th February 2000, and which, at the time the blood sample was taken, either has never left the British Islands or the Republic of Ireland; has spent six months in quarantine in either the British Islands or the Republic of Ireland and has not subsequently left those countries, or has been brought into the British Islands or the Republic of Ireland under the Council Directive 92/65/EEC and has not subsequently left those countries.[164]

In addition to the foregoing tests, not less than 24 hours and not more than 48 hours before embarkation for England the animal must have been treated by a veterinary surgeon entitled to practice veterinary medicine in the country in which the treatment is administered with medicine against *echinoccus multiloculais*[165] and ticks.[166] The animal must not have been outside the British Islands, the Republic of Ireland or any of the specified countries for the six-month period immediately preceding the date it is to be brought into England.[167]

The health status requirements of animals are exempted where the competent authority of a country or territory in Schedule 2 of the Order operates a mandatory identification system for cats or dogs

---

[162] The six-month period beings on the date that the sample was taken from the animal.

[163] The Pet Travel Scheme (Pilot Arrangements) (England) Order 1999, SI 1999/3443, Art. 6(2).

[164] The Pet Travel Scheme (Pilot Arrangements) (England) Order 1999, SI 1999/3443, Arts. 2, 6(3).

[165] The active ingredient in treating *echinococcus multilocularis* must be praziquantel.

[166] If the animal has been in Cyprus, Malta or one of the countries or territories in Schedule 6 of the 1999 Order the treatment against ticks must contain fipronil as the active ingredient.

[167] The Pet Travel Scheme (Pilot Arrangements) (England) Order 1999, SI 1999/3443, Art. 6(5) as substituted by SI 2001/6, Art. 2(6).

under which (a) the competent authority allocates a unique number to the animal; (b) a veterinary surgeon or person authorised by the competent authority to do so tattoos the animal with the unique number and registers that he has done so with the competent authority of the country or territory; (c) the competent authority issues a certificate of registration for the animal which records the unique number of the animal; (d) the number of a microchip subsequently inserted into the animal by a veterinary surgeon is recorded on the certificate of registration by the competent authority. If the animal is marked and registered in accordance with (a)–(d) then, by derogation from the requirement that the animal must be vaccinated and tested after it has been microchipped, the animal may be vaccinated and tested before it has been microchipped provided that it is marked and registered in accordance with the competent authorities' requirements before it is vaccinated and tested. The declaration required by paragraph 3 of Schedule 3 of the Order is required to be in the form set out in Article 6A(2).[168]

Two official health certificates, one relating to rabies vaccination and one relating to treatment for *enchinococcus multiculais* and ticks must accompany the animal.[169] The official health certificates[170] must:

a. be signed in relation to rabies by an official veterinary surgeon[171] of the specified county, the British Islands or the Republic of Ireland certifying that the certificate is accurate, and stamped by him with an official stamp indicating that he is an official veterinary surgeon; and

---

[168] The Pet Travel Scheme (Pilot Arrangements) (England) Order 1999, SI 1999/3443, Art. 6A, inserted by SI 2000/1298.

[169] The Pet Travel Scheme (Pilot Arrangements) (England) Order 1999, SI 1999/3443, Art. 7.

[170] "Official health certificate" means a certificate prepared and distributed by the competent authority for completion and signature by an official veterinary surgeon in relation to rabies, and by a veterinary surgeon entitled to practice veterinary medicine in the country in which the treatment is administered in the case of *echinococcus multiloculeris* and ticks: Art. 2.

[171] "Official veterinary surgeon" means in England and Wales a veterinary surgeon authorised by the Minister for these purposes, and outside England and Wales means a veterinary surgeon authorised by the competent authority to grant certification for the purposes of export of cats and dogs: Art. 2.

b. must be signed in relation to *enchinococcus multiculais* and ticks by a veterinary surgeon entitled to practise veterinary medicine in the country in which the treatment is administered; and

c. state the date and time of the treatment, and the treatment used; and

d. be in English, but may, in addition to the English text, contain a translation in a language of any of the specified countries.[172]

Animals from a specified island are subject to additional provisions contained in Schedule 6 of the Order.[173] The animals from those countries or territories classified as rabies-free islands must be treated for tapeworms in the country of export.[174] Save for animals from Ascension Island, the Falkland Islands or St Helena, which may be transported by sea, all others must be transported by air.[175] Before transport to England, the container in which the animal is transported must be sealed by an official authorised by the competent authority of the exporting country with the official seal of that authority. If the seal is broken during transport an appropriately appointed official must replace it.[176] On arrival in England, the carrier must examine the seal on the animal's container. If the seal is unbroken, or correctly re-sealed and its number corresponds to the number of the seal entered on the certificate, the carrier must check the microchip and the prescribed documentation.[177] If the seal is missing or is broken, but not re-sealed or if the seal does not correspond to the number of the seal entered on the certificate, the carrier must ensure that the animal is taken into quarantine.[178] If the

---

[172] The Pet Travel Scheme (Pilot Arrangements) (England) Order 1999, SI 1999/ 3443, Art. 7(2)(a), (2)(b), (4) and (6) respectively.

[173] The Pet Travel Scheme (Pilot Arrangements) (England) Order 1999, SI 1999/ 3443, Art. 7A. These provisions have been added by SI 2001/6, Arts. 2(1), 8.

[174] The Pet Travel Scheme (Pilot Arrangements) (England) Order 1999, SI 1999/ 3443, Sch. 6, para. 3.

[175] The Pet Travel Scheme (Pilot Arrangements) (England) Order 1999, SI 1999/ 3443, Sch. 6, para. 5.

[176] The Pet Travel Scheme (Pilot Arrangements) (England) Order 1999, SI 1999/ 3443, Sch. 6, para. 6(1), (2).

[177] In the case of a cat from Australia, a certificate is required certifying that the cat had not been on a holding where Henra virus had been confirmed during 60 days prior to departure: The Pet Travel Scheme (Pilot Arrangements) (England) Order 1999, SI 1999/3443, Sch. 6, para. 1, 7(2).

[178] For the provisions relating to quarantine, see pp. 55-58 and 208-211.

Minister is satisfied that the animal was not exposed to risk of infection of rabies during its journey, he may subsequently release the animal from quarantine.[179] Where the animal is brought in by sea, the carrier must check the microchip and prescribed documentation. If the carrier is satisfied that the documentation is correct and that, during the voyage, the animal had no contact with any other animal, and had not been put ashore at any point, the carrier may release the animal to its owner.[180]

Before bringing an animal into England, a carrier[181] must have checked, for each animal that it carries, the appropriate certificates and declaration required by this Order and must satisfy itself that (a) the animal has been implanted with a microchip; (b) the number of the microchip corresponds with the number of the microchip recorded in all three certificates; (c) the certificates relating to rabies, *echinococcus multilocularis* and ticks show that (i) they are current; (ii) they have been signed by an official veterinary surgeon in relation to rabies and by a veterinary surgeon entitled to practise veterinary medicine in the country in which the treatment is administered in relation to *echinococcus multilocularis* and ticks; and (iii) the animal has been vaccinated against rabies, has been blood tested and has been treated against *echinococcus multilocularis* and ticks; and (d) that the certificate relating to the animal's place of residence in the previous six months has been

---

179 The Pet Travel Scheme (Pilot Arrangements) (England) Order 1999, SI 1999/ 3443, Sch. 6, para. 7.
180 The Pet Travel Scheme (Pilot Arrangements) (England) Order 1999, SI 1999/ 3443, Sch. 6, para. 8.
181 "Carrier" means any undertaking carrying goods or passengers for hire by land, sea or air: The Pet Travel Scheme (Pilot Arrangements) (England) Order 1999, SI 1999/3443, Art. 2. The Minister may approve a carrier if he is satisfied that: (a) the carrier complies with the requirements in Schedule 5 of the Order; (b) the written procedures and contingency plans required in Schedule 5 are adequate; and (c) the carrier will comply with this Order, the written procedures required in Schedule 5 and any conditions of the approval. The approval must specify (a) where checks must be carried out; (b) the routes to be used by the approved carrier to bring an animal into England; and (c) any other conditions the Minister considers appropriate. The carrier must provide such information to the Minister as he may reasonably require: Art. 8. Approvals must be in writing, may be made subject to conditions and may be amended, suspended or revoked by notice in writing at any time, and in particular may be suspended or revoked if the Minister is reasonably of the opinion that the provisions of the Order are not being complied with or that the written procedures and contingency plans produced under Schedule 5 have not been complied with: Art. 12.

signed by the person accompanying the animal.[182] The checks must be carried out in the place and in the manner specified in the approval.

If the checks are carried out before the animal is taken on to the means of transport, it is an offence for the approved carrier to bring an animal into England unless the carrier has carried out the checks mentioned in the previous paragraph and is satisfied that the animal complies with those requirements.[183]

If the checks are carried out during transport or after an animal has landed in England, the approved carrier must keep possession of the animal at the place of arrival until it has carried out the required checks and it is satisfied that the animal has been correctly treated.[184] However, if the carrier is not satisfied that the animal has been identified, vaccinated and blood-tested, it must ensure that the animal is transferred immediately to quarantine[185] facilities.[186]

If, after carrying out the relevant checks, whether the checks are carried out before the animal is taken on to the means of transport, during transport or after landing, the carrier is satisfied that an animal may be brought into England, it must (i) in the case of an animal being brought in by a foot passenger or a passenger of an aircraft, issue a certificate to the person accompanying the animal, signed and dated by a representative of the carrier, and attach a label to the collar of the animal or to its carrying cage if there is one, showing the date of importation and stating that the animal complies with the provisions of the pet travel scheme; or (ii) in the case of an animal being brought in by car or other motor vehicle, give the person a sticker or hanger suitable for displaying on the windscreen and indicating that the vehicle is carrying an animal which has been checked and found to comply with the provisions

---

[182] The Pet Travel Scheme (Pilot Arrangements) (England) Order 1999, SI 1999/3443, Art. 9(1).

[183] The Pet Travel Scheme (Pilot Arrangements) (England) Order 1999, SI 1999/3443, Art. 9(3).

[184] The Pet Travel Scheme (Pilot Arrangements) (England) Order 1999, SI 1999/3443, Art. 9(4)(a).

[185] For the provisions relating to quarantine, see pp. 55-58 and 208-211.

[186] The Pet Travel Scheme (Pilot Arrangements) (England) Order 1999, SI 1999/3443, Art. 9(4)(b).

of the pet travel scheme.[187]

A person bringing an animal into England must display the sticker or hanger given by the carrier in a prominent position in the windscreen until the vehicle leaves the confines of the port of arrival in the case of a ferry crossing or, in the case of the Channel Tunnel,[188] the Folkestone Terminal at Cheriton.[189] A foot passenger on a ferry or a passenger on an aircraft bringing an animal into England must not remove the label attached by the carrier to the collar or carrying cage until he leaves the confines of the port or airport of arrival.[190] A person bringing an animal into England must produce on demand by an officer of the Minister or the local authority the two certificates and one declaration required and, in the case of a foot passenger, the certificate of entry given by the carrier, and must make the animal available for checking: (a) in the case of transport by ferry, in the port area; (b) in the case of transport through the Channel Tunnel, in the Tunnel system; and (c) in the case of air transport, in the airport.[191]

An officer of the Minister or a local authority may stop any vehicle displaying a windscreen sticker or hanger indicating that an animal is being carried, or any other vehicle in which he reasonably suspects that a cat or dog is being carried, or any person in possession of an animal or whom he suspects to be in possession of an animal, at any of the three specified places. These are (a) in the case of transport by ferry, in the port area; (b) in the case of transport through the Channel Tunnel, in the Tunnel System; or (c) in the case of air transport, in the airport. At such places he may carry out any checks and searches that may be necessary to ensure that the provisions of the Order are being complied with.[192]

---

[187] The Pet Travel Scheme (Pilot Arrangements) (England) Order 1999, SI 1999/ 3443, Art. 9(5).

[188] I.e. the Tunnel System as defined in section 1(7) of the Channel Tunnel Act 1987.

[189] The Pet Travel Scheme (Pilot Arrangements) (England) Order 1999, SI 1999/ 3443, Art. 10(1).

[190] The Pet Travel Scheme (Pilot Arrangements) (England) Order 1999, SI 1999/ 3443, Art. 10(2).

[191] The Pet Travel Scheme (Pilot Arrangements) (England) Order 1999, SI 1999/ 3443, Art. 10(3). "Airport" means the aggregate of the land, buildings and works comprised in an aerodrome within the meaning of the Civil Aviation Act 1982.

[192] The Pet Travel Scheme (Pilot Arrangements) (England) Order 1999, SI 1999/ 3443, Art. 11.

Chapter 4

PET ANIMALS

Introduction

This chapter brings together the law which particularly affects pet animals in a number of ways. Most of it relates to dogs which, by their popularity and nature, have generated more legislation than other kinds of pets.

Necessarily other chapters contain law which also affects pets. In particular, these are: Chapter 6 on dangerous wild animals, which are sometimes kept as pets; the powers to deal with rabies on pages 55 to 58 and 208 to 211 in Chapters 3 and 9, which should be read in conjunction with the provisions on pages 58 to 65; and the passages in Chapter 8 covering abandonment of animals (page 132), operations on animals (pages 141 to 144), killing or injuring animals (pages 194 to 196) and Chapter 12 covering experiments on dogs and cats.

Matters relating especially to horses (and allied kinds of animals) may be found on other pages as follows: riding stables (pages 100 to 104), docking and nicking (page 135) and public performances (pages 214 to 215).

Dog Registration

The licensing scheme was abolished under the Local Government Act 1988.[1] However, section 37 allows the establishment of a dog registration and administration scheme in the future.[2]

Dog Licences

Anyone who uses a dog for taking, killing or pursuing game,[3]

---

[1] Local Government Act 1988, ss. 38(1), (4), 41, Sch. 7 Pt. V.
[2] The functions of the Secretary of State in relation to the Local Government Act 1988 are, so far as exercisable in relation to Wales, transferred to the National Assembly of Wales: The National Assembly for Wales (Transfer of Functions) Order 1999, SI 1999/672. References to "Secretary of State" should be read and construed accordingly.
[3] "Game" means hares, pheasants, partridges, grouse, heath or moor game and black game (Game Act 1831, s. 2).

woodcock, snipe, rabbits or deer must take out a game licence.[4] But this is not needed for pursuing and killing hares by coursing with greyhounds or by hunting them with beagles or other hounds, nor for pursuing and killing deer by hunting with hounds.[5]

Trespassing by Dogs

If a dog of its own accord enters land without permission but does no more, its owner is not liable under civil law for trespass.[6] But the owner is so liable if he deliberately sends a dog on to someone else's land in pursuit of game,[7] although he himself did not enter the land,[8] or if he allows a dog to roam at large knowing it to be addicted to destroying game.[9]

Except as noted below, where a trespassing dog causes damage by killing or injuring[10] livestock,[11] a keeper of the dog is liable for the damage.[12] A number of aspects of this liability need examination.

In the cases listed below no liability arises; but otherwise it matters not what active or passive role is played by the keeper of the dog. It is enough that he is its keeper and that the dog does the damage. There is no liability:

a. if the damage to livestock is due wholly to the fault of the person whose livestock it is;[13] or

---

[4] Game Licenses Act 1860, s. 4. For game licences generally, see pp. 116-121.
[5] Game Licences Act 1860, s. 5, Exceptions 3 and 4.
[6] *Mitten v Faudryre* (1626) Poph 161; *Mason v Keeling* (1700) 1 Ld Raym 606.
[7] Possibly he is also liable if the dog is so sent for a different purpose and causes damage.
[8] *R v Pratt* (1855) 4 E & B 860.
[9] *Read v Edwards* (1864) 17 CBNS 245.
[10] Injury can include indirect injury, e.g. dog barking at foals which injured themselves (*Campbell v Wilkinson* (1909) 43 ILT 237), and poultry ceasing laying as a result of shock (*Ives v Brewer* (1951) 95 Sol Jo 286).
[11] "Livestock" means cattle, horses, asses, mules, hinnies (offspring of she-ass by stallion), sheep, pigs, goats and deer not in a wild state; the domestic varieties of fowls, turkeys, ducks, geese, guinea-fowls, pigeons, peacocks and quails, and while in captivity only, pheasants, partridges and grouse (Animals Act 1971, s. 11).
[12] Animals Act 1971, s. 3. For the circumstances in which the dog may justifiably be killed or injured to protect livestock, see pp. 80-82.
[13] Animals Act 1971, s. 5(1).

b. if the livestock was killed or injured on land on to which it had strayed and:

   i. either the dog belonged to the occupier of that land, or

   ii. its presence on that land was authorised by him.[14]

The meaning of "keeper" is described at some length. A person is a keeper of a dog if he either owns it, or has it in his possession, or is the head of a household[15] of which a member under 16 years old owns the animal or possesses it. Such a person remains the keeper of the dog until someone else fulfilling these qualifications succeeds him as keeper.[16] But a person who takes possession of a dog to prevent it causing damage or to restore it to its owner does not, just because of that possession, become its keeper.[17]

A few words on the meaning in law of "possession" and "possessing" may be helpful at this point. The words must be construed in a popular and not a narrow sense; a person would be regarded as having possession of a dog, not only when he or she is actually with it and controlling it, but also when the dog is in some place, e.g. a building or a vehicle, over which the person has control. If, however, the person does not realise that the dog is, or may be, in that place, the person cannot be said to be in possession of it.[18]

Where damage is caused by two or more dogs acting together, the law regards each dog as causing the whole of the damage, and consequently the owner of each will be responsible for the whole damage.[19]

---

[14] Animals Act 1971, s. 5(4).
[15] Presumably, and despite modern trends, in the common case of a household with husband, wife and children the husband is assumed to be its head. But proof of the fact could be difficult, and establishing the identity of the head in many households of different composition more so.
[16] Animals Act 1971, s. 6(3).
[17] Animals Act 1971, s. 6(4). But he should nevertheless take reasonable care of the dog; otherwise, if the dog causes damage or injury, he may be liable under the laws of negligence or nuisance.
[18] *Lockyer v Gibb* [1966] 2 All ER 653; *Warner v Metropolitan Police Commissioner* [1968] 2 All ER 356.
[19] *Arneil v Paterson* (1931) 145 LT 393. I.e. the keeper of any one of the dogs can be sued for the whole cost of the damage.

If a dog worries livestock[20] on agricultural land,[21] its owner, and, if it is in the charge of anyone else, that person also, is guilty of an offence.[22] The phrase "worrying livestock" is defined as meaning:

1. Attacking livestock; or

2. Chasing it[23] in such a way as may be reasonably expected to cause it injury[24] or suffering or, in the case of females, abortion or loss or diminution in their produce; or

3. Being at large (i.e. not on a lead or otherwise under close control) in a field or enclosure in which there are sheep.[25]

But 3. does not apply to the following dogs:

1. A dog owned by, or in the charge of, the occupier of the field or enclosure, or the owner of the sheep, or a person authorised[26] by either of those persons;

2. A police dog;

3. A guide dog;

4. A trained sheep dog;

5. A working gun dog;

6. A pack of hounds.[27]

However, there will be no offence:

---

[20] "Livestock" here means bulls, cows, oxen, heifers, calves, sheep, goats, swine, horses, asses, mules, domestic fowls, turkeys, geese and ducks (Dogs (Protection of Livestock) Act 1953, s. 3(1)).

[21] "Agricultural land" means land used as arable, meadow or grazing land or for the purpose of poultry or pig farming, market gardens, allotments, nursery grounds or orchards (Dogs (Protection of Livestock) Act 1953, s. 3(1)). This can include a cricket field on which sheep are grazing (*Williams v Richards* (1970) 114 Sol Jo 864).

[22] Dogs (Protection of Livestock) Act 1953, s. 1(1). I.e. he can be prosecuted and fined, as opposed to being sued on a claim for damages as earlier described.

[23] Actual pursuit need not be proved; it is enough for the dog to run among the livestock so as to alarm them (*Stephen v Milne* 1960 SLT 276).

[24] As to injury, see note 10 on p. 67.

[25] Dogs (Protection of Livestock) Act 1953, s. 1(2).

[26] The authorisation is not required to be in writing.

[27] Dogs (Protection of Livestock) Act 1953, s. 1(2A).

a. by the owner if he proves[28] that at the time in question the dog was in the charge of some other person whom he reasonably believed to be a fit and proper person to be in charge of it;[29] or

b. if at the material time the livestock were trespassing on the land in question and the dog was owned by, or in the charge of, the occupier of that land or a person authorised[30] by him, except in a case where the authorised person[31] causes the dog to attack the livestock.[32]

If a police officer reasonably believes that a dog found on land has been worrying livestock[33] there, and the land appears to him to be agricultural land,[34] and no person is present who admits to being the owner of the dog or in charge of it, then the officer may, in order to find out the owner, seize and keep the dog until the owner has claimed it and paid all the expenses of its detention.[35]

For the purpose of preventing the worrying of cattle,[36] a local authority[37] may make regulations requiring that dogs generally or any class of dogs shall, during all or any of the hours between sunset and sunrise, be kept under control as described in the regulations.[38] It is an offence without lawful authority or excuse to break the regulations, or to aid, abet, counsel or procure a breach of them.[39]

---

[28] It is enough for the owner to satisfy the court of the probability of existence of the facts in defence a. (*R v Carr-Briant* [1943] 2 All ER 156).
[29] Dogs (Protection of Livestock) Act 1953, s. 1(4).
[30] The authorisation is not required to be in writing.
[31] The Act is phrased so as to refer at this point only to the authorised person though it seems odd that the occupier of the land should not be coupled with him.
[32] Dogs (Protection of Livestock) Act 1953, s. 1(3).
[33] For the definition of "livestock", see note 20 on p. 69.
[34] For the definition of "agricultural land", see note 21 on p. 69.
[35] Dogs (Protection of Livestock) Act 1953, s. 2(2). The dog is then treated as though seized as a stray (Dogs (Protection of Livestock) Act 1953, s. 2(3)), for which see pp. 77-79.
[36] "Cattle" includes horses, mules, asses, sheep, goats and swine. (Control of Dogs Order 1930 (S.R. & O. 1930/399), Art. 2(2).)
[37] This is the county council, or, in London, the borough council or the Common Council of the City of London or the council or county boroughs in Wales (Animal Health Act 1981, s. 50 (1)–(3)).
[38] Control of Dogs Order 1930, Art. 2(1).
[39] Control of Dogs Order 1930, Art. 6 (as amended by SI 1992/901); Animal Health Act, 1981, s.73(a).

Dangerous Dogs[40]

If it appears to a magistrates' court that a dog is dangerous and not kept under proper control,[41] they may order it to be kept by the owner[42] under proper control or to be destroyed. The penalty for non-compliance is a fine which at the date of this publication is not to exceed £400,[43] but notice of the penalty must be given to the owner.[44] The magistrates have a wide discretion to impose specific means as to the control of the dog,[45] whether by muzzling, keeping on a lead, exclusion from named places or otherwise.[46] Similarly, if the dog is male and it appears to the court that to neuter the dog would make it less dangerous then the court may make such an order.[47] "Proper control" is not limited to public places, but extends to the owner's private property to which other people have a right of access.[48] Any question as to whether the dog is under control is one of fact, not law.[49] The court is under no obligation to make a control order in the first instance and may order the dog to be destroyed.

Where a dog is proved to have injured cattle or poultry or chased sheep, it may be dealt with as a dangerous dog.[50] "Dangerous" includes dangerous to animals,[51] and a dog may be dangerous

---

[40] With the exception of s. 1, the provisions of the Dangerous Dogs Act 1991 are, so far as exercisable in relation to Wales, transferred to the National Assembly of Wales: The National Assembly for Wales (Transfer of Functions) Order 1999, SI 1999/672. References to "Secretary of State" hereafter should be read and construed accordingly.

[41] The need for proper control is not limited to public places but extends to places where the dog is on the owners' private property to which other people have a right of access (*Philip v Wright* (1940) SLT 22).

[42] It is thought that "owner" has its ordinary meaning here and not any extended meaning as is given to the keeper of a dog in another context.

[43] Dogs Act 1871, s. 2.

[44] *Haldane v Allen* (1956) JC 41.

[45] Dangerous Dogs Act 1991, s. 3(5)(b).

[46] Dangerous Dogs Act 1991, s. 3(5).

[47] Dangerous Dogs Act 1991, s. 3(6), which provides for such an order to be made under the Dogs Act 1871, s. 2.

[48] *Philip v Wright* 1940 JC 9.

[49] *Wren v Pollock* (1876) 40 JP 646.

[50] Dogs Act 1906, s. 1(4).

[51] *Williams v Richards* (1970) 114 Sol Jo 864. Though a dog which killed two tame white rabbits in a neighbour's garden was held to be not dangerous, it being in the nature of dogs to wound and kill little animals (*Sansom v Chief Constable of Kent* [1981] Crim LR 617). Dogs will be deemed dangerous if dangerous to other dogs (*Briscoe v Shattock* [1999] 1 WLR 342).

though not ferocious.[52] An order may be made though the owner did not know that the dog was dangerous.[53]

When a destruction order is made, the court may also appoint a person to undertake the destruction and require any person to deliver the dog up for destruction. Failure to comply with a destruction order or to deliver a dog up for destruction is an offence. The magistrates may disqualify the owner for a specified period[54] in addition to imposing a fine.

An order to destroy a dog may be made without giving the owner the option of keeping it under proper control.[55] If the owner does not comply with a control order, court proceedings must be started again when the court can make a destruction order, although a destruction order cannot be made on a summons for non-compliance with the original order.[56] An appeal can be made to the Crown Court against a destruction order[57] but not apparently against a control order.

The Dangerous Dogs Act 1991 has imposed further procedures when dealing with dangerous dogs. Two types of dog are named in the Act, namely the pit bull terrier[58] and the Japanese Tosa. By an order of the Secretary of State, any other type of dog may be designated if it is a type appearing to him to be bred for fighting or having the characteristics of a type bred for that purpose.[59] The Dogo Argentino and Fila Braziliero have been so designated.[60]

It is an offence[61] to breed, or breed from, such a dog,[62] sell or

---

[52] This seems to be a matter of degree; a dog with a propensity only to bite small children, postmen or any other class of persons will be dangerous but could not be described as ferocious (*Keddle v Payn* [1964] 1 All ER 189).

[53] *Parker v Walsh* (1885) 1 TLR 583.

[54] Dangerous Dogs Act 1991, s. 1(3).

[55] *Pickering v Marsh* (1874) 43 LJMC 143.

[56] *Rhodes v Heritage* [1951] 1 All ER 904.

[57] Dogs Amendment Act 1938, s. 1(1); Courts Act 1971, s. 56(2), Sch. 9, Pt. I.

[58] The court may use the American Dog Breeder's Association standard to determine whether the dog is in fact a pit bull terrier together with the animal's behavioural characteristics (*R v Crown Court at Knightsbridge, ex p Dunne; Brook v DPP* [1993] 4 All ER 491).

[59] Dangerous Dogs Act 1991, s. 1(1)(c).

[60] Dangerous Dogs (Designated Types) Order 1991, SI 1991/1743.

[61] From 12th August 1991.

[62] Dangerous Dogs Act 1991, s. 1(2)(a).

exchange such a dog or offer, advertise[63] or expose such a dog for sale or exchange,[64] to make or offer to make a gift of such a dog or offer, advertise or expose such a dog as a gift.[65] Likewise it is an offence for such a dog to be in a public place,[66] without it being muzzled and kept on a lead[67] and to abandon such a dog so as to allow it to stray.[68] It is a defence to show that the sale, exchange, gift or otherwise was done with a view to removing the dog from the United Kingdom.[69]

Separate offences are committed by the owner[70] or the person for the time being in charge[71] of a dog which is dangerously out of control[72] in a public place,[73] or where he allows the dog to enter a place which is not a public place and, while it is there, it injures any person or there are reasonable grounds for apprehension that it will

---

[63] "Advertisement" includes any means of bringing a matter to the attention of the public and "advertise" is construed accordingly.

[64] Dangerous Dogs Act 1991, s. 1(2)(b).

[65] Dangerous Dogs Act 1991, s. 1(2)(c).

[66] "Public place" means any street, road or other place, enclosed or not, to which the public have access for payment or otherwise and includes the common parts of a building containing two or more separate dwellings (Dangerous Dogs Act 1991, s10(2)). It has been held that a dangerous dog (not muzzled or on a lead) in a private motor vehicle which is on the highway is treated as being in a public place and falls within the meaning of section 10(2) (*Bates v DPP* (1993) 157 JP 1004). Notwithstanding lack of public use, if the area is in public ownership and open to the public it may be inferred that such an area is a public place (*Cummings v DPP* (1999) *The Times* 26 March 1999).

[67] "Muzzled" means securely fitted with a muzzle sufficient to prevent the dog biting any person: Dangerous Dogs Act 1991, s. 7(1)(a). "Kept on a lead" means securely held in that manner by a person who is not less than 16 years old: Dangerous Dogs Act 1991, s. 7(1)(b). Voluntary intoxication is not a defence to the offence of allowing a dog to be at large in a public place without being muzzled or kept on a lead: *DDP v Kellet* (1994) 158 JP 1138.

[68] Dangerous Dogs Act 1991, s. 1(2)(d), (e).

[69] Dangerous Dogs Act 1991, s. 1(4).

[70] Where a dog is owned by a person who is less than 16 years old, the owner, for the purposes of this offence, will include the head of the household, if any, of which that person is a member: Dangerous Dogs Act 1991, s. 6.

[71] It is a defence for an owner to show that the dog was in the charge of a person whom he reasonably believed to be a fit and proper person: Dangerous Dogs Act 1991, s. 3(2). Cf *R v Hubbart* [1999] Crim LR 568.

[72] A dog is regarded as dangerously out of control on any occasion on which there are grounds for reasonable apprehension that it will cause injury to any person, whether or not it does so, except where the dog is being used for a lawful purpose by a constable or person in the service of the Crown: Dangerous Dogs Act 1991, s. 10(3).

[73] For the definition of "public place" see note 66 above.

do so. A more serious offence is committed if that dog injures a person[74] whilst being out of control.[75]

The court has a discretion to make a destruction order,[76] in addition to fining or imprisoning the person guilty of any of the offences described above. Additionally, on conviction the person may also be disqualified for such period as the court thinks.[77] The Dangerous Dogs (Amendment) Act 1997 gives the court power to make contingent destruction orders.[78] The effect of a contingent order is that where:

a. a person is convicted of an offence relating to prohibited fighting dogs, other specified dangerous dogs or dogs dangerously out of control;[79]

b. the court does not order the destruction of the dog;[80] and

c. in the case of an offence relating to fighting dogs, the dog is exempted from that prohibition in the Dangerous Dogs Act 1991, s. 1(3),

the court must order that unless the dog is exempted from that prohibition within the requisite period, the dog must be destroyed.[81]

The owner of the dog must be given an opportunity to be heard before an order is made[82] for the destruction of the dog, even though the destruction is mandatory[83] and any failure to give notice of the hearing to the owner constitutes a breach of natural justice.[84]

---

[74] The act of a dog causing injury to a person is itself conduct giving grounds for reasonable apprehension of injury; there is no requirement for the apprehension to precede the injury (*Ratiq v DPP* (1997) 161 JP 412).

[75] Dangerous Dogs Act 1991, s. 3(1).

[76] Dangerous Dogs (Amendment) Act 1997, ss. 1–3.

[77] Dangerous Dogs Act 1991, s. 4(1).

[78] Dangerous Dogs Act 1991, s. 4A, inserted by the Dangerous Dogs (Amendment) Act 1997, s. 2.

[79] Dangerous Dogs Act 1991, s. 1, 3(1) or (3).

[80] Dangerous Dogs Act 1991, s. 4(1)(a).

[81] Dangerous Dogs Act 1991, s. 4A(1), inserted by the Dangerous Dogs (Amendment) Act 1997.

[82] I.e. under Dangerous Dogs Act 1991, s. 4(1)(a).

[83] *R v Ealing Magistrates Court, ex p Fanneran* (1996) 160 JP 409.

[84] *R v Trafford Magistrates Court, ex p Riley* (1995) 160 JP 418.

The Justice of the Peace need not make an order if he is satisfied that (a) the dog will not constitute a danger to public safety; and (b) the dog was born before 30th November 1991 and is subject to the prohibition in section 1(3), that there is good reason why the dog has not been exempted from that prohibition.[85] However he must make a destruction order if there is no good reason.[86]

A dog seized under the powers described in the Dangerous Dogs Act 1991[87] may be destroyed[88] by order from a Justice of the Peace where it appears to him that:

a. no person has been or is to be prosecuted for an offence,[89] or an order in respect of that dog, because no owner can be found or for any other reason; and

b. the dog cannot be released into the custody or possession of its owner without the owner contravening the prohibition in the Dangerous Dogs Act 1991, s. 1(3).

In order to keep a type of dog deemed to be dangerous, the owner must hold a certificate of exemption. In order to acquire such a certificate, the following must apply:

a. the police must be provided with such information concerning the dog as may reasonably be required by the Secretary of State[90] for the purpose of establishing

   i. that the dog is one to which section 1 of the Act applies; and

   ii. the address at which the dog is kept; and

   iii. the name, age and gender of the dog;[91]

---

[85] Dangerous Dogs Act 1991, s. 4B(2), inserted by the Dangerous Dogs (Amendment) Act 1997.

[86] Dangerous Dogs Act 1991, s. 4B(3), inserted by the Dangerous Dogs (Amendment) Act 1997.

[87] Sections 5(1) or (2).

[88] Dangerous Dogs Act 1991, s. 4(B), inserted by the Dangerous Dogs (Amendment) Act 1997, s. 3.

[89] Under the Dangerous Dogs Act 1991.

[90] Note that, at the time of publication, the functions of the Secretary of State were being transferred to the Minister for the Department for Environment, Food and Rural Affairs.

[91] The Dangerous Dogs Compensation and Exemption Scheme Order 1991, Art. 6.

b. the dog must be neutered and provided with permanent
    identification in such form as may be prescribed by the Agency[92]
    in order that it may be readily ascertained that the relevant
    operation has been performed on it;[93]

c. an insurance policy must be taken out to insure against third
    party death or personal injury to anyone;[94]

d. payment of a fee[95] to the Agency.

Breeding from the four named breeds of fighting dogs has been
prohibited from 12th August 1991. No puppies under the Dangerous
Dogs Compensation and Exemption Scheme Order 1991, Art. 5
born after 30th November 1991 can be exempt. Therefore the
certificate of exemption must be in force and the requirements
specified therein complied with, in respect of all such dogs whether
adult or puppy.

Ferocious Dogs

Except in the Greater London area, it is an offence for a person in
any street,[96] to cause the obstruction, annoyance or danger of the
residents or passengers, to "suffer to be at large"[97] any unmuzzled
ferocious[98] dog, or to set on or urge any dog or other animal to
attack, worry or put in fear any person or animal.[99] Similar
offences are created for the Metropolitan Police District.[100]

Dogs involved in offences against badgers may be destroyed by
court order and their owners disqualified from keeping dogs.[101]

---

92   "Agency" means the person or body for the time being designated by the Secretary
     of State to discharge those functions, namely, the Index of Exempt Dogs.
93   The Dangerous Dogs Compensation and Exemption Scheme Order 1991, Art. 7.
94   The Dangerous Dogs Compensation and Exemption Scheme Order 1991, Art. 8.
95   For the current fee for a certificate of exemption under Art. 9, see Dangerous Dogs
     (Fee) Order 1997, SI 2297/1152.
96   The word "street" extends to and includes any road, square, court, alley, thoroughfare
     or public passage (Town Police Clauses Act 1847, s. 3).
97   A dog on a lead is not "at large" (*Ross v Evans* (1959)).
98   For comment on the distinction between "ferocious" and "dangerous", see note 52
     on p. 72.
99   Town Police Clauses Act, 1847, s. 28; Public Health Act, 1875, s. 171; Local
     Government Act, 1972, s. 180, Sch. 14, paras. 23, 26.
100 Metropolitan Police Act. 1839, s. 54 para. 2.
101 Protection of Badgers Act 1992. See pp. 166 *et seq.*

Stray Dogs

A police officer may seize any dog found in a highway or place of public resort[102] which he has reason to believe[103] is a stray dog, and detain it until the owner has claimed it and paid all expenses incurred in its detention.[104] The power of seizure extends to private property where the owner or occupier consents to the seizure.[105] If the dog wears a collar with an address, or the owner is known, the police must serve on the person whose address is given or the owner (as the case may be) written notice that the dog has been seized and is liable to be sold or destroyed if not claimed within seven clear days after service of the notice.[106] The dog must be properly fed and maintained during detention by the person having charge of it.[107]

After seven days,[108] and if the owner has not claimed the dog and paid all expenses, the dog may be sold, or destroyed in a manner so as to cause as little pain as possible, but not given or sold for purposes of vivisection.[109]

The police must keep a register of dogs seized and record particulars. It is open to public inspection at all reasonable times for a fee of 5p.[110]

Anyone who finds or keeps a stray dog must at once either return it to its owner or take it to the nearest police station, telling the police where it was found.[111] If the finder wants to keep the dog, he may, after taking it to the police station, take it away with him

---

[102] A "place of public resort" has been said to mean a place to which the public goes as a matter of fact, as distinct from a matter of right (*Kitson v Ashe* (1899) 1 QB 429) notwithstanding that a charge is made for admission (*Glynn v Simmonds* [1952] 2 All ER 47).

[103] The officer must not only have reasonable cause to believe but must also actually believe (*R v Banks* [1916] 2 KB 621).

[104] Dogs Act 1906, s. 3(1).

[105] Dogs Act 1906, s. 3(1), (1A) (amended and added respectively by the Local Government Act 1988, s. 39(3)).

[106] Dogs Act 1906, s. 3(2).

[107] Dogs Act 1906, s. 3(8).

[108] That is, 7 days after the original detention of the dog or, if a notice has been served, 7 days after service of it.

[109] Dogs Act 1906, s. 3(4), (5).

[110] Dogs Act 1906, s. 3(6), (7).

[111] Dogs Act 1906, s. 4(1).

after giving his name and address. The police will give him a certificate of particulars of the dog, of its finding and of the finder, and he must keep the dog for at least one month.[112] At the same time the police serve a seven-day notice in the same way as if they had found the dog (assuming they know the owner or have an address for the dog). If the owner claims it within the seven days, he is entitled to it; otherwise the finder is entitled to keep it.[113]

If the finder does not want to keep the dog, the police detain it as if it was a stray seized by them.[114] The finder may be fined for not complying with the foregoing requirements.[115]

The finder may alternatively take the dog to the local authority's dog warden. Again the finder may chose whether or not to keep the dog. If he decides to keep the dog then he must supply the dog warden with his particulars who in turn will record a description of the dog, any information on the dog's collar, and particulars about how it was found. The finder (if regarded by the warden to be suitable) will be entitled to keep the dog if the warden's enquiries are to no avail or if the owner fails to collect the dog. The dog warden is responsible for warning the finder of his obligations to keep the dog for at least one month (if unclaimed by the owner) and of his liability to prosecution for failure of his obligations.[116] If on the other hand the finder does not wish to keep the dog then it will be retained by the warden and will be treated as seized by him.[117]

Where a warden seizes a dog whether on public or private land[118] he is obliged to serve the owner with a notice, not dissimilar to the type served by the police,[119] if the owner can be identified. If the dog is claimed by the owner then it will be released to him on paying a prescribed fee of £25 and the expenses of its detention by

---

[112] Dogs Act 1906, s. 4(2)(a).
[113] *Halsbury's Laws of England*, 4th Ed. (Revised), Vol. 2, para. 386.
[114] Dogs Act 1906, s. 4(2)(b).
[115] Dogs Act 1906, s. 4(3).
[116] Environmental Protection Act 1990, s. 150.
[117] Environmental Protection Act 1990, s. 150(2).
[118] If the dog is seized on private land then the warden must have the prior consent of the owner or occupier. Environmental Protection Act 1990, s. 149(1), (2).
[119] See above.

the warden.[120] If the dog has not been collected within seven days of seizure, or within seven days of the owner receiving the notice, the warden may sell or give the dog to a suitable person or a dog's home. Alternatively, it may be destroyed, but may not be used for experimentation.[121] As before, the warden must keep records, in addition to which details of any seven-day notice served, the return of the dog to its owner or its disposal must be noted. The register is available for public inspection without charge.[122]

Dog Collars

Every dog while in a highway or place of public resort[123] must wear a collar with the name and address of its owner inscribed on it or on a plate or badge attached to it. But a collar is not needed for:

a. a pack of hounds; or

b. any dog while being used for sporting purposes, for the capture or destruction of vermin, or for the driving or tending of cattle or sheep; or

c. any dog while being used on official duties by the Armed Forces, Customs and Excise officers or the police; or

d. any dog while being used in emergency rescue work; or

e. any dog registered with the Guide Dogs for the Blind Association.[124]

If this requirement is not complied with, the dog may be seized by the local authority's dog warden and treated by them as a stray.[125] Its owner, any person in charge of it and any person allowing the dog to be in the places described are each guilty of an offence unless they had lawful authority or excuse.[126]

---

[120] Environmental Protection Act 1990, s. 149(5); Environmental Protection (Stray Dogs) Regulations 1992, Reg. 2.

[121] Environmental Protection Act 1990, s.149(6).

[122] Environmental Protection Act 1990, s. 149(8); Environmental Protection (Stray Dogs) Regulations 1992, Reg. 3.

[123] For the meaning of "a place of public resort", see note 102 on p. 77.

[124] Control of Dogs Order 1992, SI 1992/901, Art. 2(2).

[125] Control of Dogs Order 1992, SI 1992/901, Art. 4.

[126] Control of Dogs Order 1992, SI 1992/901 Art. 3; Animal Health Act 1981, s. 73(a).

Killing or Injuring Dogs

Without legal justification it is a civil wrong[127] to kill or injure
another person's dog.[128] A notice that trespassing dogs will be shot
is no defence.[129] Legal justification can arise in three ways:

1. To protect livestock,[130] a person is entitled to kill or injure
    another's dog if:

    i.   the livestock or the land on which it is belongs to him[131] or
         to any person under whose express or implied authority he
         is acting;[132] and

    ii. in a case where the livestock was killed or injured on land on
         to which it had strayed, either the dog belonged to the
         occupier of that land or its presence there was authorised by
         him;[133] and

    iii. either the dog is worrying[134] or about to worry livestock and
         there are no other reasonable means of ending or preventing
         the worrying;[135] or

    iv. the dog has been worrying livestock, has not left the vicinity,
         is not under the control of any person, and there are no
         practicable means of ascertaining to whom it belongs;[136]
         and

    v.   within 48 hours of the killing or injuring the person doing it

---

[127] I.e. the dog's owner may sue for damages.

[128] *Vere v Lord Cawdor and King* (1809) 11 East 568. As to when it is a crime see pp.
136-139. There is always a risk that injury to the animal can give rise to prosecution
under Protection of Animals Act 1911, s. 1(1) (*Isted v CPS* [1998] Crim LR 194).

[129] *Corner v Champneys* (1814) cited in 2 Marsh at 584.

[130] For the meaning of "livestock" see note 20 on p. 69.

[131] For this purpose the livestock belongs to the person who owns it or has it in his
possession, and land belongs to the person who occupies it (Animals Act 1971, s.
9(5)).

[132] Animals Act 1971, s. 9(2)(a).

[133] Animals Act 1971, s. 5(4), 9(2)(b).

[134] There is no definition of "worrying" in the Animals Act 1971 which contains these
provisions. For the definition in another Act, which is suggested as a guide, see
p. 69.

[135] Animals Act 1971, s. 9(3)(a).

[136] Animals Act 1971, s. 9(3)(b). A belief on reasonable grounds that either condition
iii. or iv. was satisfied is enough (Animals Act 1971, s. 9(4)).

gave notice[137] of it to the officer in charge of a police station;[138]

2. A dog attacking a human being may be shot in self defence,[139] and presumably by one person when it is attacking another. Whether shooting is justified when the dog is running away after an attack is uncertain in the present state of the law;[140]

3. The third justification arises when a dog attacks domestic animals which are not livestock if:

    i. at the material time the dog was actually attacking the animals or, if left at large, would renew the attack so that the animals would be left in real and imminent danger unless renewal was prevented; and

    ii. either there was in fact no practicable means other than shooting of stopping the present attack or such renewal, or that, having regard to all the circumstances in which he found himself, the shooter acted reasonably in regarding the shooting as necessary.[141]

It is doubtful whether there is a defence to a civil claim for killing or injuring another's dog because it is attacking wild animals (except game) on one's land or property. The position in relation to the protection of game is discussed on pages 130 to 131, but even then it would be better to err on the side of restraint.[142]

A person must not so use his land as to tempt other people's dogs to destruction; thus, if he sets traps baited with strong smelling meat so near his neighbour's yard, or so near a highway where dogs may lawfully pass, that dogs are irresistibly drawn to the traps, he

---

[137.] Written notice is not stipulated, but will be advisable in case of later proceedings. A copy of the notice should be receipted by the police officer and endorsed by him with the time and date of receipt.

[138] Animals Act 1971, s. 9(1)(b).

[139] *Morris v Nugent* (1836) 7 C & P 572.

[140] See *Halsbury's Laws of England*, 4th Edn., Vol. 2 (Reissue), para. 387 n. 14.

[141] *Cresswell v Sirl* [1947] 2 All ER 730.

[142] *Vere v Lord Cawdor and King* (1809) 11 East 568.

may be sued for damages by the owner of any dog caught.[143]

Boarding Kennels

Boarding kennels for cats and dogs must be licensed by the local council.[144] For this purpose the keeping of such kennels is defined as the carrying on at any premises (including a private dwelling) of a business of providing accommodation for other people's cats and dogs.[145] But if the accommodation is provided in connection with a business of which the provision of such accommodation is not the main activity, a licence is unnecessary.[146] Nor is a licence necessary if cats or dogs are kept on premises pursuant to a requirement under the diseases of animals legislation.[147]

In deciding whether to grant a licence the council, as well as being able to withhold it for other reasons, must pay regard particularly to the need to secure that the animals will be suitably accommodated, fed, exercised and protected from disease and fire, and that a proper register of animals is kept with their dates of arrival and departure and their owners' names and addresses. A licence will contain conditions to these ends and the council may add other conditions.[148]

A fee for the licence will be charged; there is no maximum.[149] It covers the year in which it was granted or the next following year.[150] An applicant aggrieved by the refusal of a licence or by any

---

143 *Townsend v Wathen* (1808) 9 East 277. He would probably also be liable to prosecution under Criminal Damage Act 1971, s. 3, for possessing articles with intent to damage or destroy, or under Protection of Animals Act 1911, s. 1(1)(a), for which see pp. 146-147.

144 Animals Boarding Establishments Act 1963, s. 1(1), (2). This is the district council, the London borough council or the Common Council of the City of London in whose area the kennels are (Animals Boarding Establishments Act 1963, s. 5(2) (amended by the Local Government Act 1972, ss. 179(1), (3), 272(1), Sch. 30)). In Wales, this is the county or county borough council (Local Government (Wales) Act 1994, Sch. 16 para. 42).

145 Animals Boarding Establishments Act 1963, s. 5(1), (2).

146 Animals Boarding Establishments Act 1963, s. 5(1), proviso (a). E.g. a vet who provides board as a sideline to his practice.

147 Animals Boarding Establishments Act 1963, s. 5(1), proviso (b). Examples of such a requirement appear in Chapter 9.

148 Animals Boarding Establishments Act 1963, s. 1(3).

149 Animals Boarding Establishments Act 1963, s. 1(2).

150 Animals Boarding Establishments Act 1963, s. 1(5), (6). I.e. the licence runs, at the applicant's choice, from the day it is granted to the end of the current year, or from the beginning of the next year to the end of that year.

of its conditions may appeal to a magistrates' court who will adjudicate.[151]

The council may authorise in writing any of its officers or any vet to inspect licensed kennels and they have powers of entry and inspection at all reasonable times on producing their authority.[152] It is an offence wilfully[153] to obstruct or delay the exercise of these powers,[154] or to keep kennels without a licence, or to fail to comply with a condition of a licence.[155] On convicting a person of an offence under the regulating Act[156] or other named Acts,[157] the court may cancel his licence and may, whether he has a licence or not, disqualify him from keeping kennels for as long as it thinks fit.[158] Such a person cannot therefore be granted a licence while disqualified; nor may anyone else while disqualified from keeping a pet shop,[159] from keeping a dog or from having the custody of animals.[160]

When the licence holder dies, the licence is treated as having been granted to his personal representatives to remain in force for three months after the death. The council may extend and re-extend the three months if satisfied that that is necessary for winding up the

---

[151] Animals Boarding Establishments Act 1963, s. 1(4).

[152] Animals Boarding Establishments Act 1963, s. 2(1).

[153] This means deliberately and intentionally, and not by accident or inadvertence (*R v Senior* (1899) 1 QB 283, at p. 299). Cf *Lewis v Cox* [1985] QB 509 where "wilfully obstructs" was held to be where a police officer in execution of his duty is actually prevented by the person from carrying on his duty or makes it more difficult for the police to perform such duties and if he intentionally does the act realising that it would have an obstructive effect, regardless of underlying motives: *Halsbury's Laws of England,* 4th Ed., Vol. 2 (Reissue), para. 391 note 16.

[154] Animals Boarding Establishments Act 1963, s. 2(2).

[155] Animals Boarding Establishments Act 1963, s. 1(8).

[156] I.e. the Animal Boarding Establishments Act 1963.

[157] These are: the Protection of Animals Act 1911 (for which see pp. 132-150); the Protection of Animals (Scotland) Act 1912; and the Pet Animals Act 1951 (for which see pp. 84-89).

[158] Animals Boarding Establishments Act 1963, s. 3(3). There is a right of appeal to the Crown Court against an order for cancellation or disqualification; the magistrates may suspend the order pending the appeal (Animals Boarding Establishments Act 1963, s.3(4)).

[159] See p. 88.

[160] Animals Boarding Establishments Act 1963, s. 1(2). For cases where a person may be disqualified from having the custody of animals, see pp. 148-150.

deceased's estate and that no other circumstances make it undesirable.[161]

Dog Breeding

Dog breeding kennels must also be licensed by the local council.[162] For this purpose the keeping of such kennels is defined as the carrying on at premises of any nature (including a private dwelling) of a business of breeding dogs with a view to their being sold in the course of such business, whether by their keeper or any other person.[163] The definition of "breeding establishment for dogs" has been enlarged to include premises where there is a business of breeding dogs for sale (whether by him or any other person).[164] A person will be treated as carrying on a business of breeding dogs for sale at the premises where:

a. a person keeps a bitch at any premises at any time during any period of twelve months; and

b. the bitch gives birth to a litter of puppies at any time during that period; and

c. four or more other litters are born during the period to bitches falling within the following categories:

   i. the aforementioned bitch;

   ii. any other bitch kept by the person at the premises at any time during the period;

   iii. any bitch kept by any relative[165] of his at the premises at any such time;

   iv. any bitches kept by him elsewhere at any such time; and

---

[161] Animals Boarding Establishments Act 1963, s. 1(7).
[162] For the identity of the local council, see note 144 on p. 82. Shaw's form Cat. No. DB2 for form of application for licence.
[163] Breeding of Dogs Act 1973, s. 5(1).
[164] Breeding of Dogs Act 1973, s. 4A(2) (as inserted by the Breeding and Sale of Dogs (Welfare) Act 1999, s. 7).
[165] "Relative" means the person's parent or grandparent, child or grandchild, sibling, aunt or uncle or niece or nephew or someone with whom he lives as a couple: Breeding of Dogs Act 1973, s. 4A(6) (as inserted by the Breeding and Sale of Dogs (Welfare) Act 1999, s. 7).

v. any bitches kept (anywhere) by any person at any time under a breeding arrangement[166] made with him.[167]

But if the person shows that none of the puppies born to bitches falling within i.–iii. or v. was sold during the period (whether by him or by any other person) he will not be treated as carrying on a business of breeding dogs for sale at the premises.[168]

The rules for this kind of licensing are not dissimilar to those applying to the licensing of boarding kennels.[169] However there are certain differences. These are:

1. In addition to the cases in which a person may be disqualified from holding a licence or may have it cancelled which are mentioned on page 87, a person may have this action taken against him for an offence under the regulating Act[170] itself.[171] Such disqualification may have regard to any dog of any description which was in the offender's custody at the time when the offence was committed or has been in his custody at any time since that time. The order may require any person who has custody of the dog to deliver it up to a specified person and (if he does) also require the offender to pay specified amounts to specified persons for the care of the dog from the time when it is delivered up until permanent arrangements are made for its care or disposal;[172]

---

[166] "Breeding arrangement" means a contract or other arrangement under which the person agrees that another person may keep a bitch of his on terms that, should the bitch give birth, the other person is to provide him with either (a) one or more of the puppies; or (b) the whole or part of the proceeds of selling any of them: Breeding of Dogs Act 1973, s. 4A(6) (as inserted by the Breeding and Sale of Dogs (Welfare) Act 1999, s. 7).

[167] Breeding of Dogs Act 1973, s. 4A(3), (4) (as inserted by the Breeding and Sale of Dogs (Welfare) Act 1999, s. 7).

[168] Breeding of Dogs Act 1973, s. 4A(5) (as inserted by the Breeding and Sale of Dogs (Welfare) Act 1999, s. 7).

[169] See pp. 82-84.

[170] The Breeding of Dogs Act 1973.

[171] Breeding of Dogs Act 1973, s. 3(3) (inserted by the Breeding and Sale of Dogs (Welfare) Act 1999, s. 5).

[172] Breeding of Dogs Act 1973, s. 3(8) (inserted by the Breeding and Sale of Dogs (Welfare) Act 1999, s. 5). A person who is subject to a disqualification order may, at any time after the end of the period of one year beginning with the date of the order, apply to the court which made the order, or any magistrates' court acting for the same petty sessions area, for a direction determining the disqualification

2. On receipt of an application by a person for the grant of a licence in respect of any premises, if a licence has not been previously granted to the person in respect of the premises, the local authority shall arrange for the inspection of the premises by a vet and by an officer of the authority, and, in any other case, the local authority shall arrange for the inspection of the premises by the vet or by an officer of the authority (or both).[173] A report is prepared following the inspection which the council must consider before determining whether to grant a licence;[174]

3. In addition to the need to determine that the dogs will be suitably accommodated, fed, exercised and protected from disease and fire, and that all appropriate steps will be taken to secure adequate welfare standards during transportation, the council have regard to and make appropriate conditions to ensure that:

  i. bitches are not mated if they are less than one year old;

  ii. bitches do not give birth to more than six litters of puppies each;

  iii. bitches do not give birth to puppies before the end of the period of twelve months beginning with the day on which they last gave birth to puppies;

  iv. accurate records in a form prescribed by regulations[175] are kept at the premises and made available for inspection there by any officer of the local authority, or any vet authorised by the local authority to inspect the premises;[176]

---

from such date as the court considers appropriate: Breeding of Dogs Act 1973, s. 3(8) (inserted by the Breeding and Sale of Dogs (Welfare) Act 1999, s. 5). The court is obliged to notify the local authority and may grant or refuse the application, with or without a costs order. Where an application is refused, no further application in respect of the disqualification will be entertained if made before the end of the period of one year beginning with the date of the refusal: Breeding of Dogs Act 1973, s. 3(11) (inserted by the Breeding and Sale of Dogs (Welfare) Act 1999, s. 5).

[173] Breeding of Dogs Act 1973, s. 2A (inserted by the Breeding and Sale of Dogs (Welfare) Act 1999, s. 1).

[174] Breeding of Dogs Act 1973, s. 2B (inserted by the Breeding and Sale of Dogs (Welfare) Act 1999, s. 1).

[175] Breeding of Dogs (Licensing Records) Regulations 1999, SI 1999/3192.

[176] Breeding of Dogs Act 1973, s. 4(1)(f)–(i) (inserted by the Breeding and Sale of Dogs (Welfare) Act 1999, s. 2).

4. Whilst the cost of inspecting the premises must be met by the council, the local authority may charge such reasonable sum as the council may fix.[177]

The Breeding of Dogs Act 1991, grants local authority officers and vets greater powers of entry and inspection of breeding kennels not covered by licence under the Breeding of Dogs Act 1973, provided they first acquire a warrant from the magistrates.[178]

The keeper of a licensed breeding establishment[179] is guilty of an offence and liable to imprisonment, a fine or both,[180] if:

a. he sells a dog otherwise than at a licensed breeding establishment or a licensed pet shop;[181]

b. he sells a dog otherwise than to the keeper of a licensed pet shop knowing or believing that the person who buys it intends that it should be sold (by him or another person);

c. he sells a dog which is less than eight weeks old otherwise than to the keeper of a licensed pet shop;

d. he sells to the keeper of a licensed pet shop a dog which was not born at a licensed breeding establishment;

e. he sells to the keeper of a licensed pet shop a dog which, when delivered, is not wearing a collar with an identification tag or badge.[182]

---

[177] Breeding of Dogs Act 1973, s. 3 (inserted by the Breeding and Sale of Dogs (Welfare) Act 1999, s. 6).

[178] The Breeding of Dogs Act 1991, s. 1.

[179] "Licensed breeding establishment" means a breeding establishment for dogs the keeping of which by its keeper (or, where more than one, each of its keepers) is licensed under the Breeding of Dogs Act 1973: Breeding and Sale of Dogs (Welfare) Act 1999, s. 8(5).

[180] Breeding and Sale of Dogs (Welfare) Act 1999, s. 9(1).

[181] "Licensed pet shop" means a pet shop the keeping of which by its keeper (or, where more than one, each of its keepers) is licensed under the Pet Animals Act 1951.

[182] Breeding and Sale of Dogs (Welfare) Act 1999, s. 8(1). "Identification tag or badge", in relation to a dog, means a tag or badge which clearly displays information indicating the licensed breeding establishment at which it was born and any other information required by regulations. Breeding and Sale of Dogs (Welfare) Act 1999, s. 8(5). The tag or badge must also display the date of birth of the dog, and an identification number, if any, allocated to the dog by the licensed breeding establishment at which it was born: Sale of Dogs (Identification Tag) Regulations 1999, SI 1999/3191, Reg. 2.

Additionally, his licence may be cancelled, or he may be disqualified from keeping a licensed breeding establishment or keeping any dog specified by the court, as previously considered at 1. on page 85.

Pet Shops

A person keeping a pet shop must be licensed by the local council.[183] The regulating rules are similar to those for boarding kennels and dog breeding kennels. The keeping of a pet shop is defined to mean the carrying on at premises[184] of any nature (including a private dwelling) of a business of selling animals[185] as pets[186] and includes the keeping of animals in any such premises with a view to their being sold in the course of such a business, whether by their keeper or any other person.[187] This definition is qualified in two ways. First, a person is not treated as keeping a pet shop only because he keeps or sells pedigree animals[188] bred by him or the offspring of an animal kept by him as a pet. The second qualification arises where a person carries on a business of selling animals as pets in conjunction with a business of breeding pedigree animals, and the local council are satisfied that the animals so sold by him (in so far as they are not pedigree animals bred by him) are animals which were acquired by him with a view to being used, if suitable, for breeding or show purposes but have later been found by him not to be suitable or required for such use. In that situation the council may direct that the person shall not be treated as keeping a pet shop by reason only of his carrying on a business of selling animals as pets.[189]

---

[183] Pet Animals Act 1951, s. 1(1). For the identity of the local authority, see note 144 on page 82. Shaw's form Catalogue No PA22 for form of application for licence.

[184] "Premises" includes open land as well as buildings.

[185] "Animal" includes any description of vertebrate (Pet Animals Act 1951, s. 7(3)).

[186] The phrase "selling animals as pets" is itself defined; for cats and dogs, as including selling wholly or mainly for domestic purposes; and, for all animals, as including selling for ornamental purposes (Pet Animals Act 1951, s. 7(2)).

[187] Pet Animals Act 1951, s. 7(1). A person keeping animals on premises for short periods (48 hours in this particular case) for the purpose of exporting them nevertheless keeps a pet shop within the definition, even though the public did not go to the premises to buy animals (*Chalmers v Diwell* (1976) Crim LR 134).

[188] A pedigree animal means an animal of any description which is by its breeding eligible for registration with a recognised club or society keeping a register of animals of that description (Pet Animals Act 1951, s. 7(3)).

[189] Pet Animals Act 1951, s. 7(1), provisos.

The conditions which can attach to a licence include one that mammals will not be sold at too early an age,[190] but there will be no condition about keeping a register.[191] A person is disqualified from having a licence and may have any licence held cancelled for offences under the regulating Act[192] or the Protection of Animals Acts.[193] The fee, the right of appeal, the duration of the licence, the powers of inspection and the creation of offences are the same as those for boarding kennels.[194]

Additional offences are created for: carrying on a business of selling animals[195] as pets[196] in any part of a street or public place;[197] selling an animal as a pet to a person whom the seller has reasonable cause to believe to be under the age of 12.[198]

A keeper of a licensed pet shop will be guilty of an offence if he sells a dog which, when delivered to him, was wearing a collar with an identification tag or badge from a licensed breeding establishment, but is not wearing a collar when delivered to the person to whom he sells it.[199]

Guard Dogs

Although perhaps guard dogs may not be regarded as pet animals, it is convenient to consider in this chapter the law which affects them.

Following a number of accidents in which dogs guarding property savaged people, the Guard Dogs Act was passed in 1975 and is partly in force. For the purposes of the Act a guard dog is defined as a dog which is being used to protect premises, or property kept

---

[190] No specific ages are given, the intention being presumably that young mammals (but not other animals) are not to be separated too early from their mothers, the ages depending on the species.

[191] Pet Animals Act 1951, s. 1(3).

[192] Pet Animals Act 1951, s. 5(3). For these Acts, see pp. 132-150.

[193] I.e. the Pet Animals Act 1951.

[194] Pet Animals Act 1951, ss. 1(2), (4)–(7), 4, 5(4). For boarding kennels, see pp. 82-84.

[195] For the meaning of "animal", see note 185 on p. 88.

[196] For the meaning of "selling animals as pets", see note 186 on p. 88.

[197] Pet Animals Act 1951, s. 2.

[198] Pet Animals Act 1951, s. 3.

[199] Breeding and Sale of Dogs (Welfare) Act 1999, s. 8(4).

on the premises,[200] or a person guarding the premises or such property.[201]

It is an offence to use, or permit the use of, a guard dog at any premises unless a person (called "the handler") who is capable of controlling the dog is present on the premises, and the dog is under the control of the handler at all times while it is being used as a guard dog, except while it is secured so that it is not at liberty to roam the premises.[202] The handler's duty to control the dog is only relaxed if another handler has control of it or if it is secured so that it cannot roam.[203] A guard dog is not to be used at all unless a notice warning of its presence is clearly shown at each entrance to the premises.[204]

The following provisions of the Act are not operative at the time of writing.

It will be an offence for a person to keep a dog at guard dog kennels unless he holds a licence for the kennels.[205] "Guard dog kennels" are defined as a place where a person in the course of business keeps a dog which (notwithstanding that it is used for other purposes) is used as a guard dog elsewhere, other than a dog which is used as a guard dog only at premises belonging to its owner.[206] It will also be an offence for anyone to use, or permit the use of, a guard dog at premises if he knows, or has reasonable cause to suspect, that the dog (when not being used as a guard dog) is kept at unlicensed kennels.[207]

---

[200] "Premises" means land (other than agricultural land and land within the curtilage of a dwelling house) and buildings, including parts of buildings other than dwelling houses (Guard Dogs Act 1975, s. 7). "Agricultural land" means land used as arable, meadow or grazing land, or for the purpose of poultry farming, pig farming, market gardens, allotments, nursery grounds or orchards (Guard Dogs Act 1975, s. 7; Dogs (Protection of Livestock) Act 1953, s. 3(1)). A "curtilage" is briefly, the garden and more immediate surrounds of a house.

[201] Guard Dogs Act 1975, s. 7.

[202] Guard Dogs Act 1975, s. 1(1). It has been ruled that these requirements are met if the handler is on the premises with the dog under his control or if, in his absence, the dog is secured as described in the text (*Hobson v Gledhill* (1977), *The Times,* October 13, 1977).

[203] Guard Dogs Act 1975, s. 1(2).

[204] Guard Dogs Act 1975, s. 1(3).

[205] Guard Dogs Act 1975, s. 2(1).

[206] Guard Dogs Act 1975, s. 7.

[207] Guard Dogs Act 1975, s. 2(2).

Licences will be obtained from local councils [208] by completing a form and paying a fee. They will be issued subject to condition,[209] and will come into force on the date given on them; they will last for 12 months unless cancelled by a court order. This cancellation can be ordered if the holder of the licence is convicted of an offence against the 1975 Act or against a number of other Acts,[210] but the cancellation can be suspended pending an appeal.[211]

An applicant for a licence or the holder of one, as the case may be, will be able to appeal to a magistrates' court against the following decisions of the local council:

1. A refusal to grant a licence;

2. The conditions attached to it, unless they are conditions laid down by the Government;

3. A refusal to vary the conditions on the request of the licence holder;

4. A revocation of the licence.[212]

When hearing an appeal the court may give directions to the local council about the licence or its conditions[213] which must be obeyed.[214]

---

[208] Guard Dogs Act 1975, s. 7. For the identity of local councils, see note 144 on p. 82.

[209] The conditions will be those (if any) which the Government lays down and any others which the district council may choose to add (Guard Dogs Act 1975, ss. 3(2), 7).

[210] These are: the Protection of Animals Act 1911 (see pp. 132-150); the Protection of Animals (Scotland) Act 1912; the Pet Animals Act 1951 (see pp. 84-89); the Animal Boarding Establishments Act 1963 (see pp. 82-84); and the Breeding of Dogs Act 1973, as amended by the Breeding and Sale of Dogs (Welfare) Act 1999 (see pp. 84-88).

[211] Guard Dogs Act 1975, s. 3(1)–(5).

[212] Guard Dogs Act 1975, s. 4(1). Government regulations are to be made about revoking licences, varying conditions and a number of other ancillary matters (Guard Dogs Act 1975, s. 6).

[213] In effect, these directions will be the court's decision on the appeal which is to be carried out by the council, e.g. to remove a condition appealed against.

[214] Guard Dogs Act 1975, s. 4(2).

Control of Dogs on Roads

The Dogs (Fouling of Land) Act 1996 gives local authorities[215] the power to designate land by order,[216] either specifically or by description, on which dog fouling can be controlled.[217] The local authority may designate any land which is open to the air[218] and to which the public are entitled or permitted to have access with or without payment.[219]

The local authority is obliged to publish in a local newspaper[220] circulating in the area of the land to be designated a notice which identifies the land to be designated, states the effect of the designation, and (where a map is referred to) where it may be inspected free of charge during the prescribed period for representations.[221]

The provisions do not apply to the following types of land:

1. Land comprised in or running alongside a highway which comprises a carriageway unless the driving of motor vehicles on the carriageway is subject, otherwise than temporarily, to a speed limit of 40 miles per hour or less;[222]

---

[215] "Local authority" means (a) in relation to England, any unitary authority or any district council so far as it is not a unitary authority, and (b) in relation to Wales, the council of any county or county borough: Dogs (Fouling of Land) Act 1996, s. 7(1). "Unitary authorities" are (a) any county council so far as it is the council for the area for which there are no district councils, (b) the council of any district comprised in an area for which there is no county council, (c) any London borough council, (d) the Common Council of the City of London, and (e) the Council of the Isles of Scilly: Dogs (Fouling of Land) Act 1996, s. 7(2). The Secretary of State has the power to make or order regulation under the Dogs (Fouling of Land) Act 1996. The functions within the Dogs (Fouling of Land) Act 1996 are, so far as exercisable in relation to Wales, transferred to the National Assembly of Wales: The National Assembly for Wales (Transfer of Functions) Order 1999, SI 1999/672. References to "Secretary of State" should be read and construed accordingly.

[216] The Dogs (Fouling of Land) Regulations 1996, SI 1996/2762, sets out the form of the order for the designation, revocation and amendment and the procedure to be followed.

[217] Dogs (Fouling of Land) Act 1996, s. 2(1), (2).

[218] Land "open to air" is land which is open to the air on at least one side: Dogs (Fouling of Land) Act 1996, s. 1(5).

[219] Dogs (Fouling of Land) Act 1996, s. 1(1).

[220] The Regulations do not require the local authority to notify individually land owners or occupiers whose land may be the subject of the designation.

[221] Representations may be made in writing within 28 days of date of the publication. The address to which representation may be made will be contained in the notice.

[222] Dogs (Fouling of Land) Act 1996, s. 1(2).

2. Land used for agriculture or woodlands;

3. Land which is predominantly marshland, moor or heath; and

4. Common land to which the public are entitled or permitted access otherwise than by virtue of the Law of Property Act 1925, s. 193(1);[223]

5. Where a private Act of Parliament confers powers for the regulation of any land, the person entitled to exercise those powers may, by notice in writing given to the local authority in whose area the land is situated, exclude the application of the 1996 Act to that land.[224]

Unless a person has reasonable excuse, or the owner, occupier or person with control of the land has consented, a person in charge of a dog[225] is guilty of an offence if that dog defecates at any time on designated land and that person does not forthwith remove[226] the faeces.[227] A person not being aware of the defecation (whether by not being in the vicinity or otherwise), or not having a device or other suitable means of removing the faeces, does not have a reasonable excuse for failing to remove the faeces. However, being registered as a blind person may be relevant when the court considers whether or not there was reasonable excuse.

Whilst the local authority may operate a fixed penalty scheme,[228] it is not obliged to do so. The maximum fine on conviction for failure to comply with an order is currently £1,000.

---

[223] Dogs (Fouling of Land) Act 1996, s. 1(3).

[224] Dogs (Fouling of Land) Act 1996, s. 1(4).

[225] A person who habitually has a dog in his possession must be taken to be in charge of it at any time unless at that time some other person is in charge of the dog: Dogs (Fouling of Land) Act 1996, s. 3(4)(a).

[226] Placing the faeces in a receptacle which is provided for the purpose or for the disposal of waste is sufficient to satisfy the requirement: Dogs (Fouling of Land) Act 1996, s. 3(4)(b).

[227] Dogs (Fouling of Land) Act 1996, s. 6.

[228] Dogs (Fouling of Land) Act 1996, s. 3, 4. The Dog Fouling (Fixed Penalties) Order 1996 prescribes the form for the fixed penalty notice.

Chapter 5

HORSES

Introduction

This chapter brings together the law that relates particularly to horses. There are other matters relating to horses on the following pages: the passages in Chapter 3 relating to importation and exportation (pages 40 to 46), and welfare during transportation (pages 32 to 38); in Chapters 3 and 9 covering rabies on pages 55 to 58 and 208 to 211 respectively; in Chapter 8 on abandonment of animals (page 132), and operations on animals (pages 141 to 144); and in Chapter 10 on public performances (pages 214 to 215).

Cruel Tethering

It is an offence of cruelty[1] to tether any horse, ass or mule under such conditions or in such manner as to cause that animal unnecessary suffering.[2]

Docking and Nicking

The docking[3] or nicking[4] of horses'[5] tails is prohibited except in a case where a member of the Royal College of Veterinary Surgeons after examination of the horse has certified in writing that the operation is in his opinion necessary for its health because of disease or injury to its tail. Otherwise, both the person who performs the operation and anyone who causes or permits it commits offences.[6]

---

[1] Created by Protection Against Cruel Tethering Act 1988, s. 1.
[2] Protection of Animals Act 1911 s. 1(1)(f) (added by the Protection Against Cruel Tethering Act 1988, s. 1).
[3] "Docking" means the deliberate removal of any bone or any part of a bone from the tail of a horse (Docking and Nicking of Horses Act 1949, s. 3).
[4] "Nicking" means the deliberate severing of any tendon or muscle in the tail of a horse (Docking and Nicking of Horses Act 1949, s. 3).
[5] "Horse" includes stallion, gelding, colt, mare, filly, pony, mule and hinny (offspring of a she-ass by a stallion) (Docking and Nicking of Horses Act 1949, s.3).
[6] Punishment is by fine, imprisonment or both.

Equestrian Competition

Save for competitions[7] reserved for the purpose of permitting the improvement of a breed of horse,[8] a regional competition with a view of selecting horses, or historic or traditional events,[9] all other equestrian competitions, and the conditions governing a horse's participation therein, must not discriminate between horses which are registered or originate in the United Kingdom and horses which are registered or originate in another Member State.[10] In particular, the rules of any competition should have regard to the following:

1. The requirements for entering the competition, in particular the minimum or maximum requirements; and

2. The judging of the competition; and

3. The prize money and profits which may accrue from the competition.[11]

Where a horse registered or originating in another Member State is refused entry to a competition, the organiser of the competition must write to the owner, or his authorised representative, setting out the grounds on which such refusal is based.[12]

Farriery

It is an offence, punishable by a fine, for a person, not registered[13] with the Farriers Registration Council,[14] to carry out any

---

[7] "Competition" means any equestrian competition, including horse racing, show-jumping, eventing, dressage, events reserved for horse-drawn vehicles and showing classes: Horses (Free Access to Competitions) Regulations 1992, Reg. 2.

[8] "Horse" means domestic animals of the equine or asinine species or crossbreeds of those species: Horses (Free Access to Competitions) Regulations 1992, Reg. 2.

[9] Horses (Free Access to Competitions) Regulations 1992, Reg. 3(2).

[10] Horses (Free Access to Competitions) Regulations 1992, Reg. 4(1). Member State means a country belonging to the European Community.

[11] Horses (Free Access to Competitions) Regulations 1992, Reg. 4(2).

[12] Horses (Free Access to Competitions) Regulations 1992, Reg. 5.

[13] The process by which a farrier is registered, issues of misconduct and removal from the register are not dealt with here, but see generally Farriers (Registration) Act 1975, ss. 7, 14, Sch. 3, 15.

[14] The creation, composition and functions of the Council are not dealt with here, but see generally Farriers (Registration) Act 1975, ss. 1–6, 8–15 and the Schedules.

farriery.[15] The purpose of such registration is to prevent and avoid suffering by and cruelty to horses[16] arising from the shoeing of horses by unskilled persons; to promote the proper shoeing of horses; to promote the training of farriers and shoeing[17] smiths; to prohibit the shoeing of horses by unqualified persons.[18] An offence is not committed by the following persons:

1. A person serving under articles of apprenticeship which satisfy certain prescribed terms and conditions, if carried out in the course of his apprenticeship;

2. A person attending a training course[19] approved by the Council which is conducted at an approved institution as part of his course of training;

3. A veterinary surgeon or veterinary practitioner;

4. A person undergoing training as a veterinary surgeon in respect of any farriery carried out by him under the supervision of a veterinary surgeon, veterinary practitioner or a registered person;

5. A person rendering first-aid in case of emergency to a horse;[20]

6. A person who having had his name removed from the register has not yet been given notice of such removal;[21]

---

[15] Farriers (Registration) Act 1975, s. 16(1)(a). "Farrier" means any work in connection with the preparation or treatment of the foot of a horse for the immediate reception of a shoe thereon, the fitting by nailing or otherwise of a shoe to the foot or the finishing off of such work to the foot: Farriers (Registration) Act 1975, s. 18. This definition appears not to cover filing, rasping or trimming a horse's hoof in order to keep it in good condition, at least not when a shoe is not immediately thereafter fitted, even though these are operations commonly and properly entrusted to farriers: *Halsbury's Laws of England,* 4th Ed., Vol. 2 (Reissue), para. 423, note 1.

[16] "Horse" includes pony, mule, donkey or other equine animal: Farriers (Registration) Act 1975, s. 18.

[17] "Shoeing" has the same meaning as farriery: Farriers (Registration) Act 1975, s. 18.

[18] See Farriers (Registration) Act 1975 long title.

[19] For provisions relating to training courses and training institutions see Farriers (Registration) Act 1975, ss. 11, 12.

[20] Farriers (Registration) Act 1975, s. 16(1), provisos.

[21] Farriers (Registration) Act 1975, s. 16(2)(a), proviso. A person who is judged to be guilty of serious misconduct in any professional respect, a person who was not in fact qualified for registration at the time he was registered, and a person convicted of an offence of cruelty to animals (for which see generally, Chapter 8 Part B) may be removed from the register, or his resignation may be suspended for a specific period: *Halsbury's Laws of England,* 4th Ed., Vol. 2 (Reissue), para. 423.

7. A person who having applied for registration on the register has not had his application finally determined.[22]

It is an offence, punishable by a fine, for a person to use or adopt the style, title or description "farrier" or "shoeing smith" or any other style, title or description which is likely to cause any other person to believe that he is so registered.[23] These provisions do not apply to a person falling within exemption 6. or 7. above.[24]

Finally, it is an offence, punishable by a fine, for a person to wilfully[25] procure or attempt to procure the entry of his name in the register by making or producing or causing to be made or produced any false or fraudulent representation or declaration, either orally or in writing.[26]

Horse Passports

Where a horse[27] born on or after 1st January 1998 is registered with a recognised organisation,[28] the owner must apply in writing[29] to that organisation for a horse passport[30] for that horse.[31] The owner of a horse born before 1st January 1998 may, likewise, apply for a horse passport provided that it is already registered in the

---

[22] Farriers (Registration) Act 1975, s. 16(2)(b), proviso (added by the Farriers (Registration) (Amendment) Act 1977, ss. 1(1), Schedule).

[23] Farriers (Registration) Act 1975, s. 15A(1) (added by the Farriers (Registration) (Amendment) Act 1977, ss. 1(1), 2(3), Schedule).

[24] Farriers (Registration) Act 1975, s15A(1), proviso (added by the Farriers (Registration) (Amendment) Act 1977, ss. 1(1), 2(3), Schedule).

[25] For the meaning of "wilfully" see note 153 on p. 83.

[26] Farriers (Registration) Act 1975, s. 5.

[27] "Horse" means a domestic animal of the equine or asinine species or crossbreeds of those species: Horse Passport Order 1997, Art. 2(1).

[28] "Recognised organisation" means an organisation recognised by the Minister for DEFRA under the Horses (Zootechnical Standards) Regulations 1992 or an international association or organisation registered with the Minister as one which manages horses for competition or racing in Great Britain: Horse Passport Order 1997, Art. 2(1), 4. The functions of the Minister under the Horses (Zootechnical Standards) Regulations 1992 have been, so far as they relate to Wales, transferred to the National Assembly for Wales: National Assembly for Wales (Transfer of Functions) Order 2000, SI 2000/253.

[29] Horse Passport Order 1997, Art. 2(3).

[30] "Horse passport" means an identification document which has been issued by a recognised organisation in the prescribed form: Horse Passport Order 1997, Art. 2(1).

[31] Horse Passport Order 1997, Art. 5(1).

studbook[32] of a recognised organisation.[33]

On receipt of the application, the recognised organisation is obliged to issue a horse passport (in the prescribed format)[34] having first completed sections I to IV.[35] Where the horse was born before 1st January 1998 and the studbook shows more than one owner, the recognised body must complete section I with the details of previous owners, if applicable, before the passport is issued.[36] The owner of a registered horse may register it with more than one recognised organisation by sending the passport to the second (or subsequent) organisation for endorsement.[37] Likewise, where the owner wishes to de-register that horse from a registered organisation he must return the horse passport for cancellation of registration.[38] Once a horse passport has been issued, no person may apply for a replacement horse passport from a further organisation unless the original has been surrendered to and cancelled by the originating recognised organisation.[39] Whenever

---

[32] "Studbook" means any book, register, file or data medium which is maintained by a recognised organisation and in which horses are entered or registered with mention of all their known ascendants: Horse Passport Order 1997, Art. 2(1).

[33] Horse Passport Order 1997, Art. 5(3). The horse passport which is issued shall be sufficient identification for the purposes of the identification document requirement under the provisions of Article 8 of Council Directive 90/427/EEC (on the zootechnical and genealogical conditions governing intra-Community trade in equidae): Horse Passport Order 1997, Art. 15.

[34] See Horse Passport Order 1997, Schedule. The horse passport must conform to the provisions of the Schedule, and must be in English and French. Additionally, it may also contain a translation of the passport (in whole or in part) into such other language or languages as the recognised organisation thinks fit: Horse Passport Order 1997, Art. 5(4). Any replacement passport must be marked with the word "duplicate". See Horse Passport Order 1997, Art. 13 for details relating to the loss or damage of a horse passport.

[35] Horse Passport Order 1997, Art. 5(2). No person other than a person authorised by the recognised organisation which issued the horse passport, may amend sections I to VI of the horse passport: Horse Passport Order 1997, Art. 5(6). Likewise it is an offence, punishable by a fine, for any person other than a person authorised by the recognised organisation to complete sections I to VI of the horse passport: Horse Passport Order 1997, Art. 16(1).

[36] Horse Passport Order 1997, Art. 5(5).

[37] Horse Passport Order 1997, Art. 6(1). The owner of a horse born before 1st January 1998, which has been registered with one recognised organisation, has 28 days (from the date of receipt of the horse passport) in which to send it to any other organisation with which he wishes to register it.

[38] Horse Passport Order 1997, Art. 6(2).

[39] Horse Passport Order 1997, Art. 6(4). The further recognised organisation must ensure that all details included in the original horse passport relating to the identity of the horse and veterinary treatment contained in sections II to VII are included in the replacement horse passport: Horse Passport Order 1997, Art. 6(6).

a horse is sold, for which a horse passport has been issued, the similar procedures must be complied with, i.e. notification to the recognised organisation(s), within 28 days, of the new owner's details and any further registration with recognised organisations or de-registration.[40]

If the owner of a semi-feral breed[41] makes an application for registration to a recognised organisation, sections III and IV (relating to description and identification of the horse) need not be completed at the time of registration. However, the owner must return the horse passport to the recognised organisation for completion of the sections before:

a. the horse reaches 12 months old; or

b. the horse is sold by auction for the second time; or

c. the horse is moved to other premises for competition purposes; or

d. the horse is moved out of Great Britain; or

e. the horse is moved to the premises of a new keeper; or

f. the horse is moved on any other occasion specified by the recognised organisation; or

g. within 14 days of the horse being moved to other premises for veterinary treatment.[42]

Otherwise, the provisions are the same as for other breeds of horses.

Upon receipt of the horse passport, or whenever the horse receives veterinary treatment, the owner shall ensure that any veterinary

---

[40] Horse Passport Order 1997, Art. 11.
[41] "Semi-feral breed" means a breed registered with one of the following recognised organisations: the Dales Pony Society; the Dartmoor Pony Society; the Eriskay Pony Society; the Exmoor Pony Society; the Fell Pony Society; the Highland Pony Society; the New Forest Pony Breeding and Cattle Society; the Shetland Pony Studbook Society; the Welsh Pony and Cob Society (only horses registered in Section A and B of the Society's studbook): Horse Passport Order 1997, Art. 2(1).
[42] Horse Passport Order 1997, Art. 7.

surgeon who has, to his knowledge, treated the horse or is giving treatment (as applicable), enters in the horse passport all details of treatment listed in sections V to VII of the Schedule.[43]

Riding Establishments

It is illegal to keep a riding establishment without a licence from the local authority.[44] The keeping of a riding establishment[45] is defined to mean the carrying on of a business of keeping horses[46] for either or both of the following purposes:

1. The purpose of the horses being let out on hire for riding;

2. The purpose of their being used in providing, in return for payment, instruction in riding.

But excluded from the definition and therefore not needing a licence, is the carrying on of such a business:

a. where the premises[47] where the horses employed for the purpose of the business are kept are occupied by or under the management of the Secretary of State for Defence, i.e. military establishments; or

b. solely for police purposes; or

c. by the Zoological Society of London; or

d. by the Royal Zoological Society of Scotland.[48]

---

[43] Horse Passport Order 1997, Art. 10. It is an offence, punishable by a fine, for any person other than a veterinary surgeon to make an entry in sections V to VIII of a horse passport: Horse Passport Order 1997, Art. 16(2).

[44] Riding Establishments Act 1964, s. 1(1). "Local authority" means the council of a district or the Common Council of the City of London and in Wales means the council of a county or county borough: Riding Establishments Act 1964, s. 6(4) (amended by the Local Government Act 1972, ss. 251(2), 272(1), Sch. 29 Part II, para. 42, Sch. 30 and Local Government (Wales) Act 1994, s. 22(3), Sch. 9, para. 7).

[45] A person is deemed to keep a riding establishment at the premises (which includes land) where the horses employed for the purpose of the business concerned are kept: Riding Establishments Act 1964, ss. 6(3), 6(4).

[46] "Horse" includes any mare, gelding, pony, foal, colt, filly or stallion and also any ass, mule or jennet: Riding Establishments Act 1964, s. 6(4).

[47] "Premises" includes land: Riding Establishments Act 1964, s. 6(4).

[48] Riding Establishments Act 1964, s. 6(1).

Also excluded are universities providing approved courses for veterinary students.[49]

The rules about licensing of riding establishments are similar to those for dog breeding kennels, pet shops, and boarding kennels which were examined in the previous chapter, but they are more detailed and provide also for provisional licences to be issued. Application must be made to the local authority.[50] A number of pre-conditions must be fulfilled before a licence can be granted; these are:

1. The applicant must be at least 18 years old or an incorporated body;

2. The applicant must not be disqualified from keeping a riding establishment[51] or a pet shop[52] or boarding kennels,[53] or from having the custody of animals;[54]

3. The payment of such fee determined by the local authority;

4. The riding establishment must be in the area of the local authority;

5. The riding establishment must have been inspected by a vet[55] whose report must contain sufficient particulars to enable the local authority to decide whether they are suitable and must describe their condition and the condition of any horses or thing found there;[56]

6. In deciding whether to grant a licence the local authority must

---

[49] Riding Establishments Act 1964, s. 6(2).
[50] Riding Establishments Act 1964, s. 1(2) (amended by Local Government Act 1974, ss. 35(1), (2), Sch. 6, para. 18).
[51] See p. 104.
[52] See p. 88.
[53] See p. 82.
[54] Riding Establishments Act 1964, s. 1(2) (amended by the Protection of Animals (Amendment) Act 1988, s. 3(2), (3), Schedule).
[55] I.e. a veterinary surgeon or veterinary practitioner authorised by the local authority to carry out such inspections. The inspection must be made not earlier than a year preceding the date on which the application is received by the local authority.
[56] Riding Establishments Act 1964, s. 1(3).

have regard to whether the applicant appears to be suitable and qualified to hold the licence by:

i.   experience in the management of horses; or

ii. being the holder of an approved certificate;[57] or

iii. employing in the management of the riding establishment a person qualified as in i. or ii.;

7. Before granting a licence the local authority must also consider in particular the need to secure that a number of other matters will be in order. These (in brief) concern: health, shoeing and suitability of the horses for hire or instruction (if applicable); suitability of their accommodation; adequacy of their food and water supply, shelter, bedding material, exercising, grooming and resting; precautions against disease and provision of first aid equipment and medicines; fire precautions; adequacy of accommodation for forage, bedding, stable equipment and saddlery.[58]

Even if all the foregoing matters are satisfactory, the local authority nevertheless have a discretion to refuse a licence on any other grounds.[59] If a licence is issued, it will be subject to compulsory conditions dealing with, briefly: unfit horses not to be returned to work unless covered by a vet's certificate; supervision or hiring of horses by responsible persons; riding establishments not to be left in charge of anyone under 16; licence holder to be insured against his liability for injury to other persons; licence holder to keep a

---

[57] "Approved certificate" means any one of the following certificates issued by the British Horse Society, namely, Assistant Instructor's Certificate, Instructor's Certificate and Fellowship; or Fellow of the Institute of the Horse; or any other certificate approved by the Secretary of State: Riding Establishments Act 1964, s. 6(4) (inserted by Riding Establishments Act 1970, s. 5). No order has been made. The functions of the Secretary of State in relation to this sub-section, so far as exercisable in relation to Wales, transferred to the National Assembly of Wales: The National Assembly for Wales (Transfer of Functions) Order 1999, SI 1999/672.

[58] Riding Establishments Act 1964, s. 1(4) (substituted by the Riding Establishments Act 1970, s. 2(1)(ii)).

[59] That is to say, that the local authority may attach such conditions to the licence as it appears to it to be necessary or expedient to do so in order to secure all the objects specified in pre-condition 7: Riding Establishments Act 1964, s. 1(4).

register of horses under four years old and make it available for inspection by an authorised officer of the local authority at all reasonable times. These conditions apply whether or not they are written into the licence.[60]

The provisions dealing with the duration of a licence, the right of appeal against its refusal or its conditions (except the compulsory conditions which are not appealable) and the continuation of the licence after the holder's death are the same as those for boarding kennels already mentioned in Chapter 4.[61]

If the local authority is not satisfied that it would be justified in granting an ordinary licence, it may grant a provisional licence for a period of three months.[62] This may be extended for a further three months if applied for before the first period expires; but riding establishments cannot be licensed in this way for more than six months in any year.[63] There is no right of appeal against refusal of a provisional licence. Otherwise the provisions relating to a full licence apply equally to a provisional licence.[64]

Officers of any local authority and vets, if authorised in both cases in writing by a local authority, may enter and inspect premises which are licensed, for which a licence has been sought or which are suspected of being used as a riding establishment. They may be required to produce their authorisations; obstruction of them is an offence.[65]

A number of other offences related to riding establishments exist. These are, briefly: keeping an unlicensed riding establishment, except of course when a licence is not required;[66] breach of a condition of a licence by a licence holder; using a horse when that is likely to cause it suffering; supplying defective equipment for use with a horse which is likely to cause it suffering or an accident

---

[60] Riding Establishments Act 1964, s. 1(4A) (inserted by the Riding Establishments Act 1970, s. 2(1)(ii)).
[61] Riding Establishments Act 1964, s. 1(5), (6), (8). See pp. 82-84.
[62] Riding Establishments Act 1970, s. 1(1).
[63] Riding Establishments Act 1970, s. 1(2).
[64] Riding Establishments Act 1970, s. 1(3).
[65] Riding Establishments Act 1964, s. 2(1), (2), (4).
[66] See pp. 100-101.

to its rider; failing to provide curative care for a horse; knowingly permitting a person disqualified from keeping riding establishments to control or manage riding establishments; concealing a horse with intent to avoid its inspection; using a horse under four years old or a mare heavy with foal or within three months after foaling; and giving false information to obtain a licence.[67]

The local authority has powers to prosecute proceedings for any offence under either the 1964 or 1970 Act, save that for prosecution of proceedings against a person operating an unlicensed riding establishment or a breach of the pre-conditions 1.–7. above the local authority must first obtain a vet's report.[68] On conviction of any of these offences, or of offences under other named Acts dealing with animals,[69] the magistrates' court may cancel the offender's licence and may, whether or not he holds a licence, disqualify him from keeping a riding establishment for such time as the court thinks fit.[70] The operation of the court's orders for cancellation or disqualification may be suspended while an appeal[71] is made.[72]

Welfare of Horses at Markets

The Welfare of Horses at Markets (and Other Places of Sale) Order 1990 is intended to set and enforce welfare standards for horses[73] whilst they are exposed for sale in a market[74] or while they are

---

[67] Riding Establishments Act 1964, ss. 1(9) (amended by Riding Establishments Act 1970, s. 2(2)), 3 (amended by Riding Establishments Act 1970, s. 3).
[68] Riding Establishments Act 1964, s. 5.
[69] These Acts are: the Protection of Animals Act 1911 (see generally Section B of Chapter 8); the corresponding Protection of Animals (Scotland) Act 1912; the Pet Animals Act 1951 (see pp. 84-89) and the Animal Boarding Establishments Act 1963 (see pp. 82-84).
[70] Riding Establishments Act 1964, s. 4(3).
[71] Appeal lies, presumably, to the Crown Court.
[72] Riding Establishments Act 1964, s. 4(4).
[73] "Horse" means a horse, pony, ass, hinny or mule: Welfare of Horses at Markets (and Other Places of Sale) Order 1990, Art. 3(1).
[74] "Market" means a market place, sale-yard, fairground, highway, or any other premises or place to which horses are brought from other places and exposed for sale and includes any lairage adjoining a market and used in connection with it and any place adjoining a market used as a parking area by visitors to the market for parking vehicles. "Highway" includes a road or lane and any place over which members of the public have a right to pass or repass with or without vehicles: Welfare of Horses at Markets (and Other Places of Sale) Order 1990, Art. 3(1).

awaiting removal after being exposed for sale; or whilst they are kept temporarily in a market (without being exposed for sale) pending completion of their inland transit in Great Britain.[75] The Order burdens various persons, authorities and organisations with differing responsibilities and it is convenient to take each of these groups in turn.

(1) All persons
There are various restrictions imposed on persons generally not to permit certain happenings. How liable that person is will depend upon his immediacy to the particular offence, and may include any one or all of the following: the owner or person in charge of the horse, the market operator,[76] or such other person as the local authority or inspector[77] considers reasonably culpable. Thus, no person may permit an unfit horse to be exposed for sale in a market, nor shall they permit a mare[78] to be exposed for sale if it is likely to give birth whilst at the market.[79] Likewise, no person may cause or permit any injury or unnecessary suffering to a horse in a market. However, it will be the duty of the person in charge of the horse to ensure that the horse is not, nor is it likely to be, caused injury or unnecessary suffering by reason of:

a. the horse being exposed to the weather;[80]

b. inadequate ventilation being available for the horse;

c. the horse being hit or prodded by any instrument or other thing;

---

[75] Welfare of Horses at Markets (and Other Places of Sale) Order 1990, Art. 4.
[76] "Market operator" means the person for the time being responsible for managing the reception or the sale of horses in a market: Welfare of Horses at Markets (and Other Places of Sale) Order 1990, Art. 3(1).
[77] "Inspector" means a person appointed to be an inspector for the purposes of the Animal Health Act 1981 by the Minister or by a local authority and, when used in relation to a person appointed by the Minister, includes a veterinary inspector: Welfare of Horses at Markets (and Other Places of Sale) Order 1990, Art. 3(1).
[78] "Mare" includes a female in foal for the first time: Welfare of Horses at Markets (and Other Places of Sale) Order 1990, Art. 3(1).
[79] Welfare of Horses at Markets (and Other Places of Sale) Order 1990, Art. 5.
[80] A horse that has been clipped such that it is insufficiently protected from the weather by its natural coat may not be kept or caused to be kept at the market unless it is kept in covered accommodation or provided with suitable protective clothing: Welfare of Horses at Markets (and Other Places of Sale) Order 1990, Art. 14.

d. the horse being tethered in an unsuitable manner; or

e. any other cause.[81]

The Order is contravened if a foal[82] is brought to a market without it being at the foot of its dam, nor may it be separated from its dam whilst they await removal from the market after being exposed for sale; or when they are being kept in a market (without being exposed for sale there) pending completion of their inland transit within Great Britain. The foal at the foot of its dam may not be exposed for sale separately from its dam.[83]

Provision is made to restrict the types of handling, the use of force to control horses in markets and to prevent obstruction. Thus, it is an offence, within a market, to lift off the ground or drag a horse along the ground by its head, neck, ear, leg or tail. [84] Similarly, no person may use excessive force to control any horse and, in particular, he may not use any instrument that is capable of inflicting an electric shock, nor any stick, whip, goad or other instrument or thing to hit or prod any horse.[85] No person may drive, ride or lead any horse over any ground or floor, the nature of which is likely to cause the horse to slip[86] and any person who knowingly obstructs any horse being driven or led through the market is guilty of an offence.[87]

Where a horse has been identified as being unfit (which includes being likely to give birth) by an inspector and has been moved to a pen for the accommodation of unfit horses, no person may remove that horse without the approval of a veterinary inspector and in accordance with any conditions subject to which the approval is given.[88]

---

81 Welfare of Horses at Markets (and Other Places of Sale) Order 1990, Art. 6.
82 "Foal" means a horse under the age of four months: Welfare of Horses at Markets (and Other Places of Sale) Order 1990, Art. 3(1).
83 Welfare of Horses at Markets (and Other Places of Sale) Order 1990, Art. 7.
84 Welfare of Horses at Markets (and Other Places of Sale) Order 1990, Art. 8.
85 Welfare of Horses at Markets (and Other Places of Sale) Order 1990, Art. 9.
86 Welfare of Horses at Markets (and Other Places of Sale) Order 1990, Art. 9(3).
87 Welfare of Horses at Markets (and Other Places of Sale) Order 1990, Art. 10(1). A further offence is committed if a person wantonly or unreasonably annoys any horse in a market: Welfare of Horses at Markets (and Other Places of Sale) Order 1990, Art. 10(2).
88 Welfare of Horses at Markets (and Other Places of Sale) Order 1990, Art. 17(3).

General offences (punishable by a fine) arise where, without such lawful authority or excuse,[89] any person:

a. defaces, obliterates or removes any mark applied by an inspector to a horse;

b. (where an unfit horse is conditionally released to him by a veterinary inspector) fails to comply with any provision or with any condition imposed by a veterinary inspector;

c. contravenes or knowingly causes or permits any contravention or non-compliance with any provisions of the Order.[90]

(2) Local authority
Save where provided in (1) and (3)-(6), the local authority must execute and enforce the provisions of the Order. [91] There is likely to be an overlap with the obligations to be found in (4) if the local authority is responsible for the upkeep of a market or for the provision of fixed facilities there.

(3) Market operator
The market operator is obliged to ensure the security and welfare standards for any horse at its market. Briefly, these include adequate facilities for the penning and separation of horses; the provision of lighting and bedding; the accommodation of unfit horses; giving all reasonable assistance to an inspector as he may require for the purpose of facilitating his duties; and providing such information as he possesses as to the ownership of any horse at the market to an inspector if requested so to do.[92]

(4) Market authorities
The market authority[93] is responsible for the fabric of the market,

---

[89] The burden of proving lawful authority or excuse lies with the defendant. The burden is on the balance of probabilities.
[90] Welfare of Horses at Markets (and Other Places of Sale) Order 1990, Art. 19.
[91] Welfare of Horses at Markets (and Other Places of Sale) Order 1990, Art. 20.
[92] Welfare of Horses at Markets (and Other Places of Sale) Order 1990, Arts. 11, 13, 16 and 17(5) respectively. The market operator is not under an obligation under Arts. 11 and 13 where there is another person in charge of the horse: Welfare of Horses at Markets (and Other Places of Sale) Order 1990, Arts. 11, 13, provisos.
[93] "Market authority" means the local authority or other person responsible for the upkeep of the market or for the provision of fixed facilities there: Welfare of Horses at Markets (and Other Places of Sale) Order 1990, Art. 3(1).

certain feeding and drinking facilities, and for the safe transfer of horses from and to vehicles.[94] Thus, the authority must ensure that all passageways, sale rings, and all pens (which includes boxes and stalls) at the market are constructed and maintained in a manner which is not likely to cause injury or unnecessary suffering to horses and are free from any sharp edges or projections with which horses may come into contact. Similarly, any covered accommodation in the market in which horses are kept must be capable of being adequately ventilated.[95]

Likewise, the authority must ensure that there is an adequate supply of wholesome water together with adequate facilities in the form of troughs, buckets, drinking bowls or other drinking devices for watering horses.[96]

(5) Inspector
The inspector is appointed for the purposes (amongst other things) of ensuring that the provisions of the Welfare of Horses at Markets (and Other Places of Sale) Order 1990 are being complied with.[97] Under the Order an inspector[98] (rather than a veterinary inspector)[99] may:

a. restrict access to pens clearly marked for accommodation of unfit horses;

b. move any horse which he reasonably believes is unfit within the confines of the market to such accommodation or to any other suitable place in the market;

c. mark, or cause to be marked, any horse for the purposes of identification.[100]

---

[94] The authority must ensure that any fixed ramps used for the loading or unloading of horses into or out of vehicles have anti-slip surfaces; and side rails or some other means of protection designated and constructed so as to prevent a horse from falling off them: Welfare of Horses at Markets (and Other Places of Sale) Order 1990, Art. 15(c).

[95] Welfare of Horses at Markets (and Other Places of Sale) Order 1990, Art. 15(a), (e).

[96] Welfare of Horses at Markets (and Other Places of Sale) Order 1990, Art. 15(b), (d).

[97] For the general powers of inspectors see Animal Health Act 1981, s. 63.

[98] See note 77 on p. 105.

[99] I.e. one appointed by the Minister as a veterinary inspector: Welfare of Horses at Markets (and Other Places of Sale) Order 1990, Art. 3(1).

[100] Welfare of Horses at Markets (and Other Places of Sale) Order 1990, Arts. 16(b), 17(1), 18 respectively.

The veterinary inspector may treat any horse, or cause it to be treated, and take, or cause to be taken, any steps that he considers necessary to prevent the suffering of any horse. He may require the market operator to detain the horse in the accommodation allocated for unfit horses for such period as he considers necessary for the treatment of the horse or otherwise to protect it from suffering. The veterinary inspector's reasonable costs for the foregoing may be recovered by the Minister from the owner of the horse as a civil debt.

(6) Owner, duly authorised agent or person in charge of a horse
In addition to the provisions in (1) above, further obligations are imposed on this class of persons. Where performed by the market operator, a person in charge of a horse is required to ensure that, within the market the horse is suitably penned and, if appropriate, separated or secured in the prescribed manner.[101] Similarly, he must ensure that adequate lighting is made available for the purpose of inspecting, feeding and watering the horse and that there is adequate bedding for any foal or horse kept in the market from one day to the next.[102]

Separately, the person in charge of a horse must ensure that it receives adequate quantities of wholesome water as often as is necessary to prevent it from suffering from thirst.[103] The owner (or his duly authorised agent) is obliged to ensure that, from one day to the next during the duration of the horse's stay at the market, it has easy access to an adequate quantity of wholesome and palatable[104] food provided for in haynets, racks or troughs and an adequate quantity of wholesome water.[105]

---

[101] Welfare of Horses at Markets (and Other Places of Sale) Order 1990, Art. 11.
[102] Welfare of Horses at Markets (and Other Places of Sale) Order 1990, Art. 13.
[103] Welfare of Horses at Markets (and Other Places of Sale) Order 1990, Art. 12.
[104] I.e. palatable for the horse.
[105] Welfare of Horses at Markets (and Other Places of Sale) Order 1990, Art. 12(2). The provision of water and sustenance must be provided for before 9 pm on the day on which the horse arrives at the market or, if it arrives at the market after 9 pm, immediately on its arrival there; and thereafter once in each complete period of 12 hours (calculated from 9 pm on the day of its arrival at the market) during which the horse is kept in the market: Welfare of Horses at Markets (and Other Places of Sale) Order 1990, Art. 12(2), proviso.

Chapter 6

DANGEROUS WILD ANIMALS

The Dangerous Wild Animals Act 1976 was passed to regulate the keeping of certain kinds of dangerous wild animals. The fundamental provision of the Act is to prohibit, with exceptions, the keeping of named animals except in accordance with a licence granted by the local authority.[1] A number of the components of this provision needs to be examined in turn.

The exceptions to the prohibition are: a zoo;[2] a circus;[3] premises licensed as a pet shop;[4] and a place registered under the Animals (Scientific Procedures) Act 1986 for performing experiments.[5]

The Act is at pains to define the meaning of "keeping" in relation to the named animals. A person is a keeper of an animal if he has it in his possession;[6] for those times when an animal cannot be said to be in the possession of anybody it is treated as being in the possession of the person who last had it in his possession.[7] But a person is not to be treated as the keeper of an animal only because he has it in his possession for the purpose of: preventing it from causing damage;[8] restoring it to its owner; it undergoing veterinary

---

[1] Dangerous Wild Animals Act 1976, s. 1(1). Contravention is an offence punishable by fine (Dangerous Wild Animals Act 1976, ss. 2(5), 6(1)).

[2] Dangerous Wild Animals Act 1976, s. 5 (as amended by the Zoo Licensing Act 1981, s. 22 (1)(a)). For the meaning of "zoo" see Zoo Licensing Act 1981, s. 1(2).

[3] "Circus" includes any place where animals are kept or introduced wholly or mainly for the purpose of performing tricks or manoeuvres (Dangerous Wild Animals Act 1976, s. 7(4)). The definition includes those lodgings in which animals are kept over the winter period (*South Kesteven DC v Mackie, The Times,* 20 October 1999). An enclosure in a high street, to which a lioness was taken from a zoo for exhibition purposes, is not a circus within the definition (*Hemming* v *Graham-Jones* (1980)).

[4] For licensing of pet shops, see pp. 88-89.

[5] Dangerous Wild Animals Act 1976, s. 5 (as amended by Animals (Scientific Procedures) Act 1986, s. 27(2), Sch. 3, para. 10). See also Animals (Scientific Procedures) Act 1986, ss. 6 and 7.

[6] For some notes on the meaning of "possession", see p. 68.

[7] Dangerous Wild Animals Act 1976, s. 7(1).

[8] "Damage" includes the death of, or injury to, any person. (Dangerous Wild Animals Act 1976, s. 7(4).)

treatment; or it being transported on behalf of another person.[9]

The animals to which the Act applies are listed in its Schedule which is reproduced in Appendix D at the end of this book. It may be varied by regulations made by the Secretary of State.[10]

Licences to keep dangerous wild animals are granted by district councils.[11] They are not permitted to grant a licence unless several conditions are met. In the first place an application for a licence must:

a. specify the species of animal and the number of animals of each species proposed to be kept;[12]

b. specify the premises[13] where any animal concerned will normally be held which must be within the local authority area;

c. be made by a person who is neither under 18 years old nor disqualified from keeping any dangerous wild animal;[14] and

d. be accompanied by such fee as the authority may stipulate.[15]

In the second place, a licence is not to be granted unless the council is satisfied that:

a. it is not contrary to the public interest on the grounds of safety, nuisance or otherwise to grant it;

---

[9] Dangerous Wild Animals Act 1976, s. 7(2).
[10] Dangerous Wild Animals Act 1976, ss. 7(4), 8. The Schedule has been substituted by SI 1984/1111. This function has not been transferred to the National Assembly for Wales.
[11] Dangerous Wild Animals Act 1976, ss. 1(1), 7(4). In London the licensing authority is the Common Council of the City of London or, elsewhere, a London borough council. In relation to Wales the licensing authority is a county council or county borough council: the Local Government (Wales) Act 1994, Sch. 16, para. 50.
[12] "Kept" is to be interpreted in accordance with the definition of "keeper" (Dangerous Wild Animals Act 1976, s. 7(3)) – see above.
[13] "Premises" can include any place (Dangerous Wild Animals Act 1976, s. 7(4)).
[14] For disqualification, see p. 114.
[15] Dangerous Wild Animals Act 1976, s. 1(2). The fee should be sufficient to meet the direct and indirect costs which the council may incur as a result of the application.

b. the applicant for the licence is a suitable person to hold it;

c. the animal's accommodation will be escape-proof and suitable as regards construction, size, temperature, lighting, ventilation, drainage, cleanliness and the number of animals that can be suitably accommodated;

d. the animal will be supplied with adequate and suitable food, drink and bedding material and be visited at suitable intervals;

e. the animal will be protected in case of fire or other emergency;

f. all reasonable precautions will be taken to prevent and control the spread of infectious diseases; and

g. the animal can take adequate exercise within its accommodation.[16]

Two further conditions must be fulfilled before a licence can be granted. Unless in the council's opinion the circumstances are exceptional, the application must be made by a person who both owns and possesses,[17] or proposes both to own and possess, any animal concerned.[18] Secondly, the council must consider a report by a vet[19] on the premises where any animal will normally be held and cannot issue a licence unless, viewed in the light of that report, they consider the premises suitable.[20]

Even if all these pre-requisites are met, the grant or refusal of a licence is, subject to the right of appeal mentioned later, entirely within the council's discretion. If a licence is issued, it must include conditions about a number of matters detailed in the Act (including insurance against liability for damage[21] caused by the animal) to which the council may add their own conditions.[22] With

---

[16] Dangerous Wild Animals Act 1976, s. 1(3).
[17] For some notes on the meaning of "possession", see p. 68.
[18] Dangerous Wild Animals Act 1976, s. 1(4).
[19] The vet's fee will be part of the cost of the licence to be charged to the applicant; see note 15 on p. 111. For costs of inspection of premises, see p. 114.
[20] Dangerous Wild Animals Act 1976, s. 1(5).
[21] "Damage" includes the death of, or injury to, any person (Dangerous Wild Animals Act 1976, s. 7(4)).
[22] Dangerous Wild Animals Act 1976, s. 1(6), (7).

some limitations, the council may at any time vary or revoke the conditions, or add new conditions; unless a variation or new condition is requested by the licence-holder, he must be given reasonable time to comply with it.[23]

Contravention of or non-compliance with a condition is an offence. In addition to the licence-holder, the offence may be committed by any other person who is entitled to keep any animal under the authority of the licence and who was primarily responsible for the contravention or non-compliance. Neither may be convicted if he proves that he took all reasonable precautions to avoid committing the offence.[24]

At the choice of the applicant, the licence will last from the day it is granted to the end of the current calendar year or from the beginning of the next year to the end of that year.[25] Unless previously cancelled,[26] the licence then expires, but if a further licence is applied for beforehand it continues in force pending the grant or refusal of the application. A new licence will run from the expiry date of the previous licence.[27] Personal representatives of a deceased licence holder have the benefit of the licence for 28 days from death; if they apply for a new one within that time, the original licence continues in force until the application is determined.[28]

There is a right of appeal to a magistrates' court [29] against:

a. the council's refusal to grant a licence;

b. a condition of the licence whether imposed when it was granted or later;

c. the variation or revocation of a condition.[30]

Powers of entry to and inspection of premises connected with a

---

[23] Dangerous Wild Animals Act 1976, s. 1(9), (10).
[24] Dangerous Wild Animals Act 1976, s. 2(6), (7).
[25] Dangerous Wild Animals Act 1976, s. 2(2).
[26] See p. 114.
[27] Dangerous Wild Animals Act 1976, s. 2(3).
[28] Dangerous Wild Animals Act 1976, s. 2(4).
[29] In Scotland, to the sheriff (Dangerous Wild Animals Act 1976, s. 2(8)).
[30] Dangerous Wild Animals Act 1976, s. 2(1).

licence are given to vets and others with written authorisation from the council.[31] To obstruct or delay them is an offence.[32] The reasonable costs of the inspection may be charged to the applicant for the licence or, if it has been issued, to the licensee.[33]

If a dangerous wild animal is kept[34] without a licence, or a condition of a licence is contravened or not complied with, the council in whose area the animal is may seize it and keep it or destroy or otherwise dispose of it. No compensation is payable.[35] The council's costs are recoverable in the first case from the animal's keeper and, in the second case, from the licence-holder.[36]

In addition to fining a person for an offence against the Act, the court may cancel his licence and, whether he is a licence holder or not, disqualify him from keeping any dangerous wild animal to which the Act applies for such period as the court thinks fit. These sanctions can also be imposed for convictions for offences against certain other Acts[37] relating to animals. The court's order of cancellation or disqualification may be suspended pending an appeal.[38]

In concluding this chapter, the point is made that there is no exception to or mitigation of the 1976 Act's requirements when only few very young animals of the kind described are kept. For example, a newly born tiger requires a licence as much as a cage of adult tigers.

---

[31] Dangerous Wild Animals Act 1976, s. 3(1).

[32] Dangerous Wild Animals Act 1976, s. 3(4).

[33] Dangerous Wild Animals Act 1976, s. 3(3).

[34] "Kept" and "keeping" must be interpreted in accordance with the definition of "keeper" given on pp. 110-111 (Dangerous Wild Animals Act 1976, s. 7(3)).

[35] Dangerous Wild Animals Act 1976, s. 4(1).

[36] Dangerous Wild Animals Act 1976, s. 4(2), (3).

[37] These Acts are: the Protection of Animals Acts 1911 to 1964 (see pp. 132-150); the Protection of Animals (Scotland) Acts 1912 to 1964; the Pet Animals Act 1951 (see pp. 88-89); the Animal Boarding Establishments Act 1963 (see pp. 82-84); the Riding Establishments Acts 1964 and 1970 (see pp. 100-104); and the Breeding of Dogs Act 1973 as amended by the Breeding and Sale of Dogs (Welfare) Act 1999 (see pp. 84-88).

[38] Dangerous Wild Animals Act 1976, s. 6. The appeal lies, presumably, to the Crown Court.

Chapter 7

ANIMALS AS GAME

Introduction

In the Acts of Parliament dealing with game there are different definitions of the word or no definition at all. So far as four-legged animals are concerned, only hares, rabbits and deer are involved, but not all in the same way. The differences will appear when the relevant Acts are considered.

Where an animal is thus treated as game, a dead or tame animal of that kind is, when appropriate in the context, likewise treated.[1]

The Game Acts, when regulating dealings with game, generally use the words "take or kill". "Taking" has been interpreted to mean catching, as in a snare, with a view to keeping or killing,[2] and this word will be used in this chapter to mean both killing and taking.

Prohibited Times for Taking Game

Close Seasons

There is no close season, i.e. period of the year in which game must not be taken, for rabbits or hares.[3] The only close seasons for deer are for certain species, and it is an offence to take them out of season, but with certain exceptions; these matters are considered on pages 152 to 153. Close seasons for birds are considered on pages 176 to 177.

Sunday and Christmas Day

It is an offence to take hares on Sunday or Christmas Day or then to use any dog, gun, net, or other engine[4] or instrument for that

---

[1]   *Cook v Trevener* (1911) 103 LT 725.

[2]   *R v Glover* (1814) Russ & Ry 269; *Watkins v Price* (1877) 37 LT 578.

[3]   But occupiers of certain lands may not take hares and rabbits under the Ground Game Acts during certain periods of the year; see p. 123.

[4]   The word "engine" includes a snare *(Allen v Thompson* (1870) LR 5 QB 336 at 339). See also note 121 on p. 130.

purpose.[5] (In defining the meaning of game in this context the Act says that the word includes hares and particular game birds, and it is a matter for speculation whether, since deer are sometimes regarded as game, they may be included also.) It matters not that the net "or other engine or instrument" was set on another day; the person doing so is regarded by the law as using it on the prohibited days if it was then in position.[6]

At Night
It is an offence unlawfully[7] to take hares or rabbits at night[8] on any open or enclosed land, including any public road, highway or path or the sides of them and the openings, outlets or gates from any open or enclosed land leading on to any public road, highway or path.[9]

Other provisions about shooting hares and rabbits at night are described on pages 123 to 125. The offence of killing or taking deer at night is considered on page 154.

Game Licences
With the exceptions mentioned later,[10] a person must hold a game licence before he can take game. This obligation is created by two Acts of Parliament.[11] Because their wording is different and their combined scope is wide, it is worthwhile to set down the exact words used so far as they describe the acts which require a licence to be held:

1. To take or kill any game or use any dog, gun, net or other engine[12] or instrument for the purpose of searching for or

---

5   Game Act 1831, s. 3. The use of one dog, gun, etc. by two or more people acting together may constitute an offence by each (*R v Littlechild* (1871) 24 LT 233; *R v Heslop* (1871) 35 JP 661).
6   *Allen v Thompson* (1870) LR 5 QB 336.
7   Though mainly directed at common poachers, this offence may be committed by others not having the right to take the animals and, possibly, by someone acting unlawfully because he has no game licence.
8   This is from one hour after sunset to one hour before sunrise (Night Poaching Act 1828, s. 12).
9   Night Poaching Act 1828, s. 1; Night Poaching Act 1844, s. 1.
10 See pp. 118-119.
11 Game Act 1831 and Game Licences Act 1860.
12 See note 4 on p. 115.

killing or taking game;[13]

2. To take, kill or pursue, or aid or assist in any manner in the taking, killing or pursuing by any means whatever, or use any dog, gun, net or other engine for the purpose of taking, killing or pursuing game.[14]

So far as four-legged animals are concerned, hares only are mentioned in the definition of "game" in 1., and "game" (undefined) and rabbits and deer in 2.; though it may be argued that deer also are included in 1. and hares in 2.[15] It will be seen that the scope of the words used in 2. is generally wider than in 1., but the latter brings in searching for game.

Some examples taken from decided cases help to show the wide scope of these requirements. To walk about unlicensed with a dog or gun where there is game or to point a gun at game is evidence of the commission of an offence.[16]

If an unlicensed person kills game by accident and takes it away, he has committed an offence.[17] So a motorist knocking over a hare, who picks it up, puts it in the car and drives on, is guilty if he has no game licence. To take game out of a trap in which it has been accidentally caught with a view to killing or keeping it is an act which requires a licence.[18] It is up to anybody caught with game in his possession to prove that he acquired it innocently, i.e. in circumstances in which a licence was not needed.[19]

The same act may constitute an offence under both Acts of Parliament and subject the offender to the separate penalties[20] which they provide.[21]

---

[13] Game Act 1831, s. 23.
[14] Game Licences Act 1860, s. 4.
[15] In case 1., because the word "include" is used in defining game and the list of birds and animals in the definition is not therefore exhaustive and may include deer which are often regarded as game. Whilst in case 2., the word "game" is not defined and hares are generally treated as game.
[16] *R v Davis* (1795) 6 Term Rep 177.
[17] *Molton v Cheeseley* (1788) 1 Esp 123.
[18] *Watkins v Price* (1877) 33 LT 578.
[19] *Hemming v Halsey* (1823) 1 LJ (OS) KB 105.
[20] £24 (Game Act 1831, s. 23) and £50 (Game Licences Act 1860, s. 4).
[21] *Clark v Westaway* (1927) 137 LT 591.

A game licence is not needed in the following cases:

1. The taking of deer[22] in any enclosed lands by the owner or occupier, or by his direction or permission.[23] A court decision usefully illustrates two points on this exception; the court considered that the meaning of "enclosed lands" included "lands used for farming and enclosed by normal agricultural hedges" in contrast with "moorland where there are no enclosures and where the deer can run free"; secondly, the court made it clear that a game licence is not needed when a deer is shot on enclosed land with the owner's permission though the deer runs on and drops on land where the killer does not have that permission;[24]

2. The taking of rabbits by the proprietor of any warren or of any enclosed ground whatever, or by the tenant of lands,[25] either by himself or by his direction or permission;[26]

3. Shooting by the Royal Family and Her Majesty's game keepers;[27]

4. A person aiding or assisting in the taking of game in the company or presence of, and for the use of, another person who has a game licence in his own right, who is taking some active part in the sport with his own dog or gun and who is not acting "by virtue of any deputation or appointment".[28] The effect of this is to exempt beaters, loaders and other assistants from the necessity of being licensed; but such unlicensed beaters, etc., must not assist a gamekeeper since he holds his position by "deputation or appointment". Moreover, they apparently must not use or lend the use of any dog of their own, even to a licensed person who is by virtue of his licence then and there taking game. A loader may carry his employer's gun and thus aid in killing game, but he must not carry a gun of his own, and he

---

[22] For the protection of deer generally, see p. 151 *et seq.*
[23] Game Licences Act 1860, s. 5, Exception 5.
[24] *Jemmison v Priddle* [1972] 1 All ER 539.
[25] I.e. any lands, whether enclosed or not.
[26] Game Licences Act 1860, s. 5, Exception 2.
[27] Game Licences Act 1860, s. 5, Exceptions 1 and 2.
[28] Game Licences Act 1860, s. 5, Exception 3.

must not fire his own or his employer's gun;[29]

5. The actual occupier of any enclosed lands,[30] or the owner thereof who has the right of killing hares on those lands, or a person authorised by either of them, may kill hares on those lands without a game licence, but not at night.[31] Any authority so given must be in writing stating the names of the persons involved, a description of the lands in question, and be signed and witnessed by the person giving it;[32]

6. A person required by a Government Minister to kill certain animals and birds as pests need not hold a game licence for that purpose;[33]

7. An occupier of land, and certain persons who may be authorised by him in writing[34] may kill hares and rabbits on that land without a licence;[35]

8. Persons pursuing and killing hares, whether by coursing[36] with greyhounds or by hunting with beagles or other hounds, or pursuing and killing deer by hunting with hounds.[37]

Game licences are obtained at any Post Office at which money order business is transacted. The licence must show the amount of duty charged and the proper forenames and surname and place of residence of the person to whom it is issued. It will be dated on the day when it is actually issued[38] and will show the time of issue. It will be in force from that day[39] and time so that an offence committed on that day but before the time of issue is not condoned.[40]

---

[29] *Ex parte Sylvester* (1829) 9 B & C 61.
[30] For an interpretation of "enclosed lands" see exception 1 on p. 118.
[31] Hares Act 1848, ss. 1, 5; "night" lasts from one hour after sunset to one hour before sunrise (Hares Act 1848, s. 7).
[32] Hares Act 1848, s. 1, and Schedule.
[33] Agriculture Act 1947, ss. 98, 100(4). For further details of the requirement, see pp. 221-226.
[34] As to who these persons may be, see p. 121.
[35] Ground Game Act 1880, ss. 4, 8.
[36] Coursing is not confined to organised coursing (*Dolby v Halmshaw* [1936] 3 All ER 229).
[37] Game Licences Act 1860, s. 5, Exceptions 3 and 4.
[38] Game Licences Act 1860, s. 16.
[39] Game Licences Act 1860, s. 16.
[40] Game Licences Act 1860, s. 4. *Campbell v Strangeway* (1877) 37 LT 672.

It continues in force until the end of the day on which it is stated to expire,[41] but becomes null and void immediately its holder is convicted of trespassing in the daytime in search of game in England, Wales, or Scotland.[42] It is not transferable.

Game licences are issued for different periods and at different prices as follows:

To be taken out after July and before November and to expire on 31st July following   £6.00

To be taken out after July and before November and to expire on 31st October in the same year   £4.00

To be taken out after October and to expire on 31st July following   £4.00

Any continuous period of14 days (known as an occasional licence)   £2.00

A gamekeeper's licence   £4.00[43]

A gamekeeper's licence is an annual licence expiring on 31st July and obtained by his employer. It excuses the game-keeper from having an ordinary game licence but lasts only while he is employed as gamekeeper and is limited to use on land on which the employer has a right to take game. On a change of gamekeeper during the currency of the licence it may be endorsed by the issuing authority in favour of the new employee without further charge so as to operate in his favour for the remainder of the period of the licence.[44]

The holder of a £6 game licence is entitled to sell game, but only to a licensed game dealer.[45] Otherwise it is an offence for anyone to sell, or offer for sale (but not to give away), hares to anyone else, except by:

---

41 Game Licences Act 1860, s. 16.
42 Game Act 1831, s. 30; Game (Scotland) Act 1832; Game Licences Act 1860, s. 11.
43 Game Licences Act 1860, s. 2; Customs and Inland Revenue Act 1883, ss. 4, 5; Fees for Game and Other Licences (Variation) Order 1968, SI 1968/120. The Government may from time to time alter these fees (Local Government Act 1966, s. 35(2) and Sch. 3, Part II.)
44 Game Licences Act 1860, ss. 2, 7, 8, 9.
45 Game Act 1831, ss. 17, 25; Game Licences Act 1860, s. 13.

1. A licensed game dealer;[46]

2. An innkeeper selling game for consumption in his own house provided he obtains it from a licensed game dealer;[47]

3. A person directed in writing by a justice of the peace to sell game seized as having been unlawfully taken;[48] and

4. An occupier of land selling ground game taken on land in his occupation by him or persons authorised[49] by him.[50]

A gamekeeper's licence only entitles him to sell hares on the account and with the written authority of his employer. None of these restrictions applies to the sale of deer or rabbits.[51]

Hares, unless imported,[52] must not be sold or exposed for sale during the months of March to July inclusive.[53]

Ground Game

By the Ground Game Act of 1880 an occupier of land was given the right to take hares and rabbits (called "ground game" in the Act) on the land which he occupies, whether or not any other person has that right. The right is incidental to and inseparable from his occupation so that he cannot be divested of it in any way. Any agreement, condition or arrangement which purports to divest or alienate this right, or which gives him any advantage in return for him forbearing to exercise it, or which imposes any disadvantage on him in consequence of his exercising it, is void and of no effect.[54]

---

[46] Game Act 1831, s. 25.
[47] Game Act 1831, s. 26.
[48] Game Laws (Amendment) Act 1960, ss. 3(4), 4(4).
[49] As to who these persons may be, see pp. 122-123.
[50] Ground Game Act 1880, s. 4; This listing produces the rather curious result that others entitled to take hares, e.g. non-occupying owners with reserved shooting rights and shooting tenants, cannot legally sell them unless, holding a £6 game licence, he sells them to a licensed game dealer.
[51] Game Act 1831, ss. 2, 25; Game Licences Act 1860, s. 13. But see pp. 160-162 as to the sale of venison.
[52] For the import of live hares, see generally pp. 31-48.
[53] Hares Preservation Act 1892, ss. 2, 3.
[54] Ground Game Act 1880, ss. 1, 3, 7, 8.

This means that the occupier has the right to take ground game concurrently with any other person who has that right because, for example, he is the owner or the shooting tenant. The right was given to allow farming tenants without shooting rights to protect their crops. Under other legislation they may claim from their landlords compensation for crop damage caused by deer and certain birds;[55] there is no right to compensation for damage done by hares and rabbits.

The occupier's rights under the Act are not to affect in any way his ability to acquire and exercise sporting rights in the normal way. So, if gaming rights are not reserved to his landlord under the tenancy agreement and are vested in the occupier, he may take ground game without the restrictions which the Act imposes on the statutory right and which are considered later.[56] If, having only a statutory right, he takes game other than hares and rabbits, or gives permission to another to do so, without in either case the authority of the person having the right to that game, he may be prosecuted.[57]

Clearly, an occupying owner, tenant or sub-tenant of land is an occupier for the purpose of the Act. A person having a right of common is not. Nor, says the Act, shall a person be deemed to be an occupier "by reason of an occupation for the purpose of grazing or pasturage of sheep, cattle or horses for not more than nine months".[58]

This leaves in doubt the position of a grazier having other kinds of animals, or having grazing rights for more than nine months.

In addition to the occupier, one other person may be authorised by him in writing[59] to shoot ground game;[60] more than one may be so

---

55   See pp. 128-130.
56   Ground Game Act 1880, s. 2. For these restrictions, see pp. 123-124.
57   Game Act 1831, s. 12.
58   Ground Game Act 1880, s. 1, proviso (2).
59   No particular form is necessary but sensibly it should clearly show the date, the particulars of the person to whom it is given and the situation and extent of the land in question, and be signed by the occupier. It should also indicate whether or not authority to shoot is included.
60   Where there are joint occupiers, each is at liberty to exercise the right to take ground game (*Morrison v Anderson* (1913) 2 SLT 124) but if they authorise other persons, they must presumably do so jointly.

authorised to take them otherwise than by shooting.[61] If a person
acts on a verbal permission only, he is strictly a trespasser.[62] The
only persons who can be authorised in writing are:

1. One or more members of the occupier's household[63] resident[64]
    on the land in his occupation; and

2. One or more people in the occupier's ordinary service[65] on such
    land; and

3. Any one other person *bona fide* employed by the occupier for
    reward[66] in the taking and destruction of ground game.[67]

An authorised person must produce his written authority, if asked
to do so, to any person having a concurrent right to take ground
game on the land or to any person authorised by the latter in writing
to make the demand. In default, the authorised person's right to
ground game ceases.[68]

In the case of moorlands and unenclosed non-arable lands, except
detached portions of either which are less than 25 acres in extent
and adjoin arable lands, the occupier's right to take ground game
is suspended from 1st April to 31st August inclusive, and he must
not use firearms between 1st September and 10th December

---

61 Ground Game Act 1880, s. 1, proviso (1)(a) and (6).
62 *Richardson v Maitland* (1897) 4 SLT 277.
63 The household will include household servants living and boarding at the
    occupier's house but presumably not those living in other houses on the land (*Re
    Drax, Savile v Yeatman* (1887) 57 LT 475; *Ogle v Morgan* (1852) 1 De DM & G
    359).
64 Residence is a question of fact in each case. A person invited to stay for a week
    and shoot rabbits was held in a Scottish case to satisfy the condition. (*Stuart v
    Murray* (1884) 12 R 9.) It is not necessary that the occupier should reside there
    himself. (*R v North Curry (Inhabitants)* (1825) 4 B & C 953.)
65 "Ordinary service" presumably means regular service so that casual labour taken
    on for a week or two, as for harvest, would be excluded. Moreover, servants who,
    however regularly employed, do not find their customary work on the land would
    also be excluded.
66 The fact of, for example, a rabbit catcher being allowed to keep all or some of the
    rabbits taken would probably be sufficient evidence of such employment for
    reward (*Bruce v Prosser* (1898) 5 SLT 301) but a similar gift to a friend asked to
    come and shoot would hardly be so.
67 Ground Game Act 1880, s. 1. proviso (1)(b).
68 Ground Game Act 1880, s. 1, proviso (1)(c).

inclusive.[69] But a valid agreement may be made between the occupier on the one hand and the owner or shooting tenant on the other hand for the joint exercise by them between the last two dates of the right to take ground game or for its exercise for their joint benefit.[70]

The occupier, or one authorised person,[71] may use firearms to kill ground game on the occupier's land at night.[72] But, before either may do so, the occupier must have the written authority of the other person, or one of the other persons, entitled to kill and take ground game on the land.[73] Any other shooting of ground game at night by the occupier or an authorised person is an offence.[74]

In Greater London poison must not be used at any time for killing ground game.[75]

Owners' and Tenants' Rights to Game

The rights of owners and tenants to take game will vary according to their status and the kinds of relationships created between them; these relationships usually, but not always, depend on a lease or tenancy agreement made between them and particularly on the terms of the document.

The description given in the document to the animals which may be taken by landlord or tenant will be important. Use of the words "game" or "gaming rights" will provoke some uncertainty in the absence, as we have seen,[76] of a standard definition of "game". A probable interpretation would be that the word means, so far as four-legged animals are concerned, deer, hares and rabbits since

---

[69] Ground Game Act 1880, s. 1, proviso (3); Ground Game (Amendment) Act 1906, s. 2.

[70] Ground Game Act 1906, s. 3.

[71] I.e. one of the persons mentioned in items 1. to 3. in the text above who has been authorised by the occupier. It seems that this person should be that one of those persons who has been previously authorised to shoot generally. See p. 122.

[72] "Night" extends from the end of the first hour after sunset to the beginning of the last hour before sunrise.

[73] E.g. the landlord to whom the sporting rights are reserved.

[74] Ground Game Act 1880, s. 6; Wildlife and Countryside Act 1981, s. 12, Sch. 7, para. 1.

[75] Ground Game Act 1880, s. 6. As to the use of poisons generally, see pp. 136-138.

[76] On p. 115.

only these three come within the definitions used in Acts of Parliament. The common use of the words "shooting rights" or "sporting rights" is perhaps more satisfactory; they have been interpreted to mean the right to kill all things which are usually the object of sport.[77] Though not watertight, this interpretation will generally cover the kinds of animals in which landlords and tenants have particular interests.

In all the different situations the rights of the occupier, whether he be owner or any kind of tenant, to take hares and rabbits remain constant and, as described earlier,[78] cannot be altered by leases or written or verbal agreements.

The most straightforward situation is that of the owner occupier who has not let the sporting rights. He may take game whenever and however he pleases, though of course he must obey the laws about game licences,[79] protected animals,[80] prohibited times,[81] and cruelty to animals.[82]

If the owner does not occupy his land but lets it to a tenant, sporting rights may or may not be reserved[83] to the owner. When they are not reserved they pass in every case with possession of the land to that tenant.[84] (A contrary principle obtains in Scotland where the right to game is considered to be a right personal to the owner of the land.)[85] The tenant cannot however shoot hares or rabbits at night which he could do if the rights had been expressly granted to him by the owner.[86] The tenant may grant his rights to a shooting tenant. If the grant includes the right to ground game (hares and rabbits), the effect is that both have that right concurrently.[87]

---

[77] *Jeffryes v Evans* (1865) 13 LT 72; *Moore v Earl of Plymouth* (1817) 7 Taunt 614 at 627; *Houston v Marquis of Sligo* (1886) 55 LT 614.
[78] On p. 121.
[79] See pp. 116-121.
[80] See, generally, Chapter 8.
[81] See pp. 115-116.
[82] See, generally, pp. 132-150.
[83] A reservation of rights to the owner is made by words in the lease or tenancy agreement showing those rights as belonging to him, i.e. reserved out of the tenancy.
[84] *Pochin v Smith* (1887) 52 JP 237; *Anderson v Vicary* [1900] 2 QB 287.
[85] *Saunders v Pitfield* (1888) 58 LT 108.
[86] See the cases mentioned in notes 84 and 85 above.
[87] *Morgan v Jackson* [1895] 1 QB 885.

Sporting rights may be reserved to the owner in the lease or tenancy agreement or by a separate contract or simply by verbal agreement. The terms used may prohibit the owner from letting the rights; if not prohibited, they may be let. A reservation of "exclusive rights" has the effect of giving the owner all rights, except over hares and rabbits the taking of which he shares with the occupier.[88] The reservation is defended by the law making it an offence for the tenant to take game, except hares and rabbits if he is an occupier, or to permit anyone else to do so.[89]

The tenant may claim damages from the shooting tenant for injury caused to his crops by the land being overstocked with game[90] if this is due to that tenant's extraordinary non-natural or unreasonable action.[91] Within certain limitations, he may also claim compensation from his landlord for damage to crops by game.[92]

Where sporting rights are thus reserved, the owner, or any person to whom he may grant them, may exercise the rights to the same extent as, and precisely as if he was, the occupier of the land, subject to the tenant's rights to take ground game and to the possible claims by the tenant just mentioned.

The farming tenant is entitled to use the land and destroy gorse and underwood in the ordinary way[93] or to carry out any reasonable and normal operations which might be deemed advisable for the purpose of dealing with the land to the best advantage,[94] but he must not designedly drive game away.[95] On the other hand, the owner, or his tenant of shooting rights, must not trample fields of standing crops at a time when it is not usual or reasonable to do so; and if the owner or that tenant causes game to increase to an unreasonable extent, the tenant of the land can recover damages for the injury to his crops.[96] The owner is however entitled to be

---

[88]   Ground Game Act 1880, s. 3; *Stanton v Brown* [1900] 1 QB 671 and see p. 121.
[89]   Game Act 1831, s. 12.
[90]   *Farrer v Nelson* (1885) 52 LT 766.
[91]   *Seligman v Docker* [1948] 2 All ER 887.
[92]   See pp. 128-130.
[93]   *Jeffryes v Evans* (1865) 13 LT 72.
[94]   *Peech v Best* [1931] 1 KB 1 at p. 18.
[95]   *Jeffryes v Evans* (1865) 13 LT 72.
[96]   *Hilton v Green* (1862) 2 F & F 821.

reimbursed by the shooting tenant for such damages[97] but not if the grant of rights to the latter does not enable him (the shooting tenant) to shoot on the part of the land adversely affected.[98]

The last type of situation which needs consideration is when there is a shooting tenant, i.e. a person who, usually by lease or tenancy agreement, is granted sporting rights but no other rights over land. He may have these rights from: (a) the owner-occupier; or (b) an owner who has let his land but reserved the rights; or (c) an occupying tenant where the rights have not been reserved. In all these cases the shooting tenant may have either the right to shoot the game or general shooting and sporting rights.[99] Subject to this, in cases (a) and (b) he takes precisely those rights which the owner himself would have had, but in case (a) the owner keeps his right to take ground game.[100] An owner occupier or a tenant who infringes his shooting tenant's rights by pursuing or taking game commits an offence for which he may be prosecuted,[101] but a non-occupying owner who does so is merely liable to a civil claim for breach of contract. A person who has been granted exclusive sporting rights has a right of action in the courts against anyone whose acts interfere with his enjoyment of them.[102]

Unless there is something to the contrary in the agreement which grants the sporting rights, the grantor of those rights is not prevented from using the land in the ordinary and accustomed way but having regard to its character at the date of the grant.[103] Thus, in the case of farming land, he cannot be prevented from altering the course of husbandry,[104] cutting down timber or underwood, or doing any other act falling within the ordinary course of estate management.[105]

---

[97]   Agricultural Holdings Act 1948, s. 14.
[98]   *Cornewall v Dawson* (1871) 24 LT 664.
[99]   For comments on these terms, see pp. 124-125.
[100] *Halsbury's Laws of England,* 4th Ed., Vol. 2 (Reissue), para. 249. Though not so stated in *Halsbury,* it seems that in case (c) also the occupying tenant must retain his rights to ground game; see p. 121.
[101] Game Act 1831, s. 12.
[102] *Fitzgerald v Firbank* [1897] 2 Ch 96; *Nicholls v Ely Sugar Beet Factory* (1931) 145 LT 113.
[103] *Peech v Best* [1931] 1 KB 1 at 18.
[104] *Jeffryes v Evans* (1865) 13 LT 72.
[105] *Gearns v Baker* (1875) 33 LT 86.

But any act done with the intention of injuring the rights granted[106] or which makes a substantial change in the character of the land can be the subject of court action if it substantially injures the rights granted.[107]

Where an accident, such as fire, threatens damage to his shooting rights, the shooting tenant is entitled to adopt such means for the preservation of his rights as are reasonably necessary.[108]

The right to take game is a form of property and may therefore be sold, leased or, if already held under a lease, sub-let to a third person. Constraints on this arise when the person wanting to dispose of the right holds it by virtue of an agreement which prevents him from doing so or restricts him in doing it. For example, the lease of sporting rights to a shooting tenant may stipulate that he is not to sub-let or assign, or that he is only to do so with the grantor's consent.

Though verbal agreements are occasionally effective, transactions in sporting rights should always be recorded in writing to eliminate doubts about their effect. The law relating to property regularly requires the written document to be by deed.[109] This and the uncertainties which may arise as appearing from the preceding pages make it generally worthwhile to take legal advice, certainly if the rights involved are substantial.[110]

Compensation for Damage to Crops

The provisions for compensation for damage to crops are dependent upon the type of tenancy granted to the occupier. The Agricultural Holdings Act 1986 applies only to an agreement entered into before the 1st September 1995 or where the saving provisions of s. 4(1)(b)–(f) of the Agricultural Tenancies Act 1995 apply. As such the tenant is given the right to claim compensation where the

---

[106] *Jeffryes v Evans* (1865) 13 LT 72 and *Gearns v Baker* (1875) 33 LT 86; *Bird v Great Eastern Railway Co.* (1865) 13 LT 365.

[107] *Dick v Norton* (1916) 114 LT 548.

[108] *Cope v Sharpe (No.2)* (1912) 106 LT 56. For protection against dogs, see p. 130.

[109] Law of Property Act 1925, ss. 52(1), 205(1)(ix).

[110] On these matters generally, see *Halsbury's Laws of England,* 4th Ed., Vol. 2 (Reissue), para. 248 et seq.

tenant has sustained damage to his crops from any wild animals or birds which the landlord or anyone claiming under the landlord (i.e. the sporting tenant) has the right so to do.

The following conditions must be met to obtain compensation:

1. The tenant must not have written permission to kill the game;

2. The right to take game must not belong to the tenant, nor to anyone claiming under him[111] other than the landlord;

3. The tenant must give written notice[112] to the landlord[113] within one month after the tenant first became, or ought reasonably to have become, aware of the occurrence of the damage;

4. The landlord must be given reasonable opportunity to inspect the damage, and, in the case of a growing crop, before it is begun to be reaped, raised or consumed, and, in the case of a crop reaped or raised, before it is begun to be removed from the land;

5. The tenant must give written notice to the landlord of the particulars of the claim within one month after the end of the year in which the claim arises. The year ends on the 29th September or a different period of 12 months, may, by agreement between them, be substituted for that date.[114]

If the right to take the game belongs to someone other than the landlord, he is entitled to be indemnified by that person against the claim.[115] Disputes about this or about the amount of compensation are to be settled by arbitration.[116]

---

[111] E.g. a person to whom the tenant lets the sporting rights when these are not reserved to the landlord.

[112] The Act does not say what the contents of the notice are to be. It is suggested that it may be sufficient to indicate intention to make a claim, the situation of the land on which the crops have been damaged, and the kind of game causing it. The substantive claim will follow later under item 5. in the text above.

[113] The notice must be served by delivering it to the landlord, by leaving it at his proper address, or by sending it by registered letter or recorded delivery service to him. It may also be served by any of these means on the agent or employee of the landlord who is responsible for the management of the holding (Agricultural Holdings Act 1986, 93(1), (3)).

[114] Agricultural Holdings Act 1986, s. 20(3)(b).

[115] Agricultural Holdings Act 1986, s. 20(5).

[116] Agricultural Holdings Act 1986, s. 20(5). For arbitration procedure see Agricultural Holdings Act 1986, s. 84 and Sch. 11.

Since 1st September 1995 all new tenancies are treated as farm business tenancies, subject to certain saving provisions, as mentioned, and are not subject to the compensation provisions of the Agricultural Holdings Act 1986. The Agricultural Tenancies Act 1995 does not contain any statutory provision for damage caused by game. As such the tenant should ensure that the farm business tenancy agreement contains provision to reimburse him for damage which occurs where the landlord has reserved the sporting rights or granted them to a third party. The landlord, in any tenancy of the sporting rights should ensure that the agreement includes an appropriately worded form of indemnity for crop damage by game since any claim for such damage by the farming tenant will be against the landlord and not the sporting tenant.

Physical Protection of Game

One of the cases in which the criminal law allows a person to kill or injure another's dog is where the dog was chasing game and the defendant reasonably believed that his action was necessary to protect his interest in the game.[117] However, it seems that there would be no defence to a civil claim by the dog's owner in these circumstances.[118]

Nevertheless, an occupier of land may take steps to protect his game in his absence. For example, it was decided in two old court cases that he was justified in setting dog spears in his woods.[119] But he must not tempt dogs by baiting traps with strong-smelling meat near places where dogs may lawfully be.[120]

It is an offence for an owner of gaming rights to set any spring gun, man trap "or other engine"[121] calculated to destroy human life or

---

[117] Criminal Damage Act 1971, s. 5(1)–(4). In order to invoke the defence in s. 5 of "lawful excuse", the owner of the game must show some ownership in the game, i.e. that it is tamed or in captivity. Cf pp. 80-82. Section 5(4) excuses the person from criminal damage (i.e. killing the dog) where the defendant acted to protect his right or interest in property, i.e. his sporting rights whether granted by deed, licence or otherwise. Whether one could say that killing the dog protects one's right or interest is open to debate since the right *per se* is not affected by the dog attacking game, merely the game in *articulo mortis*.

[118] See *Halsbury's Laws of England,* 4th Ed., Vol. 2 (Reissue), para. 265.

[119] *Deane v Clayton* (1817) 7 Taunt 489; *Jordin v Crump* (1841) 8 M & W 782.

[120] *Townsend v Wathen* (1808) 9 East 277.

[121] This appears to mean any device similar to a spring gun or man trap, but it does not include electrified wires *(R v Munks* [1964] 3 All ER 757).

inflict grievous bodily harm so that it may destroy or inflict such harm upon a trespasser.[122] Traps for animals may be used within limitations.[123]

When fencing, barbed wire must not be put where it is likely to injure persons or animals using a road; if it is, the local authority may by notice require the occupier of the land to remove it.[124]

---

[122] Offences Against the Person Act 1861, s. 31.
[123] See pp. 144-146.
[124] Highways Act 1980, s. 164(1).

Chapter 8

PROTECTION OF ANIMALS

A. INTRODUCTION

Since the first Act of Parliament giving protection to animals was passed in 1822 measures strengthening that protection have appeared intermittently, and frequently in recent years, in the statute book until today there is a substantial body of law, both in Acts and regulations made under them, which both prohibits acts considered to be cruel or causing unnecessary suffering and regulates dealings with animals to mitigate suffering. These matters are dealt with in Part B of this chapter.

In more recent times particular animals have been selected by Parliament as being endangered and thus as meriting their own codes of protection in individual Acts; these are deer, seals and badgers which are considered in Parts C, D and E of this chapter. This process in turn gave way in 1975 to legislation in the shape of the Conservation of Wild Creatures and Wild Plants Act designed to protect a very limited number of rare animals from deliberate destruction and capture. Subsequently, the 1975 Act has been succeeded by Part I of the Wildlife and Countryside Act 1981 whose provisions are described in Part F below.

The chapter concludes with Part G on the criminal and civil law governing the killing or injuring of one person's animals by another.

Parliament has also made a number of protective laws dealing with animal boarding, breeding and riding establishments and pet shops, with performances and public exhibitions of animals, and with experiments involving animals. These are considered in Chapters 4, 5, 10 and 12.

B. PREVENTION OF CRUELTY

Abandonment

Any person, being the owner or having charge or control of any animal,[1] who without reasonable cause or excuse abandons it, whether permanently or not, in circumstances likely to cause it unnecessary suffering, is guilty of an offence of cruelty.[2] Equally, it is an offence to cause or procure such abandonment or, being the owner, to permit[3] it.[4]

Where the animal is left it must be in circumstances where suffering is likely and where there was sufficient evidence to prove that the defendant had relinquished, wholly disregarded or given up his duty to care for the animal. The permanence or otherwise of the abandonment must be more than simply "left or leaving unattended", there must be some mental element. Thus, the emphasis should be placed on the character of the "act of the abandonment" and not simply on the duration of the abandonment.[5]

Carriage of Animals

A person who conveys any animal in such manner or position as to cause it any unnecessary suffering is guilty of an offence of cruelty.[6] Likewise, if he causes or procures such a conveying or, being the animal's owner he permits it, he is guilty of an offence.[7]

There are detailed regulations about the transport of animals; these are discussed in Chapter 3.

Cruelty to Livestock

Any person who causes unnecessary pain or distress to livestock[8]

---

[1]   The word "animal" in this and later contexts in this section (unless otherwise defined) has a lengthily defined meaning which is fully set out in Appendix E at the end of the book (Protection of Animals Act 1911, s. 15; Abandonment of Animals Act 1960, s. 2).
[2]   For exceptions and consequences of conviction, see pp. 148-150.
[3]   An owner is deemed for the purpose of this offence to permit cruelty if he fails to exercise reasonable care and supervision in protecting the animal from it. (Protection of Animals Act 1911, s. 1(2); Abandonment of Animals Act, 1960 s. 1.)
[4]   Abandonment of Animals Act 1960, s. 1.
[5]   *Hunt v Duckering* [1993] Crim LR 678.
[6]   For exceptions and consequences of conviction, see pp. 148-150.
[7]   Protection of Animals Act 1911, s. 1(1)(b).
[8]   "Livestock" means any creature kept for the production of food, wool, skin or fur or for use in the farming of land or for such purpose as the Minister for the Department for Environment, Food and Rural Affairs may by order specify: Agriculture (Miscellaneous Provisions) Act 1968, s. 8(1), 50(1).

on agricultural land[9] under his control, or who permits such livestock to suffer unnecessary pain or distress of which he knows or may reasonably be expected to know, is guilty of an offence[10] unless the act is lawfully done under the Animals (Scientific Procedures) Act 1986[11] or under a licence for scientific research.[12]

Ministers[13] may, after appropriate consultation, make such provision by regulation[14] or codes of recommendation[15] with respect to the welfare of livestock situated on agricultural land as they see fit. The regulations may also provide for any breach of them to be an offence,[16] whilst failure to comply with a code of recommendation does not of itself involve any liability to proceedings but may be relied upon in a prosecution for causing unnecessary pain or distress.[17]

To determine whether an offence has been committed, an authorised person[18] may enter on land[19] (but not premises used wholly or mainly as a dwelling); he may also take samples of any substance on the land for analysis. The occupier or his employee must, if he can, comply with any request to indicate to the person where

---

9   "Agricultural land" means land used for agriculture within the meaning of the Agriculture Act 1947, s. 109(3), which is so used for the purposes of a trade or business: Agriculture (Miscellaneous Provisions) Act 1968, s. 8(1).
10   Agriculture (Miscellaneous Provisions) Act 1968, s. 1(1).
11   For the provisions of the Animals (Scientific Procedures) Act 1986 see Chapter 12.
12   Agriculture (Miscellaneous Provisions) Act 1968, s. 1(2).
13   The functions of the Minister in relation to the Agriculture (Miscellaneous Provisions) Act 1968 are, so far as exercisable in relation to Wales, transferred to the National Assembly of Wales: The National Assembly for Wales (Transfer of Functions) Order 1999, SI 1999/672. References to "Minister" hereafter should be read and construed accordingly.
14   Agriculture (Miscellaneous Provisions) Act 1968, s. 2(1).
15   Agriculture (Miscellaneous Provisions) Act 1968, s. 3(1).
16   Agriculture (Miscellaneous Provisions) Act 1968, s. 2(2). Exemptions and other matters may similarly be dealt with by regulation. The following regulations have been made: Welfare of Livestock (Deer) Order 1980, SI 1980/593; Welfare of Livestock (Prohibited Operations) Regulations 1982, SI 1982/1884 (amended by 1987/114); Welfare of Livestock (Intensive Units) Regulations 1978, SI 1978/1800 (disapplied to battery hens by SI 1987/2020); Welfare of Battery Hens Regulations 1987, SI 1987/2020; Welfare of Calves Regulations 1987, SI 1987/2021; Welfare of Pigs Regulations 1991, SI 1991/1477.
17   Agriculture (Miscellaneous Provisions) Act 1968, s.3 (4).
18   This is a person authorised in writing by the appropriate Minister. A person so authorised by the local authority may also enter to take samples (Agriculture (Miscellaneous Provisions) Act 1968, s. 6(1), (2), (4)).
19   For the definition of land see note 197 on page 159.

livestock or their food is kept and facilitate the person's access to those places. Failure to do so, or wilful obstruction, is an offence.[20]

Docking and Nicking

The docking of tails of sheep, pigs, cattle and dogs is prohibited or restricted as described below, except when the exemptions at items 1. to 3. on pages 142 to 143 apply. To cause or permit the docking is likewise prohibited and an offence.[21]

The short-tail docking of sheep is forbidden unless sufficient tail is retained to cover the vulva in the case of female sheep and the anus in the case of male sheep.[22]

The tail docking of pigs is forbidden unless the operation is performed by the quick and complete severance of the part of the tail to be removed and either:

a. the pig is less than eight days old; or

b. the operation is performed by a vet who is of the opinion that the operation is necessary for reasons of health or to prevent injury from the vice of tail biting.[23]

The prohibitions do not apply to the rendering, in an emergency, of first aid for the purpose of saving life or relieving pain, nor to the performance by a veterinary surgeon of an operation which is part of, in his opinion, the proper treatment for a disease or injury.

The tail docking of cattle[24] is prohibited,[25] as is the docking of dogs' tails without an anaesthetic after the dogs' eyes are open.[26]

---

[20] Agriculture (Miscellaneous Provisions) Act 1968, s. 6(1), (4), (6), (7).

[21] Agriculture (Miscellaneous Provisions) Act 1968, s. 2; Welfare of Livestock (Prohibited Operations) Regulations 1982, SI 1982/1884, Arts. 3 and 5.

[22] Welfare of Livestock (Prohibited Operations) Regulations 1982, SI 1982/1884, Art. 3(c). For the docking of lamb's tails without anaesthetics, see item 6. on p. 143.

[23] Welfare of Livestock (Prohibited Operations) Regulations 1982, SI 1982/1884, Art. 3(k).

[24] "Cattle" means all bovine animals (Welfare of Livestock (Prohibited Operations) Regulations 1982, SI 1982/1884, Art. 2).

[25] Welfare of Livestock (Prohibited Operations) Regulations 1982, SI 1982/1884, Art. 3(f).

[26] See item 4. on p. 143.

Dogs as Draught Animals

A person who uses any dog[27] for the purpose of drawing or helping to draw any cart, carriage, truck or barrow on any public highway is guilty of an offence punishable by a fine.[28] Likewise, an offence is committed if he causes or procures such use or, being the dog's owner, permits[29] it.

Drugs and Poisons

If any person wilfully[30] without any reasonable cause or excuse:

a. administers any poisonous or injurious drug or substance to any animal;[31] or

b. causes or procures the administration of such drug or substance; or

c. being the owner of the animal, permits[32] such administration; or

d. causes any such substance to be taken by any animal, he is guilty of an offence of cruelty.[33]

A person commits an offence[34] (except where he has the defence mentioned below) if he:

a. sells; or

b. offers or exposes for sale; or

c. gives away; or

d. causes or procures any person to sell or offer or expose for sale or give away; or

---

[27] "Dog" includes any bitch, sapling (greyhound in its first year) and puppy: Protection of Animals Act 1911, s. 15(d).

[28] For the consequences of conviction generally, see pp. 148-150.

[29] As to permitting, see note 3 on p. 133.

[30] "Wilfully" has been interpreted to mean deliberately and intentionally, and not by accident or inadvertence (R v Senior [1899] 1 QB at 290–291).

[31] The definition of "animal" in Appendix E to this book applies.

[32] As to permitting, see note 3 on p. 133.

[33] Protection of Animals Act 1911, s. 1(1)(d). For exceptions and consequences of conviction, see pp. 148-150.

[34] For consequences of conviction, see pp. 148-150.

e. is knowingly a party to the sale or offering or exposing for sale or giving away of,

any grain or seed which has been rendered poisonous except for bona fide use in agriculture.[35]

A person also commits an offence[36] (except where he has the defences mentioned below) if he:

a. knowingly puts or places; or

b. causes or procures any other person to put or place; or

c. knowingly is a party to the putting or placing of,

in or upon any land[37] or building, any poison, or any fluid or edible matter (not being sown seed or grain) which has been rendered poisonous.[38]

It is a defence in the case of the third offence above that the poison, etc. was placed for the purpose of destroying insects and other invertebrates, rats, mice or other small ground vermin where destruction is found to be necessary in the interest of public health, agriculture or the preservation of other animals, domestic or wild, or for the purpose of manuring the land, and that the accused took all reasonable precautions to prevent injury thereby to dogs, cats, fowls or other domestic animals[39] and wild birds,[40] provided that the poison is not banned by Government order; at present the use of elementary yellow phosphorus and red squill is banned in all cases and the use of strychnine except for destroying moles.[41]

A person is not guilty of the second or third offences above by reason only that he uses poisonous gas in any hole, burrow or earth for the purpose of killing rabbits, hares or other rodents, deer, foxes

---

[35] Protection of Animals Act 1911, s. 8(a).
[36] For the consequences of conviction, see pp. 148-150.
[37] For the meaning of "land" see note 197 on p. 159.
[38] Protection of Animals Act 1911, s. 8(b).
[39] A definition of these kinds if animals is given in Appendix E to this book.
[40] Protection of Animals Act 1911, s. 8, proviso.
[41] Animals (Cruel Poisons) Act 1962, ss. 1, 2; Animals (Cruel Poisons) Regulations 1963, SI 1963/1278.

or moles, or in places where a substance which, by evaporation or in contact with moisture, generates poisonous gas.[42]

Additionally, the relevant Minister[43] has powers to make an order permitting the use of a specified poison against grey squirrels and coypus and describing the way in which it is to be used. The use of that poison in the way described in the order will avoid prosecution under the third offence mentioned above.[44] An order has been made[45] approving the use of warfarin and its soluble salts for destroying grey squirrels under the conditions stipulated by the order.

It is an offence to put, or cause to be put, at any time any poison or poisonous ingredient on ground, whether open or enclosed, where game usually resort, or in any highway,[46] with intent to destroy or injure game.[47]

Where the relevant Minister concerned is satisfied that a poison cannot be used for destroying animals[48] or animals of any particular description without causing undue suffering, and that other suitable methods of destroying them exist, and are or would in certain circumstances be adequate, he may make regulations[49] prohibiting or restricting the use of that poison for destroying animals generally or particular animals.[50]

It is no criminal offence to use non-poisonous substances as bait for

---

[42] Prevention of Damage by Rabbits Act 1939, s. 4; Agriculture Act 1947, s. 98(3).

[43] The functions of the Minister were transferred to the Secretary of State for Wales by virtue of the Transfer of Functions (Wales) (No 1) Order 1978, SI 1978/272, in relation to the Agriculture (Miscellaneous Provisions) Act 1972, and in turn were transferred to the National Assembly for Wales by the National Assembly for Wales (Transfer of Functions) Order 1999, SI 1999/672. References to "Minister" hereafter should be read and construed accordingly.

[44] Agriculture (Miscellaneous Provisions) Act 1972, s. 19(1), (2).

[45] Grey Squirrel (Warfarin) Order 1973, SI 1973/744.

[46] For the meaning of "highway", see the brief non-statutory description in note 106 on p. 14.

[47] Game Act 1831, s. 3; Game Act 1970, s. 1(1)(a). "Game" in this context is defined to include hares, pheasants, partridges, grouse, heath or moor game and black game (Game Act 1831, s. 2).

[48] In this context "animal" means any mammal.

[49] Regulations so made are the Animals (Cruel Poisons) Regulations 1963, SI 1963/1278, for which see p. 137.

[50] Animals (Cruel Poisons) Act 1962, s. 2(1).

traps[51] for animals. But should the bait be of such a nature or so near a boundary as to attract animals which would not otherwise be likely to have entered the land, the occupier, or whoever set the bait or caused it to be set, may be liable to legal action for the value of the animals destroyed.[52] It is probable, even if he acted merely in defence of his property, that he could be prosecuted for possessing articles with intent to damage or destroy.[53]

The use of poisons against protected wild animals is considered on pages 187 and 188.

Fighting and Baiting of Animals

It is an offence of cruelty[54] to cause, procure or assist at the fighting or baiting[55] of any animal;[56] or to keep, use, manage, or act or assist in the management of any premises or place for the purpose, or partly for the purpose, of fighting or baiting any animal; or to permit any place to be so kept, managed or used; or to receive, or cause or procure any person to receive, money for the admission of any person to such premises or place.[57]

It is also an offence to keep or use or act in the management of any house, room, pit or other place for the purpose of fighting or baiting any animal.[58]

Separately, it is an offence to possess any instrument or appliance designed or adapted for use in connection with the fighting of any

---

51 For the use of traps, see pp. 144-147.
52 *Townsend v Wathen* (1808) 9 East 277.
53 The prosecution could be made under Criminal Damage Act 1971, s.3: *Halsbury's Laws of England*, 4th Ed., Vol. 2 (Reissue) para. 389 note 2.
54 As to punishment of offences of cruelty, see pp. 148-150.
55 "Baiting" is not defined but should be regarded as coursing or hunting an animal in an enclosed space from which it has no reasonable chance of escape. See Protection of Animals Act 1911, s. 1(3)(b) as amended by the Protection of Animals Act (1911) Amendment Act 1921, s. 1.
56 The long definition of "animal" is to be found in Appendix E at the end of the book.
57 Protection of Animals Act 1911, s. 1(1)(c).
58 Metropolitan Police Act 1839, s. 47 (amended by the Protection of Animals (Amendment) Act 1988, s. 2(1), (4)); Town Police Clauses Act 1847, s. 36 (amended by the Protection of Animals (Amendment) Act 1988, s. 2 (1), (4)); Public Health Act 1875, s. 171 (extended by the Local Government Act 1972, s. 180, Sch. 14, para. 23).

domestic fowl for the purpose of so using it or permitting its use.[59] Upon conviction, and in addition to the punishment mentioned below, the court may order the instrument or appliance to be destroyed or otherwise dealt with.[60]

Persons found guilty of any of the above offences may be fined, imprisoned or both.

Persons may be fined for the following lesser offences where:

a. they are found without lawful excuse on any premises so kept or used for the purpose of fighting or baiting any animal;[61]

b. they are present without lawful excuse when animals are placed together for the purpose of their fighting each other;[62]

c. they publish or cause to be published an advertisement for a fight between animals knowing that it is such an advertisement.[63]

Captive Birds; Decoys

An offence, punishable by special penalty,[64] is committed when a person promotes, arranges, conducts, assists in, receives money for, or takes part in, any event whatever at or in the course of which captive birds are liberated by hand or by other means whatever for the purpose of being shot immediately after their liberation.[65] The owner or occupier of any land is similarly guilty of an offence where the land is permitted to be used for the purposes of such an event.[66]

---

[59] Cockfighting Act 1952, s.1(1) (amended by virtue of the Criminal Justice Act 1982, s. 46).

[60] Cockfighting Act 1952, s. 1(2). The order does not take effect until the expiration of the 14 days allowed for appealing, or until the determination of any appeal (Cockfighting Act 1952, s. 1(2), proviso).

[61] Metropolitan Police Act 1839, s. 47 (amended by the Protection of Animals (Amendment) Act 1988, s. 2(1), (4)); Town Police Clauses Act 1847, s. 36 (amended by the Protection of Animals (Amendment) Act 1988, s. 2 (1), (4)).

[62] Protection of Animals Act 1911, s. 5A (added by the Protection of Animals (Amendment) Act 1988, s. 2(2)).

[63] Protection of Animals Act 1911, s. 5B (added by the Protection of Animals (Amendment) Act 1988, s. 2(2)).

[64] See Wildlife and Countryside Act 1981, s. 21(1).

[65] Wildlife and Countryside Act 1981, s. 8(3)(a).

[66] Wildlife and Countryside Act 1981, s. 8(3)(b).

Other offences may be committed under the Wildlife and Countryside Act 1981 (see below).

Myxomatosis

It is an offence, punishable by fine, knowingly to use or permit the use of a rabbit infected with myxomatosis to spread the disease among uninfected rabbits; but this provision does not prevent a properly authorised experiment in the disease.[67]

Operations and Anaesthetics

Any person who subjects any animal[68] to an operation which is performed without due care and humanity is guilty of an offence of cruelty,[69] as is anyone who causes or procures such an operation or, being the owner of the animal, permits[70] it.[71]

More specifically, it is an offence, subject to the exemptions mentioned below, for any person to perform, or cause or permit to be performed, any of the following operations on livestock[72] on agricultural land:[73]

1. Penis amputation and other penile operations;

2. Freeze dagging[74] of sheep;

3. Tongue amputation in calves;

4. Hot branding of cattle;[75]

---

[67] Pests Act 1954, s. 12, proviso (amended by the Animals (Scientific Procedures) Act 1986, s.27(2), Sch. 3 para. 4).

[68] The full definition of "animal" is given in Appendix E to this book.

[69] For exceptions and consequences of conviction, see pp. 148-150.

[70] As to permitting, see note 3 on p. 133.

[71] Protection of Animals Act 1911, s. 1(e).

[72] "Livestock" means any creature kept for the production of food, wool, skin or fur or for use in the farming of land or for such purpose as the Minister for the Department for Environment, Food and Rural Affairs may by order specify: Agriculture (Miscellaneous Provisions) Act 1968, s. 8(1), 50(1).

[73] "Agricultural land" means land used for agriculture within the meaning of the Agriculture Act 1947, s. 109(3), which is so used for the purposes of a trade or business: Agriculture (Miscellaneous Provisions) Act 1968, s. 8(1).

[74] Freeze dagging means treating the skin in the area of the crutch to prevent wool growth.

[75] "Cattle" means all bovine animals (Welfare of Livestock (Prohibited Operations) Regulations 1982, SI 1982/1884, Art. 2).

5. Devoicing of cockerels;

6. Castration of a male bird by a method involving surgery;

7. Any operation on a bird with the object or effect of impeding its flight, other than feather clipping;

8. Fitting any appliance which has the object or effect of limiting vision to a bird by a method involving the penetration or other mutilation of the nasal septum;

9. Removal of any part of the antlers of a deer before the velvet of the antlers is frayed and the greater part of it has been shed.[76]

10. Tooth grinding of sheep.

The prohibitions do not apply to the rendering, in an emergency, of first aid for the purpose of saving life or relieving pain, nor to the performance by a veterinary surgeon of an operation which is part of, in his opinion, the proper treatment for the disease or injury;[77] or to acts lawfully done under the Animals (Scientific Procedures) Act 1986.[78]

Further legislation regulates the use of anaesthetics in operations on animals. With the exceptions mentioned below, all operations on animals,[79] with or without instruments, involving interference with their sensitive tissues or bone structure without the use of anaesthetics so administered as to prevent any pain during the operation are deemed to be operations performed without due care and humanity and are offences of cruelty.[80] The exceptions are:

1. The making of injections or extractions by means of a hollow needle;[81]

---

[76] The Agriculture (Miscellaneous Provisions) Act 1968, s. 2; Welfare of Livestock (Prohibited Operations) Regulations 1982, SI 1982/1884, Arts. 3 and 4.

[77] Welfare of Livestock (Prohibited Operations) Regulations 1982, SI 1982/1884, Art. 4.

[78] See Chapter 12.

[79] Animals in this context do not include fowls or other birds, fishes or reptiles, but otherwise the word has the meaning given in Appendix E at the end of the book; Protection of Animals (Anaesthetics) Act 1954, s. 1(4).

[80] Protection of Animals (Anaesthetics) Act 1954, s. 1(1), 2; Protection of Animals Act 1911, s. 1(1)(e).

[81] Protection of Animals (Anaesthetics) Act 1954, s. 1(2).

2. Any experiment duly authorised under the Animals (Scientific Procedures) Act 1986;[82]

3. The rendering in emergency of first aid for the purpose of saving life or relieving pain;[83]

4. The docking of a dog's tail, or the amputation of its dew claws, before its eyes are open;[84]

5. The castration of a sheep under the age of three months, or of a goat, bull[85] or pig under the age of two months, except by the use of a rubber ring or other device to constrict the flow of blood to the scrotum unless applied within the first week of life;[86]

6. Any minor operation performed by a vet which by reason of its quickness or painlessness is customarily performed without an anaesthetic, or any minor operation, whether performed by a vet or not, which is not customarily performed only by a vet; none of these exceptions, however, permits castration, dehorning of cattle[87] or disbudding of calves except by chemical cauterisation in the first week of life, nor the docking of lambs' tails by the use of a rubber ring unless applied in the first week of life,[88] the docking of the tails of pigs more than seven days old,[89] nor the removal of antlers in velvet.[90]

The relevant Minister may alter the ages of the animals mentioned in paragraph 5. above[91] and may extend the classes of operations

---

[82] Protection of Animals (Anaesthetics) Act 1954, s. 1(2)(b), Sch. 1 para. 1 (amended by the Animals (Scientific Procedures) Act 1986, s. 27(2), Sch. 3, para. 3).

[83] Protection of Animals (Anaesthetics) Act 1954, Sch. 1, para. 2.

[84] Protection of Animals (Anaesthetics) Act 1954, Sch. 1, para. 3, 4.

[85] The relevant age for a bull was altered from 3 months to 2 months by the Protection of Animals (Anaesthetics) Act 1954 (Amendment) Order 1982, SI 1982/1626.

[86] Protection of Animals (Anaesthetics) Act 1954, Sch. 1, para. 6, 6A (substituted by the Protection of Animals (Anaesthetics) Act 1964, s. 1(1), (3) and amended by the Protection of Animals (Anaesthetics) Act 1954 (Amendment) Order 1982, SI 1982/1626).

[87] "Cattle" means bulls, cows, bullocks, heifers, calves, steers or oxen: Protection of Animals (Anaesthetics) Act 1964, s. 1(5).

[88] Protection of Animals (Anaesthetics) Act 1964, s. 1(1)(4).

[89] Agriculture (Miscellaneous Provisions) Act 1968, ss. 5, 51(1); Docking of Pigs (Use of Anaesthetics) Order 1974, SI 1974/798.

[90] Agriculture (Miscellaneous Provisions) Act 1968, ss. 5, 51(1); Removal of Antlers in Velvet (Anaesthetics) Order 1980, SI 1980/685.

[91] Protection of Animals (Anaesthetics) Act 1954, s. 1(3).

in which anaesthetics must be used so as to include other operations.[92]

The law on experiments on animals and the connected use of anaesthetics is set out in Chapter 12.

Traps

With the two exceptions mentioned below, a person commits an offence if:

a. for the purpose of killing or taking animals[93] he uses, or knowingly permits the use of, any spring trap, other than an approved trap; or

b. he uses, or knowingly permits the use of, an approved trap for animals in circumstances for which it is not approved; or

c. he sells, or exposes or offers for sale, any spring trap other than an approved trap with a view to its being used for a purpose which is unlawful under the last two paragraphs; or

d. he has any spring trap in his possession for a purpose which is unlawful under any of the foregoing paragraphs.[94]

References to an approved trap in these paragraphs mean a trap of a type and make approved by Government Ministers,[95] either generally or subject to conditions as to the animals for which or the circumstances in which it may be used.[96] A list of traps presently so approved and the conditions under which each may be used are set out in Appendix H at the end of the book.[97]

The two cases in which the acts described do not amount to an offence are:

---

[92]   Agriculture (Miscellaneous Provisions) Act 1968, ss. 5, 51(1).
[93]   The word " animals" is not defined in this context, but for its meaning generally in law, see p. 1.
[94]   Pests Act 1954, s. 8(1).
[95]   The functions of the Minister in relation to the Pests Act 1954 are, so far as exercisable in relation to Wales, transferred to the National Assembly of Wales: The National Assembly for Wales (Transfer of Functions) Order 1999, SI 1999/ 672. References to "Minister" hereafter should be read and construed accordingly.
[96]   Pests Act 1954, s. 8(3).
[97]   Spring Traps Approval Order 1995, SI 1995/2427.

1. The experimental use of a spring trap under and in accordance with a licence or authority given by Ministers to enable a trap to be developed or tested with a view to its becoming an approved trap;[98] and

2. Traps of any description detailed in an order of Ministers as being adapted solely for the destruction of rats, mice or other small ground vermin.[99] Traps of the following descriptions have been so authorised: spring traps known as break-back traps and commonly used for the destruction of rats, mice and other small ground vermin; and spring traps of the kind commonly used for catching moles in their runs.[100]

Any person who sets, or causes or procures to be set, any spring trap for the purpose of catching any hare or rabbit, or which is so placed as to be likely to catch any hare or rabbit, must inspect, or cause some competent person to inspect, the trap at reasonable intervals of time and at least once every day between sunrise and sunset; failure to do so is an offence.[101] It is also an offence if a person:

a. sets in position any snare which is of such a nature and so placed as to be calculated to cause bodily injury to any wild animal[102] coming into contact with it; and

b. while the snare remains in position fails, without reasonable excuse, to inspect it, or cause it to be inspected, at least once every day.[103]

It is an offence to use, or knowingly permit the use of, a spring trap for the purpose of killing or taking hares or rabbits elsewhere than in a rabbit hole;[104] though liability is avoided if the trap is used in

---

[98] Pests Act 1954, s. 8(4).

[99] Pests Act 1954, s. 8(5).

[100] Small Ground Vermin Traps Order 1958, SI 1958/24.

[101] Protection of Animals Act 1911, s. 10. For the consequences of conviction see pp. 148-150.

[102] For the definition of "wild animal", see p. 185.

[103] Wildlife and Countryside Act 1981, s. 11(3).

[104] This means the part of the burrow which is inside the ground and covered by a roof, and not the ground which is scraped away outside: *Brown v Thompson* (1882) 9 R 1183. However it does not mean a hole scooped out under a wire fence with no roof of soil (*Fraser v Lawson* (1882) 10 R 396).

accordance with Ministers' regulations[105] or under licence from them.[106] The licence may be embodied in a rabbit clearance order[107] or in a notice by Ministers[108] requiring action to prevent pest damage, and is revocable by notice.[109] It should be noted that a spring trap, though placed in a rabbit hole, is unlawful under offence a. on page 144 unless of an approved type.

Other restrictions on the use of traps and snares against protected and other wild animals are considered on pages 187 and 188.

Other Cases of Cruelty

If a person cruelly:

a. beats, kicks, ill-treats, over-rides, over-drives, overloads, tortures, infuriates or terrifies any animal;[110] or

b. causes or procures or, being the owner, permits[111] any animal to be so used; or

c. by wantonly or unreasonably doing or omitting to do any act, or causing or procuring the commission or omission of any act, causes any unnecessary suffering to any animal; or

d. being the owner, permits any unnecessary suffering to be caused as last described,

he is guilty of an offence of cruelty.[112]

This collection of wide-ranging offences may benefit from some commentary. In those cases where it is an explicit ingredient of the offence that the act or omission be done cruelly, the accused can be guilty without proof of his intention to commit cruelty. The questions are whether pain or suffering was inflicted and, if so,

---

[105] No such regulations have to date been made.

[106] Pests Act 1954, s. 9(3)(4).

[107] For rabbit clearance orders, see pp. 226-229.

[108] For such notice, see pp. 221-223.

[109] Pests Act 1954, s. 9(4).

[110] The full definition of "animal" is given in Appendix E to this book.

[111] As to permitting, see note 3 on p. 133.

[112] Protection of Animals Act 1911, s. 1(1)(a). For exceptions and consequences of conviction, see pp. 148-150.

whether it was inflicted without good reason; affirmative answers to both questions should lead to conviction. A simple definition of the cruelty aimed at is "the unnecessary abuse of the animal". On the other hand, if the charge is causing or procuring the commission or omission of an act, guilty knowledge must be shown; it is not enough to show that a defendant would have known of the animal's suffering had he properly performed his duties.[113]

Exceptions to Cruelty Offences

A number of offences which have been examined in the previous pages are expressed to be offences of cruelty. Where this is the case, it is provided that the following acts are permissible so as to legalise what would otherwise be offences :

1. Any act lawfully done under the Animals (Scientific Procedures) Act 1986;[114]

2. The commission or omission of any act in the course of the destruction, or the preparation for destruction, of any animal as food for mankind, unless such destruction or preparation was accompanied by the infliction of unnecessary suffering;

3. The coursing or hunting of any captive animal,[115] unless such animal is liberated in an injured, mutilated or exhausted condition; but a captive animal shall not be deemed to be coursed or hunted before it is liberated for that purpose, or after it has been re-captured, or if it is under control; nor if it is in an enclosed space from which it has no reasonable chance of escape.[116]

Wild Mammals

When considering wild mammals[117] it is an offence[118] if any person mutilates, kicks, beats, nails or otherwise impales, stabs,

---

[113] See further, *Halsbury's Laws of England,* 2nd Ed. (Reissue), paras. 407–409.
[114] See further Chapter 12.
[115] For the meaning of "captive animal", see Appendix E.
[116] Protection of Animals Act 1911, s. 1(3).
[117] "Wild mammal" means any mammal which is not a domestic or captive animal within the meaning of the Protection of Animals Act 1911; Wild Mammals (Protection) Act 1996, s. 3.
[118] For the consequences of conviction see pp. 148-150.

burns, stones, crushes, drowns, drags or asphyxiates any wild mammal with intent to inflict unnecessary suffering.

Again some further consideration may be useful. Unlike the Protection of Animals Act 1911, which does not require intent, but does require the prosecution to establish that unnecessary suffering has been caused to the animal, the Wild Mammals (Protection) Act 1986 requires intent to be established, but there is no requirement to establish that unnecessary suffering has been caused. It should further be noted that to cause unnecessary suffering in a manner other than prohibited is not an offence however much such suffering may be caused.

Exceptions to Unnecessary Suffering Offences

There are a number of exceptions to the offence of causing unnecessary suffering to wild mammals. These are:

1. Where a person attempted killing the wild mammal as an act of mercy if that person shows that the mammal had been so seriously disabled otherwise than by his unlawful act that there was no reasonable chance of it recovering;[119]

2. When killing a wild mammal in a reasonably swift and humane manner if that person shows that the wild mammal had been injured or taken in the course of either lawful shooting, hunting, coursing or pest control;[120] and

3. When doing anything which is authorised by or under any other enactment.[121]

Consequences of Conviction for Offences of Cruelty or Unnecessary Suffering

In addition to fining and/or imprisoning offenders for offences of cruelty, the court has a number of other powers. First, the court may, if satisfied that it could be cruel to keep the animal alive, direct that it be destroyed and assign it to any person for that purpose; but no such direction will be given except upon the

---

[119] Wild Mammals (Protection) Act 1996, s. 2(a).
[120] Wild Mammals (Protection) Act 1996, s. 2(b).
[121] Wild Mammals (Protection) Act 1996, s. 2(c).

evidence of a registered vet[122] unless the animal's owner assents. The court may order the owner to pay the reasonable expenses of destroying the animal.[123]

The court may also, in addition to any other punishment, deprive the offender of the ownership of the animal and may order its disposal, but only if it is shown by evidence as to a previous conviction or to the character of the owner or otherwise that the animal, if left to him, is likely to be exposed to further cruelty.[124] If convicted again of a cruelty offence, the court may disqualify him for a stated period from having custody of any animal or of any animal of a particular kind.[125] Disqualification may be suspended by the court for so long as it thinks necessary for arrangements to be made for the alternative custody of the animal or animals involved, or to allow an appeal to be made.[126] After 12 months from the date of disqualification the offender may apply to the court to remove it;[127] the court may, instead of refusing or granting the application, vary the order to make it apply to animals of a particular kind. When considering an application the court will have regard to the applicant's character and his conduct since disqualification, the nature of the offence and any other circumstances of the case.[128]

For any offence, whether of cruelty or not, the convicting court may order the offender to pay compensation up to £5,000[129] for any loss or damage resulting from that offence.[130] This does not affect

---

[122] Protection of Animals Act 1911, s. 2, proviso. Cf Veterinary Surgeons Act 1966, ss. 2, 6.

[123] Protection of Animals Act 1911, s. 2.

[124] Protection of Animals Act 1911, s. 3, proviso.

[125] Protection of Animals (Amendment) Act 1954, s. 1(1) (amended by the Protection of Animals (Amendment) Act 1988, s. 1(1). Breach of a disqualification order is an offence leading to a fine and/or imprisonment (Protection of Animals (Amendment) Act 1954, s. 2).

[126] Protection of Animals (Amendment) Act 1954, s. 1(2).

[127] If unsuccessful, he must wait at least 12 months before applying again, and so on for subsequent applications (Protection of Animals (Amendment) Act 1954, s. 1(3), proviso).

[128] Protection of Animals (Amendment) Act 1954, s. 1(3).

[129] Magistrates Courts Act 1980, s. 40 (as amended by SI 1984/447 and the Criminal Justice Act 1991, Sch. 4). A different sum may from time to time be substituted by order of the Secretary of State: Magistrates Courts Act 1980, s. 143(1)(2).

[130] Powers of Criminal Courts Act 1973, s. 35(1), (3), (4); Magistrates Court Act, s. 40(1) (as amended).

punishment for the offence[131] but may affect damages awarded in civil proceedings.[132]

A person disqualified from having the custody of animals cannot, while the disqualification lasts, obtain a licence to keep boarding kennels,[133] riding stables,[134] a pet shop[135] or dog breeding kennels.[136] Furthermore, when a person holds one of these licences and is convicted of any offence under the Protection of Animals Act 1911[137] (or the corresponding Scottish Act), the convicting court may cancel the licence and disqualify him from keeping the kind of animal establishment to which it relates.[138] The same will apply in the case of a guard dog kennel licence except that the holder may not be disqualified.[139]

Dealing with Diseased or Injured Animals

A police constable must take the following action if he finds any animal[140] so diseased or so severely injured or in such a physical condition that in his opinion, having regard to the means available for removing the animal, there is no possibility of doing that without cruelty. If the owner is absent or refuses to consent to the destruction of the animal, the constable must at once summon a registered vet if one lives without a reasonable distance. If the vet gives a certificate that the animal is mortally injured, or so severely

---

[131] E.g. fine and/or imprisonment.

[132] Powers of Criminal Courts Act 1973, s. 38.

[133] Animal Boarding Establishments Act 1963, s. 1(2).

[134] Riding Establishments Act 1964, s. 1(2)(e).

[135] Pet Animals Act 1951, s. 1(2).

[136] Breeding of Dogs Act 1973, s. 1(2) (as amended by Breeding and Sale of Dogs (Welfare) Act 1999).

[137] I.e. all offences in this chapter described as offences of cruelty and also: failure to feed and water animals in pounds (see p. 14); putting down and dealing in poisonous substances (see pp. 136-139); using dogs as draft animals (see p. 136); and failure to inspect spring traps (see p. 145).

[138] Pet Animals Act, s. 5(3); Animal Boarding Establishments Act 1963, s. 3(3); Riding Establishments Act 1964, s. 4(3); Breeding of Dogs Act 1973, s. 3(3) (as amended by Breeding and Sale of Dogs (Welfare) Act 1999). For the licensing of these establishments see pp. 82-89, 100-104.

[139] Guard Dogs Act 1975, s. 3(4); the Act's provisions about licences are not yet operative: see p. 91.

[140] In this context "animal" means any horse, mule, ass, bull, sheep, goat or pig (Protection of Animals Act 1911, s. 11(4)).

injured, or so diseased, or in such physical condition, that it is cruel to keep it alive, the constable may without the owner's consent arrange for the slaughter of the animal in such a way as to inflict as little suffering as practicable.[141] If the animal is so slaughtered on a public road, the constable may arrange for the removal of the carcase from the road.[142]

If the vet on being summoned certifies that the animal can be removed without cruelty, the person in charge of it must remove it at once with as little suffering as possible. If he does not, the constable may cause the animal to be removed at once without that person's consent.[143]

Any reasonable expenses of the constable in carrying out his duties, including the vet's expenses and regardless of whether or not the animal is slaughtered under these provisions, may be recovered[144] from the animal's owner as a civil debt.[145]

C. DEER

The Deer Act 1991[146] has consolidated and replaced the previous Deer Acts.[147]

Close Seasons

There are close seasons for four species of deer and these are as follows:

---

[141] In practice, the constable would ask the vet humanely to put down the animal. It appears that if no vet is accessible the constable is powerless to put down the animal without the owner's consent.

[142] Protection of Animals Act 1911, s. 11(1).

[143] Protection of Animals Act 1911, s. 11(2).

[144] Recovery is presumably by the police authority for which action can be taken in the magistrates' court.

[145] Protection of Animals Act 1911, s. 11(3).

[146] The functions of the Minister in relation to the Deer Act 1991, ss. 2 and 7 are, so far as exercisable in relation to Wales, transferred to the National Assembly of Wales except that in relation to s. 7(5)(b) only the function of the Secretary of State as "agriculture Minister" is transferred to the Assembly: The National Assembly for Wales (Transfer of Functions) Order 1999, SI 1999/672.

[147] In particular this Act has repealed the Deer Acts 1963, 1980 and 1987. The Act came into force on 25th October 1991.

1st May – 31st July inclusive
Red deer (*Cervus elaphus*) stag
Fallow deer (*Dama dama*) buck
Sika deer (*Cervus nippon nippon*) stag

1st November – 31st March inclusive
Roe deer (*Capreolus capreolus*) buck

1st March – 31st October inclusive[148]
Red deer (*Cervus elaphus*) hind
Fallow deer (*Dama dama*) doe
Sika deer (*Cervus nippon nippon*) hind
Roe deer (*Capreolus capreolus*) doe

It is an offence to take[149] or intentionally[150] kill deer[151] of these species, or to attempt to do so, during their respective close seasons, except where one of the following defences is available. One of these defences is available only to "an authorised person", and this means:

1. The occupier of the land on which the action is taken; or

2. Any member of the occupier's household[152] normally resident on the occupier's land, acting with the written authority of the occupier; or

3. Any person in the ordinary service[153] of the occupier on the occupier's land, acting with the written authority of the occupier; or

---

[148] Deer Act 1991, s. 2(1), (2), Sch. 1. Further species of deer with close seasons for them may be added, varied or deleted by statutory instrument by the Secretary of State (Deer Act 1991, ss. 2(4)(5), 15(1),(2)).

[149] For the meaning of "take", see p. 115.

[150] A person is not culpable by reason of accident or mistake, but is strictly liable if he deliberately commits the act.

[151] The word "deer" includes the carcase of any deer or any part of the carcase (Deer Act 1991, s. 16). It will also include deer of either sex and all ages (*R v Strange* (1843) 7 JP 629).

[152] For comment on the meaning of these words, see note 63 on p. 123. Though this is derived from the law relating to ground game, it may serve as a guide pending any courts' decisions on the words' meaning in the text above which is new law.

[153] For comment on the meaning of these words, see note 65 on p. 123. Though this is derived from the law relating to ground game, it may serve as a guide pending any courts' decisions on the words' meaning in the text above which is new law.

4. Any person having the right to take or kill deer on the land[154] on which the action is taken; or

5. Any person acting with the written authority of a person at 4. above.[155]

The defences are:

1. That farmed deer[156] are killed during the close season by their keeper or his servants or agents;[157]

2. In connection with an offence under section 2, that the deer was killed or taken, or was injured in an attempt to kill or take it, by an authorised person by means of shooting, and the act was done on any cultivated land, pasture or enclosed woodland.[158] But this defence[159] cannot be relied upon unless the authorised person shows that:

   i. he had reasonable grounds for believing that deer of the same species were causing, or had caused, damage to crops, vegetables, fruit, growing timber or any other form of property on the land;[160] and

   ii. it was likely that further damage would be so caused and such damage was likely to be serious;[161] and

---

[154] As to the landlords' and tenants' rights to take game on land, see pp. 124-128.

[155] Deer Act 1991, ss. 1(4), 7(4).

[156] "Farmed deer" are those kept on land enclosed by a deer-proof barrier for production of meat or other foodstuffs or skins or other by-products, or as breeding stock, and which are conspicuously marked to show ownership by the farmer (Deer Act 1991, s. 2(2)).

[157] Deer Act 1991, s. 2(2).

[158] Deer Act 1991, s. 7(1).

[159] The Secretary of State and the Agriculture Minister acting jointly may by order either generally or in relation to any area or any species and description of deer specified in the order add any further conditions which must be satisfied or may vary or delete any conditions so added. Note that, at the time of publication, the functions of the Secretary of State were being merged with those of the Agriculture Minister and will rest with the Minister for DEFRA. Deer Act 1991, s. 7(5)(b). The functions of the Minister in relation to this sub-section, so far as exercisable in relation to Wales, have been transferred to the National Assembly of Wales (except that only the function of the Secretary of State as "Agriculture Minister" is transferred to the Assembly): The National Assembly for Wales (Transfer of Functions) Order 1999, SI 1999/672.

[160] Deer Act 1991, s. 7(3)(a). I.e. the land on which the act was done, being land of one of three descriptions given earlier in the text.

[161] Deer Act 1991, s. 7(3)(b).

iii. his action was necessary for the purpose of preventing any such damage;[162]

3. In connection with an offence under section 2 or 3, that any of the prohibited acts was done for the purpose of preventing suffering by an injured or diseased deer;[163]

4. In connection with an offence under section 2 or 3, that any of the prohibited acts was done in pursuance of a Government Minister's requirement under section 98 of the Agriculture Act 1947;[164]

5. In connection with an offence under section 4(1)(a) or 4(1)(b), that the prohibited act was done for the purpose of removing deer from one area to another or of taking deer alive for scientific or educational purposes under the authority (in both cases) of a licence,[165] using one or more of the following methods:

   i. a net, trap, stupefying drug or muscle-relaxing agent of a type authorised by the licence;

   ii. a missile carrying or containing such a drug or agent, the missile being discharged by a means authorised by the licence.[166]

Killing Deer at Night

It is an offence to take or wilfully kill a deer at night, or to attempt to do so, except where one of the defences described at 3., 4. and 5. above is available.[167]

Use of Unlawful Methods and Illegal Possession of Objects

Subject to the defences later described, which are available in the instances below which are asterisked, the following acts done in

---

[162] Deer Act 1991, s. 7(3)(c).
[163] Deer Act 1991, s. 6(2).
[164] Deer Act 1991, s. 6(1).
[165] See p. 157 for further particulars about licences.
[166] Deer Act 1991, s. 6(3).
[167] Deer Act 1991, s. 3.

relation to deer, and attempts to commit those acts, are offences:

1. Setting in position any trap, snare, or poisoned or stupefying bait which is of such a nature and so placed as to be calculated to cause bodily injury to any deer coming into contact with it;

2. Using, for the purpose of killing or taking any deer, any trap, snare or poison or stupefying bait or net;

3. Using, for the purpose of killing or taking[168] any deer:

   i. any smooth bore gun or any cartridge for use in it;*

   ii. any rifle of a calibre less than .240 inches or a muzzle energy of less than 2,305 joules (1,700 foot pounds);

   iii. any bullet for use in a rifle, other than a soft-nosed or hollow-nosed bullet;

   iv. any air gun, air rifle, or air pistol;[169]

   v. any arrow, spear or similar missile;

   vi. any missile, whether discharged from a firearm or otherwise, carrying or containing any poison, stupefying drug or muscle-relaxing agent;[170]

4. Discharging any firearm[171] or projecting any missile from any mechanically propelled vehicle at any deer;[172] *

5. Using any mechanically propelled vehicle for the purpose of driving deer;[173] *

---

[168] For the meaning of "take" and "taking", see p. 115.

[169] The description of guns and ammunition in sub-paras a.–d. as located in Deer Act 1991, Sch. 2 may be amended by the Secretary of State (Deer Act 1991, s. 4(3)).

[170] Deer Act 1991, s. 4(2)(c).

[171] "Firearm" has the same meaning as in the Firearms Act 1968, s. 57(1) (Deer Act 1991, s. 16), namely, "a lethal barrelled weapon of any description from which any shot, bullet or other missile may be discharged". Cf *Read v Donovan* [1947] 1 All ER 37; *Moore v Gooderham* [1960] 3 All ER 575; *R v Thorpe* [1987] 2 All ER 108; *R v Singh* [1989]; *Grace v DPP* (1988) 153 JP 491; *Castle v DPP* (1998), *The Times*, 3 April 1998 if there are doubts as to whether the weapon is capable of being classified as a firearm.

[172] Deer Act 1991, ss. 4(4)(a), 16.

[173] Deer Act 1991, ss. 4(4)(b), 16.

6. Attempting to commit any of the offences described at items 3 to 5 inclusive;[174]

7. Possessing,[175] for the purpose of committing any of the offences described on pages 152 to 156 inclusive, any firearm[176] or ammunition[177] or any weapon or article which is described at items 2. or 3. above.[178]

The defences which are available in some instances are:

1. In the case of the offence at 3.i. above, that the gun[179] was used for the purpose of killing any deer if the user can show that it had been so seriously injured, otherwise than by his unlawful act,[180] or was in such a condition, that to kill it was an act of mercy;[181]

2. In the case of the offence at 3.i. above, that the gun was used as a slaughtering instrument to kill deer, provided the gun:

   i. was of not less gauge than 12 bore; and

   ii. had a barrel less than 24 inches (609.6 mm) in length; and

   iii. was loaded with a cartridge purporting to contain shot none of which was less than .203 inches (5.16 mm) in diameter (size AAA or larger);[182]

---

[174] Deer Act 1991, s. 5(1).

[175] For notes on the meaning of "possession" see p. 68.

[176] For the meaning of "firearm" see note 171 on p. 155.

[177] "Ammunition" means ammunition for any firearm and includes grenades, bombs and other like missiles, whether capable of use with a firearm or not, and any ammunition containing, designed or adapted to contain, any noxious liquid, gas or other thing: Firearms Act 1968, s. 57(2), (4); Deer Act 1991, s. 16. Cartridges containing only primer are ammunition (*R v Stubbings* [1990] Crim LR 811).

[178] Deer Act 1991, ss. 5(2), 9, 13. To secure conviction for this offence, it would be necessary for the prosecution to prove to the court's satisfaction a link between possession and commission, or intended commission, of one of the offences. See the Criminal Attempts Act 1981.

[179] This defence is in fact restricted to the use of a smooth bore gun and does not extend to cartridges for it. For cartridges which may be used with it, see items 2. and 3. below.

[180] The words "unlawful act" are not restricted to acts made unlawful by the Deer Act 1991, and will thus, it seems, embrace acts which are otherwise unlawful, e.g. the improper use of a gun without a shotgun certificate.

[181] Deer Act 1991, s. 6(4).

[182] Deer Act 1991, s. 6(5).

3. In the case of the offence at 3.i. above, that a gun of not less gauge than 12 bore was used by an authorised person[183] to take or kill deer on any land, and the gun was loaded with:

   i. a cartridge containing a single non-spherical projectile weighing not less than 350 grains (22.68 grammes); or

   ii. a cartridge as described at 2.iii. above;[184]

   But this defence cannot be relied upon unless the authorised person can show the existence of the three points described in items 2i., 2ii. and 2iii. on pages 153 and 154.

4. In the cases of the offences at 4. and 5. above, that the prohibited act was done by, or with the written authority of, the occupier of any enclosed land where deer are usually kept and was done in relation to deer on that land.[185]

Licences

As we have seen at 5. on page 154, a licence can be obtained for taking deer by certain means for the purposes there described. The licence will exempt the person to whom it is issued, and any other person acting with his written authority, from liability for acts within the terms of the licence which would otherwise be offences.

Such a licence is issued by the Nature Conservancy Council of England[186] or the Countryside Council for Wales.[187] It may be revoked by them at any time, and may be granted subject to conditions. Contravention of, or failure to comply with, any

---

[183] For the meaning of "authorised person" see pp. 152-153.

[184] Deer Act 1991, s. 7(2). The Secretary of State and the Agriculture Minister acting jointly may by order, in relation to particular areas or species of deer, alter in any way the types of guns or ammunition in item 3 (Deer Act 1991, s. 7(5)(a)). Note that, at the time of publication, the functions of the Secretary of State were being merged with those of the Agriculture Minister and will rest with the Minister for DEFRA. The functions of the Minister, so far as exercisable in relation to Wales, have been transferred to the National Assembly of Wales: The National Assembly for Wales (Transfer of Functions) Order 1999, SI 1999/672.

[185] Deer Act 1991, s. 4(5).

[186] Deer Act 1991, s. 8(1). The Nature Conservancy Council of England has adopted the name "English Nature". Its address is SCHA Headquarters, Northminster House, Peterborough, Cambridgeshire, PE1 1UA or see www.english-nature.gov.uk.

[187] Deer Act 1991, s. 8(2). The address for the Countryside Council for Wales is Plas Penrhos, Ffordd Penrhos, Bangor, Gwynedd, LL57 2LQ or see www.ccw.gov.uk.

condition is itself an offence.[188]

Powers of Court on Conviction of Offences

Offences are punishable with substantial fines, imprisonment, or both. If an offence is committed with respect to more than one deer, the maximum fine shall be determined as if there had been a separate offence against each of them.[189]

A convicting court may order the forfeiture of:

a. any deer or venison in respect of which the offence was committed or which was found in the accused's possession;[190] and

b. any vehicle,[191] animal, weapon or other thing which:

    i. was used to commit the offence; or

    ii. was capable of being used to take,[192] kill or injure deer and was found in the accused's possession.[193]

Where a person[194] is guilty of an offence under any of sections 1, 10 or 11 or if the person fails to surrender his firearm or shotgun certificate within 21 days from the date of that requirement,[195] the court may, in addition to forfeiture:

a. disqualify that person from holding or obtaining a licence to deal in game for such period as the court thinks fit; and/or

b. cancel any firearm or shotgun certificate held by him.[196]

Deer Poaching

With the purpose of preventing the poaching of deer, the following

---

[188] Deer Act 1991, s. 8(3).
[189] Deer Act 1991, s. 9(2).
[190] For notes on the meaning of "possession" see p. 68.
[191] "Vehicle" includes any aircraft, hovercraft or boat: Deer Act 1991, s. 16.
[192] For the meaning of "take" and "taking" see p. 115.
[193] Deer Act 1991, s. 13(1).
[194] This includes a body corporate: Deer Act 1991, s. 14.
[195] Deer Act 1991, s. 13(3)(c).
[196] Deer Act 1991, s. 13(2).

acts are, subject to the exemptions mentioned below, made offences by section 1:

1. To enter land[197] in search or pursuit of any deer[198] with the intention of taking, killing or injuring it;

2. While on any land:

   i. intentionally to take, kill or injure, or attempt to take, kill or injure, any deer;

   ii. to search for or pursue any deer with the intention of taking, killing or injuring it;

   iii. to remove the carcase of any deer.

But these offences are not perpetrated if the person committing the act:

a. has the consent[199] of the owner or occupier of the land; or

b. has lawful authority[200] to do it;[201] or

c. believes that he would have the consent of the owner or occupier of the land if the owner or occupier knew of his doing the act and the circumstances of it; or

d. believes that he has other lawful authority[202] to do the act.[203]

---

[197] "Land" includes buildings and other structures and land covered with water: Interpretation Act 1978, s. 5, Sch. 1.

[198] "Deer" in the context of this and ensuing offences means deer of any species and includes the carcase of any deer or any part of the carcase: Deer Act 1991, s. 16.

[199] Although written consent is not required, the possession of it is surer protection.

[200] No definition or explanation of "lawful authority" is given, but these words would cover acts by a tenant with sporting rights over the land (for which, generally, see pp. 124-128), or by Ministry officers acting under powers given to them to deal with animal diseases: see pp. 200-202.

[201] Deer Act 1991, s. 1(2).

[202] The difference between the defence and that at b. above is that the former relies only on the defendant's belief that he had lawful authority of some kind other than described at c. above; for examples, see note 200 above. For the belief to be effective as a defence, it is thought that, though the belief may be mistaken, it must be honestly and reasonably held.

[203] Deer Act 1991, s. 1(3).

If an authorised person[204] suspects with reasonable cause that another person is committing or has committed any of these offences on any land, he may require that person to give his full name and address and to leave the land at once; failure to do so is an offence.[205]

Constables[206] are given wide powers by section 12 of the Deer Act 1991 to stop, search and arrest suspected persons, to examine vehicles,[207] weapons, animals and other things for evidence, to seize and detain things which are such evidence and deer, venison,[208] vehicles, animals, weapons and other things which a court may order to be forfeited on conviction, and to enter land[209] (except a dwelling) to exercise the foregoing powers where they have reasonable cause[210] of suspecting that person or persons of committing or having committed an offence under the Deer Act 1991. Deer or venison so seized may be sold and the proceeds forfeited.[211]

Venison

The 1991 Act also regulates sales of venison and requires licensed game dealers[212] to keep records of their sales of it. Thus an offence

---

[204] "Authorised person" is defined as the owner or occupier of the land or any person authorised by the owner or occupier, and includes any person having the right to take or kill deer on the land: Deer Act 1991, s. 1(5).

[205] Deer Act 1991, s. 1(4). This provision does not enable an authorised person to eject the suspected person, but an owner or occupier of the land, or an employee acting under the orders, may eject a trespasser at common law, using only such force as is necessary.

[206] For the meaning of "constables" see note 414 on p. 194.

[207] For the meaning of "vehicle" see note 191 on p. 158.

[208] "Venison" here means any carcase (or part thereof) or any edible part of the carcase (or part thereof) which has not been cooked or canned (Deer Act 1991, s. 16).

[209] For the meaning of "land" see note 197 on p. 159.

[210] These words require that the constable has reasonable grounds for suspicion and also that he does actually suspect; see *R v Banks* [1916] 2 KB 621; *Kakkuda Ali v Jayaratne* [1951] AC 66. The existence of reasonable grounds for suspicion, and of the actual suspicion, are questions of fact for the court to decide: see *McArdle v Egan* (1933) 150 LT 412; *Kakkuda Ali v Jayaratne* [1951] AC 66. Cf *Liversidge v Anderson* [1941] 3 All ER 338; *Halsbury's Laws of England,* 4th Ed., Vol. 2 (Reissue), para. 330.

[211] Deer Act 1991, s. 12(3).

[212] "Licensed game dealer" means any person licensed to deal in game under the Game Act 1831 and the Game Licences Act 1960, or a servant of such a person: Deer Act 1991, s. 10(5).

punishable by a fine is committed if any person not being a licensed game dealer:

a. at any time during the prohibited period[213] sells[214] or offers or exposes for sale any venison;[215] or

b. has in his possession[216] for sale any venison; or

c. at any time sells or offers or exposes for sale any venison otherwise than to a licensed game dealer.

Likewise, any person who sells or offers or exposes for sale or has in his possession for sale, or purchase, or offers to purchase or receives, any venison which he knows or has reason to believe has been unlawfully taken or killed contrary to the provisions of the Deer Act 1991[217] is guilty of an offence punishable by a fine or imprisonment or both.

Every licensed game dealer who sells or offers or exposes for sale, or has in his possession for sale any venison is obliged to keep a record book[218] in which he must note full particulars of all his purchases and receipts of venison.[219] Each completed record book must be retained until the end of three years.[220] It is an offence to intentionally obstruct any authorised officer or constable making an inspection of the record book; any venison in the licensed game dealer's possession or under his control, or on his premises or in vehicles under his control; or any invoices, consignment notes, receipts or other documents which relate to entries in the record book.[221] Likewise, it is an offence to knowingly or recklessly make

---

[213] I.e. the period beginning with the expiry of the tenth day, and ending with the expiry of the last day, of the close season for the particular species of deer: Deer Act 1991, s. 10(2).

[214] "Sale" includes barter and exchange, and "sell" and "purchase" are to be construed accordingly: Deer Act 1991, s. 10(5).

[215] See note 208 above. Venison also includes imported deer.

[216] For notes on the meaning of "possession" see p. 68.

[217] I.e. Deer Act 1991, ss. 1–9.

[218] The record book must be in the form set out in the Deer Act 1991, Sch. 3, or a form substantially to the same effect: Deer Act 1991, s. 11(1). The Secretary of State may by order vary the form in which records are required to be kept (Deer Act 1991, s. 11(2)).

[219] Deer Act 1991, s. 11(1)(b), (3).

[220] Deer Act 1991, s. 11(4)(c), (5).

[221] Deer Act 1991, s. 11(4), (7)(a).

or cause to be made in the record book any entry which is false or misleading in a material particular.[222] Such offences are punishable by a fine.

Other provisions

The need for a game licence to take deer is considered on pages 116 to 121, and tenants' compensation for damage to crops by deer is looked at on pages 128 to 130. The removal of deers' antlers while in velvet is mentioned on pages 142 and 143.

D. SEALS

The protection afforded to seals by the Conservation of Seals Act 1970 is similar to that available for deer in that the use of certain kinds of guns and ammunition for killing them are prohibited, they are protected during close seasons, and licences to take them are available for limited purposes; exceptions are made in the first two cases.

Taking these aspects in order, it is an offence to use or attempt to use:

a. for the purpose of killing or taking any seal, any poisonous substance; or

b. for the purpose of killing, injuring or taking any seal, any firearm other than a rifle using ammunition having a muzzle energy of not less than 600 foot pounds and a bullet weighing not less than 45 grains.

The following defences will be available in a prosecution for offence b.:

A. In the case of killing a seal, that it had been so seriously disabled otherwise than by an act of the killer that there was no reasonable chance of its recovering;

B. That the act done was authorised by a licence granted by the Department for Environment, Food and Rural Affairs;

---

[222] Deer Act 1991, s. 11(4), (7)(b).

C. That the act was done outside the seaward limits of the territorial waters adjacent to Great Britain.

The annual close seasons for seals are as follows:

Grey seals (*Halichoerus grypus*): 1st September to 31st December inclusive.

Common seals (*Phoca vitulina*): 1st June to 31st August inclusive.

It is an offence wilfully to kill, injure or take, or attempt to kill, injure or take, these seals during their close seasons or at any time in an area which is designated by an order made by the Department for Environment, Food and Rural Affairs (DEFRA) and which prohibits these acts in it.

The following defences are available to an accused in the case of a prosecution:

1. That the killing or injuring of the seal was unavoidable and the incidental result of a lawful action;

2. That the killing or attempted killing of any seal was to prevent it from causing damage to a fishing net or fishing tackle in the accused's possession or in the possession of a person at whose request he killed or attempted to kill the seal, or to any fish for the time being in such fishing net, provided that at the time the seal was in the vicinity of such net or tackle. This defence is not available to the accused who kills or attempts to kill any seal for the purpose of protecting fish stocks generally;

3. In the case of taking or attempted taking, that the seal had been disabled otherwise than by the accused's act and it was taken or to be taken solely for the purpose of tending it or releasing it when no longer disabled;

4. The defences described in items A., B. and C. above.

DEFRA may grant licences for specific purposes to kill or take seals and, provided this is done within the terms and conditions of the licence, no offence will be committed.

The purposes are:

1. Purposes of any zoological gardens or collection;

2. Scientific or educational purposes;

3. Preventing damage to fisheries, reducing a population surplus of seals for management purposes, or using a population surplus of seals as a resource;

4. Protecting flora or fauna in special areas.

In all cases the licence will authorise a killing or taking in the area described in the licence which will also specify the means to be used and the number of seals to be killed or taken. The licence may be revoked at any time by DEFRA, and a person who contravenes, or attempts to contravene, or fails to comply with, any condition of the licence commits an offence.

Any person who, for the purpose of committing any of the offences described, has in his possession, or attempts to have in his possession, any poisonous substance or any prohibited firearm or ammunition commits an offence.

A court convicting a person of any of the offences described may order the forfeiture of any seal or seal skin in respect of which the offence was committed, or any seal, seal skin, firearm, ammunition or poisonous substance in his possession at the time of the offence.

The powers which police and other constables can use when with reasonable cause they suspect an offence are similar to those available to them in cases of offences under the Deer Act 1991. Additionally, they may without warrant search any vehicle or boat which the suspected person may be using, but their power to arrest a suspect without warrant can only be exercised if he fails to give his name and address to a constable to his satisfaction.

Seals have additional protection by virtue of the Conservation (Natural Habitats, &c.) Regulations 1994. Unless licensed, it is an offence[223]

---

[223] Conservation (Natural Habitats, &c.) Regulations 1994, SI 1994/2716 Reg. 41(2)(a).

to use for the purpose of taking or killing any seal[224] any of the following prohibited means:

1. Blind or mutilated animals as live decoys;

2. Tape recorders;

3. Electrical or electronic devices capable of killing or stunning;

4. Artificial light sources;

5. Devices for illuminating targets;

6. Sighting devices for night shooting comprising an electronic image magnifier or image converter;

7. Explosives;

8. Nets which are non-selective according to their principle or their conditions of use;

9. Traps which are non-selective according to their principle or their conditions of use;

10. Crossbows;

11. Poisons and poisoned or anaesthetic bait;

12. Gassing or smoking out;

13. Semi-automatic or automatic weapons with a magazine capable of holding more than two rounds of ammunition.[225]

It is likewise an offence to take or kill any seal from an aircraft or moving vehicle.[226]

---

[224] "Seals", here, means the bearded seal (*Erignathus barbatus*), common seal (*Phoca vitulina*), grey seal (*Halichoerus grypus*), harp seal (*Phoca groenlandica* otherwise known as *Pagophilus groenlandicus*), hooded seal (*Cystophora cristata*) and the ringed seal (*Phoca hispida* otherwise known as *Pusa hispida*): Conservation (Natural Habitats, &c.) Regulations 1994, SI 1994/2716, Sch. 3.

[225] Conservation (Natural Habitats, &c.) Regulations 1994, SI 1994/2716, Reg. 41(3).

[226] Conservation (Natural Habitats, &c.) Regulations 1994, SI 1994/2716, Reg. 41(2)(b), (5).

E. BADGERS

Special protection for badgers is given by the Protection of Badgers Act 1992. The Act consolidates previous Acts relating to the protection of badgers.[227] It starts by making it an offence for anyone wilfully[228] to kill, injure or take,[229] or to attempt to kill, injure or take, any badger.[230] Where there is evidence from which it could reasonably be concluded that at the material time the accused was attempting to kill, injure or take a badger, the burden of proof rests with the defendant to establish on the balance of probabilities the contrary. The Act later enumerates a number of defences available to those prosecuted for this offence, and these are:

1. In the case of killing or taking or attempting either, or in the case of injuring a badger in the course of taking it or attempting to kill or take it, the defendant can show that his action was necessary for the purpose of preventing serious damage to land,[231] crops, poultry or any other form of property;[232] but this defence is not available in relation to any action taken at any time if it had become apparent, before that time, that that action would prove necessary for the purpose mentioned, and either:

   i. a licence authorising that action had not been applied for as soon as reasonably practicable after the fact of the action proving necessary had become apparent; or

   ii. an application for such a licence had been determined;[233]

---

[227] Badgers Act 1973, the Badgers Act 1991 and the Badgers (Further Protection) Act 1991. Additionally, it repeals the Wildlife and Countryside Act, s. 73(4) and in Sch. 7, paras. 8 to 12; the Wildlife and Countryside (Amendment) Act 1985, s. 1; the Animals (Scientific Procedures) Act 1985, Sch. 3, para. 9; the Environmental Protection Act 1990, Sch. 9, para. 6.

[228] This means deliberately and intentionally, and not by accident or inadvertence (*R v Senior* [1899] 1 QB 283 at pp. 290–291).

[229] For an interpretation of "take", see p. 68.

[230] Protection of Badgers Act 1992, s. 1(1). "Badger" is defined to mean any animal of the species *Meles meles* (Protection of Badgers Act 1992, s. 14).

[231] "Land" is defined to include, amongst other things, buildings and other structures and land covered with water (Interpretation Act 1978, s. 5, Sch. 1).

[232] Protection of Badgers Act 1992, s. 7(1).

[233] Protection of Badgers Act 1992, s. 7(2).

2. That it was a taking or attempted taking of a badger which had been disabled otherwise than by the act of the accused, and it was taken or to be taken solely for the purpose of tending it;[234]

3. That it was a killing or attempted killing of a badger which appeared to be so seriously injured or in such a condition that to kill it would be an act of mercy;[235]

4. That it was an unavoidable killing or injuring as an incidental result of a lawful action;[236]

5. That the act was done as a regulated procedure under the Animals (Scientific Procedures) Act 1986;[237]

6. That the act was done under the authority of, and within the conditions of, a licence the provisions for which are considered further below.[238]

A person is guilty of an offence if, unless otherwise permitted by or under the Act, he intentionally or recklessly interferes with a badger sett.[239] To interfere with a badger sett is (a) to damage it or any part of it, (b) destroy it, (c) obstruct either access to it, or its entrance, (d) cause a dog to enter it or (e) disturb a badger whilst such badger is occupying it.[240] Again, a person is not guilty of such an offence if he shows that his action was necessary for the purpose of preventing serious damage to land, crops, poultry or any other form of property, but such defence is not available where in relation to the action taken it had become apparent, before that time, that the action would require a licence authorising such action and such licence had not been obtained or an application for such a licence had not been determined.[241]

Likewise a person is not guilty of an offence in the case of (a), (c)

---

[234] Protection of Badgers Act 1992, s. 6(a).
[235] Protection of Badgers Act 1992, s. 6(b).
[236] Protection of Badgers Act 1992, s. 6(c).
[237] Protection of Badgers Act 1992, s. 6(d).
[238] Protection of Badgers Act 1992, s. 10. See pp. 168-170.
[239] "Badger sett" means any structure or place which displays signs indicating current use by a badger: Protection of Badgers Act 1992, s. 14.
[240] Protection of Badgers Act 1992, s. 3. See *Lovett v Bussey* (1998) 162 JP 423.
[241] Protection of Badgers Act 1992, s. 8(1), (2).

or (e) where the accused shows that his action was the incidental result of a lawful operation and could not reasonably have been avoided.[242]

A person is not guilty of an offence in the case of (a), (c), (e) by reason of obstructing an entrance of a badger sett for the purpose of hunting foxes with hounds.[243] The exemption is conditional and requires the person[244] to act with the authority of the owner or occupier of the land and the authority of a recognised hunt.[245] Additionally, he must not do anything other than obstruct the entrance(s) nor dig into the tops or sides of the entrances. In sett stopping he must use only (i) untainted straw or hay, leaf-litter, bracken, loose soil; or (ii) a bundle of sticks or faggots, or paper sacks either empty or filled with untainted straw or hay, leaf-litter, bracken, loose soil.[246] Such materials may not be packed hard into the entrance and in the case (i) may only be placed in the entrance on the day of the hunt or after midday on the preceding day; whilst in case (ii) they may only be placed on the day of the hunt and must be removed on the same day. [247]

Licences[248] may be granted for the following purposes:

1. For scientific or educational purposes or for the conservation of badgers:

   i. to kill or take within the area and by the means specified in the licence, or to have in the licensed person's possession, the number of badgers stipulated by the licence;

   ii. to interfere with any badger sett within the area and in the manner specified in the licence;

---

[242] Protection of Badgers Act 1992, s. 8(3).

[243] Protection of Badgers Act 1992, s. 8(4).

[244] The recognised hunt is obliged to keep a register of such persons: Protection of Badgers Act 1992, s. 8(8). "Recognised hunt" means a hunt recognised by the Masters of Fox Hounds Association, the Association of Masters of Harriers and Beagles or the Central Committee of Fell Packs: Protection of Badgers Act 1992, s. 8(9).

[245] Protection of Badgers Act 1992, s. 8(4)(d).

[246] Protection of Badgers Act 1992, s. 8(5).

[247] Protection of Badgers Act 1992, s. 8(6).

[248] Such licences may neither be unreasonably withheld nor revoked. Protection of Badgers Act 1992, s. 10(9).

2. For the purpose of any zoological gardens or collection specified in the licence, to take within the area and by the means prescribed in the licence, or to sell or have in the licensed person's possession the number of badgers stipulated by the licence;

3. For the purpose of ringing and marking, to take badgers within the area described in the licence, to mark them and to attach to them any ring, tag or other marking device as specified in the licence;

4. For the purpose of preventing the spread of disease, to kill or take badgers, or to interfere with a badger sett, within the area prescribed and in the manner specified;

5. For the purpose of preventing serious damage to land, crops, poultry or any other form of property, to kill or take badgers, or to interfere with a badger sett within the area stipulated and in the manner prescribed;

6. For the purpose of any agricultural or forestry operation, to interfere with a badger sett within the specified area and by the means stipulated by the licence;

7. For the purpose of any operation (whether by virtue of the Land Drainage Act 1991 or otherwise) to maintain or improve any existing watercourse or drainage works, or to construct new works required for the drainage of any land, including works for the purpose of defence against sea water or tidal water, to interfere with a badger sett within the area specified in the licence by any means so specified;

8. For the purpose of any development,[249] to interfere with a badger sett within an area specified in the licence by the means so specified;

9. For the purpose of the preservation, or archaeological investigation, of a monument,[250] to interfere with a badger sett

---

[249] For the meaning of "development" see Town and Country Planning Act 1990, s. 55(1).

[250] The monument must be scheduled under the Ancient Monuments and Archaeological Areas Act 1979.

within an area specified in the licence by the means so specified;

10. For the purpose of investigating whether any offence has been committed or gathering evidence in connection with proceedings before any court, to interfere with a badger sett within an area specified and in the manner so licenced.

In cases 1–3 (inclusive) and cases 8–10 (inclusive) licences are granted by the Conservancy Council[251] and in the remaining cases by the Department for Environment, Food and Rural Affairs.[252] Additionally, a licence to interfere with a sett may be granted by either the Council or the Minister for the purpose of controlling foxes in order to protect livestock, game or wildlife.[253] A licence may be revoked at any time, and breach of any of its conditions is an offence.[254]

The 1992 Act creates a number of other offences related to badgers, some with special defences, and these will now be considered.

Unless permitted by or under the Act, it is an offence for any person to have in his possession[255] or under his control any dead badger or any part of, or anything derived from, a dead badger.[256] It is a defence if the person shows that:

a. the badger had not been killed; or

b. it had been killed otherwise than in contravention of the 1992 Act or of the Badgers Act 1973; or

c. the object in the person's possession or control had been sold (whether to him or any other person) and, at the time of

---

[251] Protection of Badgers Act 1992, s. 10(1). "Conservancy Council" means, in England, the Nature Conservancy Council for England (now known by its adopted name "English Nature"), and in Wales, the Countryside Council for Wales. The functions of English Nature have now been transferred to DEFRA.

[252] Protection of Badgers Act 1992, s. 10(2). The Minister is obliged to consult the Conservancy Council before exercising his functions under 5.-7. (inclusive) and may not grant a licence without first being advise by the appropriate Conservancy Council – Protection of Badgers Act 1992, s. 10(6).

[253] Protection of Badgers Act 1992, s. 10(3).

[254] Protection of Badgers Act 1992, s. 10(8).

[255] For some notes on the meaning of "possession", see p. 68.

[256] Protection of Badgers Act 1992, s. 1(3).

purchase, the purchaser had had no reason to believe that the badger had been killed in contravention of the Act.[257]

Described as offences of cruelty, the following acts are forbidden:

1. Cruelly to ill-treat any badger;

2. To use any badger tongs in the course of killing or taking, or attempting to kill or take, any badger;

3. To dig for any badger, except as permitted by or under the Act;

4. To use, for the purpose of killing or taking any badger, any firearm[258] other than a smooth bore weapon of not less than 20 bore or a rifle using ammunition having a muzzle energy of not less than 160 foot pounds and a bullet weighing not less than 38 grains.[259]

Where proceedings are brought for the act of cruelty involving digging for a badger and there is evidence from which it could reasonably be concluded that at the material time the accused was digging for a badger he will be presumed to have been digging for a badger unless the contrary is shown.[260]

It is an offence for any person to sell,[261] offer for sale, or have in his possession or under his control any live badger. Where that person has possession or control of a live badger:

a. in the course of his business as a carrier; or

b. when it has been disabled otherwise than by the act of the accused solely for the purpose of tending it, and it is necessary for that purpose for it to remain in the accused's possession or under his control; or

---

[257] Protection of Badgers Act 1992, s. 1(4).

[258] For the definitions of "firearm" and "ammunition" which are applicable, see note 171 on page 155 and note 177 on p. 156 (Protection of Badgers Act 1992, s. 14).

[259] Protection of Badgers Act 1992, s. 2(1).

[260] Protection of Badgers Act 1992, s. 2(2).

[261] The word "sale" includes hire, barter and exchange and cognate expressions are interpreted accordingly (Protection of Badgers Act 1992, s. 14).

c. the possession or control of the badger was covered by a licence
    granted under the Act,

then that person shall not be guilty of an offence.[262]

Except under licence, it is also an offence if any person marks, or
attaches any ring, tag or other marking device to, any badger.[263]

Police and other constables are given wide powers by the Act to
search suspects, vehicles and articles, to arrest suspects and to
seize and detain anything which may be evidence of an offence
under the Act or which may be forfeited by a court.[264] On conviction
of any offence under the Act and in addition to a fine or imprisonment
or both (as applicable) the court must order forfeiture of any badger
or skin in respect of which the offence was committed, and may
order forfeiture of weapons and articles connected with the
offence.[265]

Where a dog is used or present at the commission of the offence,
the court may also, in addition to any other punishment, deprive the
offender of the ownership of the animal and may order its destruction
or disposal.[266] The destruction of the dog may not be ordered by the
court during the period of appeal granted by the court or where
notice of appeal has been received during its determination.[267]
Where the court has ordered the destruction or disposal of the dog,
it may appoint a person to undertake the destruction or other
disposal of the dog and order any person having custody of the dog
to deliver it to the appointee for destruction or disposal.[268]

Where the offender has been disqualified from having custody of
a dog he may, after 12 months from the date of disqualification,

---

[262] Protection of Badgers Act 1992, s. 9.
[263] Protection of Badgers Act 1992, s. 5.
[264] Protection of Badgers Act 1992, s. 11.
[265] Protection of Badgers Act 1992, s. 12.
[266] Protection of Badgers Act 1992, s. 13(1).
[267] Protection of Badgers Act 1992, s. 13(4).
[268] Protection of Badgers Act 1992, s. 13(2)(a). Additionally the offender may be
    required to pay such reasonable expenses as determined by the court in connection
    with the destruction, disposal or keep prior to such destruction or disposal
    (Protection of Badgers Act, s. 13(2)(b)). Failure to deliver up the dog is an offence
    (Protection of Badgers Act 1992, s. 13(7)).

apply to the court to remove it.[269] When considering an application the court will have regard to the applicant's character and his conduct since disqualification, the nature of the offence and any other circumstances of the case.[270]

If any person is found on land committing any of the offences mentioned below, the owner or occupier of the land, or an employee of either of them, or a constable, may require that person to leave the land at once and to give his name and address.[271] If that person then deliberately refuses to comply with either requirement, he commits an offence. The offences in question are: killing, injuring or taking a badger, or attempting to do so; and having possession or control of a dead badger, or part of it, or anything derived from it.[272]

The powers of Government Ministers to destroy wild badgers for the purpose of combating disease are discussed on pages 200 to 202.

F. PROTECTION OF OTHER WILD ANIMALS

Introduction

The principal statute relating to the protection of wildlife is the Wildlife and Countryside Act 1981.[273] The intention of Part I of the Act is to prohibit the killing and taking of birds, other animals and

---

[269] Protection of Badgers Act 1992, s. 13(5). If unsuccessful, he must wait at least 12 months before applying again, and so on for subsequent applications (Protection of Badgers Act 1992, s. 13(6)).

[270] Protection of Badgers Act 1992, s. 13(6)(a).

[271] Protection of Badgers Act 1992, s. 1(5). Note that the Act gives no right forcibly to eject the offender from the land, but at common law the owner and occupier have the right if the offender is a trespasser, as also will the employees and a constable if (in either case) they are exercising it under the direction of the owner or occupier.

[272] Protection of Badgers Act 1992, s. 1. These offences are fully set out on pp. 166 and 168 and the defences available for them in the respective following passages. Difficulties may arise in practice because of the problem of establishing on the spot whether a defence is available which would prevent an apparent offence from being a real one and thus nullifying the rights to make the two requirements which, on the wording of the Act, depend upon an offence being committed.

[273] As amended by the Wildlife and Countryside (Amendment) Act 1985 (amending s. 28) and Wildlife and Countryside (Amendment) Act 1991 (amending ss. 5 and 11). The Water Act 1989 amended ss. 27(1) and 36(7).

plants.[274] Its provisions extend to the territorial waters[275] adjacent to Great Britain.[276] Throughout Part I various species benefit from differing levels of protection,[277] thus some birds and animals are protected by general law, others by added protection throughout the year, whilst others are protected only during close seasons. Similarly the general public is denied the right to destroy various birds or animals, whilst landowners and those benefiting from sporting rights are exempted from certain liabilities.

Wild Birds[278]

Section 1(1) makes it an offence intentionally to:

a. kill, injure or take[279] any wild bird;[280]

b. take, damage or destroy the nest of any wild bird while that nest is in use or is being built; or

c. take or destroy[281] an egg of any wild bird.

Additionally, section 1(2) makes it an offence if any person has in his possession[282] or control (a) any live or dead wild bird or any part

---

274 For the provisions relating to plants see JF Garner and BL Jones *Countryside Law* 3rd Edition 1997, Shaw & Sons, Crayford.

275 The extent of territorial waters is much disputed in international law, but the U.K. uses the rule of the 3-mile limit, measured, in general, from the low-water mark.

276 Wildlife and Countryside Act 1981, s. 27(5). "Great Britain" means England, Wales and Scotland, and excludes the Channel Islands and the Isle of Man.

277 The Secretary of State may vary the protection afforded to particular birds, wild animals and plants by statutory instrument: Wildlife and Countryside Act 1981, s. 22. This has been done by the Wildlife and Countryside Act 1981 (Variation of Schedules) Orders of 1988 (SI 1988/288), 1989 (SI 1989/906), 1991 (SI 1991/ 367), 1992 (SI 1992/320, SI 1992/2674, SI 1992/2350, SI 1992/3010).

278 "Wild bird" excludes any bird bred in captivity: Wildlife and Countryside Act 1981, s. 1(6). It means "any wild bird of a kind which is ordinarily resident in or is a visitor to Great Britain in a wild state but does not include poultry". Poultry is defined as domestic fowl, geese, ducks, guinea-fowls, pigeons, quails and turkeys. Game birds are likewise exempted from the definition of wild birds, but not so in respect to section 5 (prohibiting certain methods of killing or taking wild birds) and section 16 (permitting certain activities by official licences). "Game bird" means "any pheasant, partridge, grouse (or moor game), black (or heath) game or ptarmigan" (Wildlife and Countryside Act 1981, s. 27(1)).

279 "Take" means "capture" – see *Robinson v Everett and W & FC Bonham and Son Ltd* [1988] Crim LR 699.

280 The Schedules to the Wildlife and Countryside Act 1981 relating to wild birds are reproduced in Appendix F.

281 "Destroy" includes doing anything calculated to prevent an egg from hatching.

282 For some notes on the meaning of "possession", see p. 68.

of, or anything derived from, such a bird; or (b) an egg of a wild bird or any part of such an egg.

Some commentary is appropriate. The two subsections are distinguished by the word "intention". Given that subsection (1) uses the term "intentionally" then a person is not culpable by reason of mistake or accident. However, if a person deliberately commits the act then liability is strict. Subsection (2) does not use the term "intentionally" and is a strict liability offence, thus in *Kirkland v Robinson*[283] it was held that it was not a defence that the accused did not know that the gosshawks he had in his possession were wild birds.

It is a defence to show that (1) the bird or egg had not been killed or taken; or (2) had been killed or taken otherwise than in contravention of the Act; or (3) that the bird, egg or other thing in the accused's possession or control had been sold[284] (whether to him or any other person) otherwise than in contravention of the Act.[285] The burden of proving the defences falls on the defendant. The defendant need only prove the defence on the balance of probabilities.

Specially Protected Wild Birds

Schedule 1 to the 1981 Act lists a number of birds which enjoy additional protection. The effect of the listing means that it is an offence intentionally or recklessly[286] (i) to disturb any wild bird in Schedule 1 while it is building a nest or is in, on or near, a nest containing eggs or young; or (ii) to disturb dependent young of such a bird.[287] Certain defences[288] mentioned above will not be available to the defendant, so, in (1) the acts done must be in pursuance of orders made under sections 21 and 22 of the Animal Health Act 1981,[289] and (1) and (2) are not available to authorised

---

[283] [1986] Crim LR 643.

[284] The word "sale" includes hire, barter and exchange and cognate expressions are interpreted accordingly (Wildlife and Countryside Act 1981, s. 27(1)).

[285] Wildlife and Countryside Act 1981, s. 1(3).

[286] The words "or recklessly" inserted by Countryside and Rights of Way Act 2000, Sch. 12, para. 1.

[287] Wildlife and Countryside Act 1981, s. 1(5).

[288] See generally, Wildlife and Countryside Act 1981, s. 4.

[289] Wildlife and Countryside Act 1981, s. 4(1)(a).

persons.[290] There is however a general exception where the offender shows, again on the balance of probabilities that:

a. the wild bird had been disabled otherwise than by his unlawful act and was taken for the sole purpose of tending it and thereafter releasing it when no longer disabled; or

b. he killed the wild bird because it was so seriously disabled otherwise than by his unlawful act and that it had no reasonable chance of recovery from its disability; or

c. the act made unlawful by the provisions of section 1 was the incidental result of a lawful operation and could not reasonably have been avoided.[291]

Game Birds

Schedule 2 to the 1981 Act lists a number of birds which receive less protection than the general protection set out on pages 174 to 175. Before considering the listed birds it should be noted that, during the close season, the goldeneye, pintail and (in parts of northwest Scotland only) the greylag goose may be hunted despite the fact that they are listed in Schedule 1 of specially protected birds.

The modification to the basic offences means that it is not an offence to kill or take any bird listed in Part I of Schedule 2 or to injure it in an attempt to kill it, outside the close season in question.[292] The close seasons are:

1. Capercaillie and (except in Scotland) woodcock — 1st February–30th September;

2. Snipe — 1st February–1st August;

3. Wild duck and wild geese in or over any area below high-water mark of ordinary spring tides — 21st February–31st August;

4. All other Schedule 2 Part I wild birds — 1st February–31st August.[293]

---

[290] Wildlife and Countryside Act 1981, s. 4(3).
[291] Wildlife and Countryside Act 1981, s. 4(2).
[292] Wildlife and Countryside Act 1981, s. 2(1).
[293] Wildlife and Countryside Act 1981, s. 2(4).

The Secretary of State has the power under section 2(5) to make orders varying the close season with respect to the whole or any part of Great Britain. He may also make temporary orders for a period of up to 14 days at a time protecting birds listed in Part II of Schedule 1 or Part II of Schedule 2.[294] Such orders may be made after consulting a representative of shooting interests and are intended for periods of exceptionally severe weather (usually in the case of wildfowl) or other temporary crisis for the birds.[295]

The killing or taking of Schedule 2 birds on Sundays or on Christmas Day in Scotland is not permitted. In England and Wales no Sundays are prohibited, although the Secretary of State has power to prohibit them, by order for such specified areas.[296]

Pests

All pest species are no longer separately scheduled under Schedule 2 Part II.[297] It is now the case that it is permissible for an authorised person[298] to kill or injure, whilst attempting to kill or take, any wild bird formerly listed[299] or their eggs for a variety of purposes

---

[294] Wildlife and Countryside Act 1981, s. 2(6).

[295] Wildlife and Countryside Act 1981, s. 2(7).

[296] Wildlife and Countryside Act 1981, s. 2(3). The following Wild Birds (Sundays) Orders were made under the Protection of Birds Act 1954 and are presumed to remain effective in the prescribed areas: SI 1955/1286 – Caernarvon, Carmarthen, Devon, Isle of Ely, Montgomery, Norfolk, Pembroke, and York, North Riding and York, West Riding, Doncaster, Great Yarmouth and Leeds; SI 1956/1310 – Brecknock, Cardigan, Denbigh and Merioneth; SI 1957/429 – Cornwall, Glamorgan and Somerset; SI 1963/1700 – Anglesey.

[297] The birds were removed by SI 1992/3010.

[298] An "authorised person" means the owner or occupier, or any person authorised by the owner or occupier, of the land on which the action is authorised, where an occupier, in relation to land other than foreshore, includes any person having any right of hunting, shooting, fishing or taking game or fish. Additionally, "authorised person" includes any person authorised in writing by the local authority, or by any of the Nature Conservancy Councils, a water authority or a sewage undertaker, a district board in Scotland, a local sea fisheries committee, the National Rivers Authority for the area within which the action authorised is taken: Wildlife and Countryside Act 1981, s. 27(1), as amended by the Environmental Protection Act 1990, s. 132(1)(a), Sch. 9, para. 11(7)(a) (effected by SI 1991/685); Water Act 1989, s. 190(1), Sch. 25, para. 66(1) (effected by SI 1989/1146), s. 190(3), Sch. 27, Pt. I and s. 194(3) (effected by SI 1989/1530).

[299] The birds are the crow, collared dove, great black-backed gull, lesser black-backed gull, herring gull, jackdaw, jay, magpie, feral pigeon, rook, house sparrow, starling and woodpigeon.

including the protection of serious damage of livestock, foodstuffs, crops, vegetables, or fruit and the preservation of public health or nature conservation, or air safety, under general licence.[300] The licences are annual but apply to all authorised persons, so that there is no need for individual applications to be made.

Areas of Special Protection

The Secretary of State may, by order, specify areas of special protection for wild birds.[301] Such an order can extend the protection given to Schedule 1 birds to all, or specified, wild birds[302] in the area of special protection, to their nests, young and eggs. The order can also make it an offence to disturb such a bird whilst it builds a nest, or is in, on or near a nest containing eggs or young; or where such dependent young are disturbed.[303]

Before such an order is made the Secretary of State must give particulars of the intended order, whether by written notice to every owner and occupier of any land in the proposed area or, where in his opinion this is impractical, by advertisement in a newspaper circulated in the locality in which the area is situated.[304] The Secretary of State may not make an order unless (a) all the owners and occupiers have consented; or (b) no objections have been received within three months of the notice being given or the publication of the advertisement; (c) any objections have subsequently been withdrawn.[305]

The effect of the order is to impose greater liability[306] on those

---

[300] Wildlife and Countryside Act 1981, s. 16.
[301] Wildlife and Countryside Act 1981, s. 3(1).
[302] With the consequent effect that a higher fine may be imposed.
[303] Wildlife and Countryside Act 1981, s. 3(1).
[304] Wildlife and Countryside Act 1981, s. 3(4).
[305] Wildlife and Countryside Act 1981, s. 3(5).
[306] Indeed the offence will be treated as falling within section 7(3A) and a special penalty will be imposed where an offence is committed (a) under section 1(1) or (2) in respect of (i) a bird included in Schedule 1 or any part of, or anything derived from, such a bird, (ii) the nest of such a bird, or (iii) an egg of such a bird or any part of such an egg; (b) any offence under s. 1(5) or 5; or (c) any offence under s. 6 in respect of (i) a bird included in Schedule 1 or any part of, or anything derived from such a bird, or (ii) an egg of such a bird or any part of such an egg; (d) any offence under s. 8: inserted by Countryside and Rights of Way Act 2000, Sch. 12, para. 4.

persons entering the area of special protection who do not have a legal or equitable title to the land.[307] The making of an order under section 3 does not effect the exercise by any person of any right vested in him, whether as owner, lessee or occupier of any land in the area or by virtue of licence or agreement.[308]

Prohibited Methods of Taking and Killing Wild Birds

In an attempt to curb the methods of indiscriminate species destruction and to an extent to give such birds as may be hunted a fair chance, section 5 of the 1981 Act[309] sets out a catalogue of prohibited methods. In general, it is an offence to (a) set in position any spring, trap, gin, snare, hook and line, any electrical device for killing, stunning or frightening or any poisonous, poisoned or stupefying substance;[310] or (b) use for the purposes of killing or taking any wild bird any of the articles mentioned in (a), whether or not of such a nature and so placed as to kill, injure or take, or any net, baited board, bird-lime or substance of a like nature to bird lime. However, an authorised person will not have committed an offence if he can show that the article in (a) was set for the lawful killing or taking of wild animals in the interests of public health, agriculture,[311] forestry, fisheries or nature conservation and that he can show that he took all reasonable precautions to prevent injury to the wild birds.[312]

---

[307] An order may exclude the general public from an area, except as may be provided by the order: Wildlife and Countryside Act 1981, s. 3(1)(b).

[308] Wildlife and Countryside Act 1981, s. 3(3).

[309] Wildlife and Countryside Act 1981, s. 5(1) as amended by the Wildlife and Countryside (Amendment) Act 1991, s. 1.

[310] As noted at para. 8-4145 of *Stones Justices Manual* (1999). This section distinguishes between a substance poisonous *per se*, a substance with which poison had been mixed (so that it became a poisoned substance) and a substance which was intended to and had the effect of stupefying; if there is doubt about which of these categories applies to a substance, separate information should be laid; see *Robinson v Hughes* [1987] Crim LR 644.

[311] Though not defined in this context, the word "agriculture" is defined in Agricultural Holdings Act 1986, s. 98(1) and Agricultural Tenancies Act 1995, s. 38(1) as including horticulture, fruit growing, seed growing, dairy farming and livestock breeding and keeping, the use of land as grazing land, meadow land, osier land, market gardens and nursery grounds, and the use of land for woodlands where that use is ancillary to the farming of land for other purposes. This serves as a guide, but no more, to its meaning in its present context.

[312] Wildlife and Countryside Act 1981, s. 5(4) but such defence is not available where the article is set to kill or take those animals listed in Wildlife and Countryside Act 1981, Sch. 6.

Generally, certain types of instruments may not be used to kill or take any wild birds, namely, (i) a bow or crossbow, (ii) any automatic or semi-automatic weapon, (iii) any shot-gun of which the barrel has an internal diameter at the muzzle of more than 1.25 inches, (iv) any device illuminating a target or any sighting device for night shooting, (v) any form of artificial lighting or any mirror or other dazzling device, (vi) any explosive other than ammunition for a firearm, (vii) any gas or smoke not falling within (a) and (b) above, or (viii) any chemical wetting agent.[313] Again, an authorised person may use lawfully the instruments (i) – (vi) for the purpose of killing birds that were formerly listed in Schedule 2 Part II[314] provided that such use is in the interests of public health, agriculture, or air safety, viz. under the general licence considered above.

The use of any sound recording or any live bird or other animal which is tethered or secured by means of braces or which is blind, maimed[315] or injured is prohibited for the purposes of killing or taking any wild bird.[316] Likewise, the use of any mechanically propelled vehicle in immediate pursuit of a wild bird for the purpose of killing or taking it is prohibited.[317]

There are a number of general exemptions, thus, a cage trap (such as a Larcen trap) or net may be used by an authorised person for the purpose of taking a bird included in what was formerly Schedule 2 Part II. Similarly, nets may be used in a decoy for the purpose of taking wild duck provided that it can be shown that it has been in use since immediately before the passing of the Protection of Birds Act 1954 and a cage trap or a net may be used to take game birds for the sole purpose of breeding. In both cases these exceptions do not make it lawful to use any net taking birds in flight or the use of a net not propelled by hand to capture birds on the ground.

---

[313] Wildlife and Countryside Act, 1981, s. 5(1)(c).
[314] See note 299 on p. 177 for the birds so listed.
[315] There must be permanent deprivation of a member or mutilation or crippling for the bird or animal to be "maimed". Thus, jackdaws who had their primary wing feathers clipped but which would grow back at the moulting stage were not "maimed" within the meaning of the Act (*Holden v Lancaster Justices* (1998) 162 JP 789): *Stones Justices Manual* (1999) para. 8-4145, note 3.
[316] Wildlife and Countryside Act, 1981, s. 1(e).
[317] Wildlife and Countryside Act, 1981, s. 1(f).

A licence granted by the appropriate authority[318] may entitle the holder to set any article or take or kill any wild bird by any prohibited means.[319]

Trading in Live and Dead Birds, and their Eggs

The trade in wild birds, whether live or dead, and their eggs is restricted by the Wildlife and Countryside Act 1981 and the Regulations arising under the Act. There is a complete prohibition in the trade of wild birds and their eggs save for certain birds listed in Schedule 3 and those that may be traded under licence. Thus, unless authorised under a licence granted by the Department of Transport, Environment and the Regions,[320] it is an offence for any person (1) to sell, offer or expose for sale or have in his possession, or transport for the purpose of sale, any live wild bird (including those which have been bred in captivity) other than a bird[321] included in Part I of Schedule 3, or an egg of a wild bird or any part of such an egg; or (2) to publish or cause to be published any advertisement likely to be understood as conveying that he buys or sells, or intends to buy or sell, any of those things.[322]

A general licence (WLF 100095) allows for the sale, subject to conditions, of all wild birds,[323] save for those listed in Annex A of Council Regulation (EC) 338/97, and those listed in Part I of Schedule 3. Certain birds are excluded from the provisions of the general licence and require individual licences. These are as listed overleaf:

---

[318] See Wildlife and Countryside Act 1981, s. 16(9) for a definition of "appropriate authority".

[319] Wildlife and Countryside Act 1981, s. 16(1).

[320] Licences to sell wild birds (apart from those covered by EC Regulations 338/97) may be issued under s. 16(4).

[321] The bird must be ringed in accordance with the Wildlife and Countryside (Ringing of Certain Birds) Regulations 1982, SI 1982/1220.

[322] Wildlife and Countryside Act 1981, s. 6(1).

[323] The general licence does not allow for the sale of the eggs of those species. There are three conditions attached to the general licence: (i) the bird must have been bred in captivity and documentary evidence must accompany the sale of the bird; (ii) the bird must be ringed with an individually numbered close ring; and (iii) the owner must, if so requested by a DEFRA official or police official, make the bird available for a blood sample to be taken, for the purposes of confirming its ancestry. For further details see www.defra.gov.uk.

Brent goose	*Branta bernicla*
Goldeneye	*Bucephala clangula*
Long-tailed duck	*Clangula hyemalis*
Bewick's swan	*Cygnus bewickii*
Mute swan	*Cygnus olor*
Velvet scoter	*Melanitta fusca*
Common scoter	*Malanitta nigra*
Goosander	*Mergus merganser*
Red-breasted goosander	*Megus serrator*
Ruddy duck	*Oxyura jamaicensis*

Similarly, it is an offence for any person not for the time being registered in accordance with regulations made by the Secretary of State to (a) sell, offer or expose for sale or have in his possession, or transport for the purpose of sale, any dead wild bird other than a bird included in Part II or III of Schedule 3 to the Act, or any part of, or anything derived from, such a wild bird; or (b) to publish or cause to be published any advertisement likely to be understood as conveying that he buys or sells, or intends to buy or sell, any of those things.[324] There are currently two general licences in effect: WLF 100092, permits the sale of feathers and parts of wild birds included in Part III of Schedule 3, and WLF 100096, permits the sale of certain dead birds (being any dead wild bird other than those included in Part I of Schedule 2, Parts II and III of Schedule 3, or barnacle geese and the Greenland race of white fronted geese).[325]

Equally, it is an offence for any person to show, or cause or permit to be shown, for the purposes of any competition or in any premises where a competition is being held (i) any live wild bird other than one included in Part I of Schedule 3 to the Act, or (ii) any live bird one of whose parents was such a wild bird unless licenced.[326]

Any person convicted of any of the foregoing offences in respect of a bird included in Schedule 1 or in respect of any part of, or

---

[324] Wildlife and Countryside Act 1981, s. 6(2).
[325] Michael Bradley Taylor (Ed) *Wildlife Crime, A Guide to Wildlife Law Enforcement in the United Kingdom* 1996, London, The Stationery Office, p. 15.
[326] Wildlife and Countryside Act 1981, s. 6(3).

anything derived from, such a bird, or an egg of such bird or any part of such an egg, is liable to a special penalty.[327]

Any person authorised in writing by the Secretary of State,[328] including a wildlife inspector,[329] may at any reasonable time and, if required to do so, upon producing evidence that he is authorised, enter and inspect any premises where a registered person keeps any wild birds, for the purpose of ascertaining whether an offence under these provisions is being, or has been, committed on those premises.[330] The intentional obstruction of such a person exercising such a power, including a wildlife inspector,[331] is an offence.[332]

Captive Birds

If any person keeps or has in his possession or under his control any bird included in Schedule 4 which has not been registered and ringed or marked in accordance with regulations[333] made by the Secretary of State, he is guilty of an offence and liable to a special penalty.[334]

If any person keeps or has in his possession or under his control any bird included in Schedule 4 within (a) five years of having been convicted of an offence under Part I of the Act for which a special penalty is provided, or (b) within three years of having been convicted of any other offence under Part I relating to the protection

---

[327] Wildlife and Countryside Act 1981, s. 6(4).

[328] Note that, at the time of publication, the functions of the Secreatary of State were in the process of being transferred to the Minister for DEFRA.

[329] Wildlife and Countryside Act 1981, s. 19ZA introduced by the Countryside and Rights of Way Act 2000, Sch. 12, para. 8. For the provisions of enforcement by wildlife inspectors and the power to take samples see Wildlife and Countryside Act 1981, ss. 19ZA and 19ZB respectively.

[330] Wildlife and Countryside Act 1981, s. 6(9).

[331] Wildlife and Countryside Act 1981, s. 19ZA introduced by the Countryside and Rights of Way Act 2000, Sch. 12, para. 8. For the provisions of enforcement by wildlife inspectors and the power to take samples see Wildlife and Countryside Act 1981, ss. 19ZA and 19ZB respectively.

[332] Wildlife and Countryside Act 1981, s. 6(10).

[333] See: Wildlife and Countryside (Registration and Ringing of Certain Captive Birds) Regulations 1982, SI 1982/1221; the Wildlife and Countryside (Registration and Ringing of Certain Captive Birds) (Amendment) Regulations 1991, SI 1991/478; the Wildlife and Countryside Act 1981 (Variation of Schedule 4) Order 1994, SI 1994/1151; and the Wildlife and Countryside (Registration and Ringing of Certain Captive Birds) (Amendment) Regulations 1994, SI 1994/1152.

[334] Wildlife and Countryside Act 1981, s. 7(1).

of birds or other animals, or any offence involving their ill-treatment, he is guilty of an offence.[335] If any person knowingly disposes of or offers to dispose of any bird included in Schedule 4 to any person within those periods after that person's conviction for either of the offences, he is guilty of an offence[336]

Any person authorised in writing by the Secretary of State, including a wildlife inspector,[337] may at any reasonable time and, if required to do so, upon producing evidence that he is authorised, enter and inspect any premises where any birds included in Schedule 4 are kept, for the purpose of ascertaining whether an offence under these provisions is being, or has been, committed on the premises.[338] The intentional obstruction of such a person exercising such a power is an offence. [339]

Any person who keeps or confines any bird in any cage or other receptacle which is not sufficient in height, length and breadth to permit it to stretch its wings freely is guilty of an offence and liable to a special penalty.[340] This bar does not apply to poultry, nor to the keeping and confining of any bird while it is in the course of conveyance by whatever means, or while it is being shown for exhibition or competition purposes for a period not exceeding 72 hours, or while it is undergoing veterinary examination or treatment.[341]

Any person who promotes, arranges, conducts, assists in, receives money for or takes part in any event at or in the course of which captive birds are liberated for the purpose of being shot immediately after their liberation, or who, as the owner or occupier of land, permits it to be used for such an event, is guilty of an offence and liable to a special penalty.[342]

---

[335] Wildlife and Countryside Act 1981, s. 7 (3).
[336] Wildlife and Countryside Act 1981, s. 7 (4).
[337] Wildlife and Countryside Act 1981, s. 19ZA introduced by the Countryside and Rights of Way Act 2000, Sch. 12, para. 8. For the provisions of enforcement by wildlife inspectors and the power to take samples see Wildlife and Countryside Act 1981, ss. 19ZA and 19ZB respectively.
[338] Wildlife and Countryside Act 1981, s. 7 (6).
[339] Wildlife and Countryside Act 1981, s. 7 (7).
[340] Wildlife and Countryside Act 1981, s. 8(1).
[341] Wildlife and Countryside Act 1981, s. 8(2).
[342] Wildlife and Countryside Act 1981, s. 8(3).

Protection of Wild Animals

Since the expression "wild animals" frequently recurs in the pages following, it will be convenient at this point to examine the scope of its meaning. The words "wild animal" are defined to mean any animal (other than a bird) which is or (before it was killed or taken) was living wild.[343] The word "animal", as a part of this expression, will itself have a wide meaning: first, any reference in the Act to an animal of any kind is to include, unless the context otherwise requires, a reference to an egg, larva, pupa, or other immature stage of an animal of that kind.[344] Secondly, as a matter of general law, the term "animals" includes all creatures not belonging to the human race.

Specially Protected Wild Animals

As with the provisions relating to wild birds, the Schedules to the 1981 Act name different kinds of wild animals as meriting special protection.[345] Their names are given in Appendix F at the end of the book. They are regarded[346] as animals in danger of extinction in Great Britain or likely to become so endangered unless conservation measures are taken. Thus, unlike the provisions relating to wild birds, where all such birds are given protection, only those wild animals considered to require special protection are listed. The Secretary of State may by means of orders[347] add further names to, or remove names from, this list.[348]

Apart from the defences next mentioned, it is an offence for any person intentionally to kill, injure or take any wild animal[349] included in Schedule 5 set out in Appendix F, or to attempt to do so.[350]

---

[343] Wildlife and Countryside Act 1981, s. 27(1).

[344] Wildlife and Countryside Act 1981, s. 27(3).

[345] Wildlife and Countryside Act 1981, Sch. 5.

[346] Judged by the principal criteria used in Wildlife and Countryside Act 1981, s. 22(3) used for altering the listing.

[347] The Secretary of State must first seek the advice of the Nature Conservancy Councils before issuing such orders: Wildlife and Countryside Act 1981, ss. 22(3), 24(1)–(3).

[348] Wildlife and Countryside Act 1981, s. 22(3), (4)(a).

[349] In proceedings for the offence, the animal is to be presumed to have been wild unless the contrary is shown: Wildlife and Countryside Act 1981, s. 9(6).

[350] Wildlife and Countryside Act 1981, ss. 9(1), 18(1).

The defences available[351] are:

1. That the act was done in pursuance of a requirement by a Government Minister under section 98 of the Agriculture Act 1947;[352]

2. That the act was done under, or in pursuance of an order made under, the Animal Health Act 1981;[353]

3. That the defendant can show that the animal taken had been disabled otherwise than by his unlawful act[354] and that it was taken solely for the purpose of tending it and releasing it when no longer disabled;[355]

4. That the defendant can show that the animal killed had been so seriously disabled otherwise than by his unlawful act that there was no reasonable chance of its recovering;[356]

5. That the defendant can show that the act was the incidental result of a lawful operation and could not reasonably have been avoided.[357] But, in the case of anything done to a bat (except in the living area of a dwelling house), this defence will not be available unless the defendant had notified the Nature Conservancy Council[358] of what act he intended to do and allowed them a reasonable time to advise him as to whether that should be done and, if so, the method to be used;[359]

6. That the animal was killed or injured by an authorised

---

[351] It should be noted that in some instances a defence will apply to all acts which may be the subject of this offence, i.e. killing, injuring, taking and attempts, whereas in other instances a defence applies only to one or two of the acts.

[352] Wildlife and Countryside Act 1981, s. 10(1)(a). For details of this requirement, see pp. 221-226.

[353] Wildlife and Countryside Act 1981, s. 10(1)(b). For the provisions of the Animal Health Act 1981 and its orders, see Chapters 3 and 9, and especially pp. 200-202.

[354] The words "unlawful act" are not restricted to acts made unlawful by the Wildlife and Countryside Act 1981 and will thus, it seems, embrace acts which are otherwise unlawful, e.g. the improper use of a gun without a shotgun certificate.

[355] Wildlife and Countryside Act 1981, s. 10(3)(a).

[356] Wildlife and Countryside Act 1981, s. 10(3)(b).

[357] Wildlife and Countryside Act 1981, s. 10(3)(c).

[358] For the appropriate address see notes 186 and 187 on p. 157.

[359] Wildlife and Countryside Act 1981, s. 10(5).

person[360] who can show that his action was necessary for the purpose of preventing serious damage to livestock,[361] foodstuffs for livestock, crops, vegetables, fruit, growing timber or any other form of property or to fisheries.[362] But this defence will not be available for any action taken at any time if it had become apparent, before that time, that the action would prove necessary for one of the purposes mentioned and

i. either a licence[363] authorising the action had not been applied for as soon as reasonably practicable after the fact of the action proving necessary had become apparent; or

ii. an application for such a licence had been determined;[364]

7. That the act was done under and in accordance with the terms of a licence issued to the defendant;

8. That the act was not done intentionally.[365]

Prohibited Methods of Killing or Taking Wild Animals

The Wildlife and Countryside Act 1981 contains a long list of

---

360 An "authorised person" means the owner or occupier, or any person authorised by the owner or occupier, of the land on which the action is authorised, where, an occupier, in relation to land other than foreshore, includes any person having any right of hunting, shooting, fishing or taking game or fish. Additionally, "authorised person" includes any person authorised in writing by the local authority, or by any of the Nature Conservancy Councils, a water authority or a sewage undertaker, a district board in Scotland, a local sea fisheries committee, the National Rivers Authority for the area within which the action authorised is taken: Wildlife and Countryside Act 1981, s. 27(1) (as amended by the Environmental Protection Act 1990, s. 132(1)(a), Sch. 9, para. 11(7)(a) (effected by SI 1991/685); Water Act 1989, s. 190(1), Sch. 25, para. 66(1) (effected by SI 1989/1146), s190(3), Sch. 27, Pt. I and s. 194(3) (effected by SI 1989/1530)).

361 "Livestock" includes any animal which is kept for: the provision of food, wool, skins or fur; the purpose of its use in carrying on any agricultural activity; or the provision or improvement of shooting or fishing: Wildlife and Countryside Act 1981, s. 27(1).

362 Wildlife and Countryside Act 1981, s. 10(4).

363 For licences see pp. 192-193.

364 Wildlife and Countryside Act 1981, s. 10(6). This is a rather involved qualification of the defence which must in some circumstances render it nugatory. An application for a licence should be submitted as soon as possible, and the defence will then not be vitiated for any action taken thereafter, irrespective of the outcome of the application.

365 It is a necessary ingredient of the offence that it is done intentionally – see p. 185.

methods of killing or taking wild animals which are prohibited. Some of these are applicable to all wild animals, and others only to those named. The list, divided in this way, is reproduced in Appendix G at the end of the book, which also makes reference to a list of the named animals.[366] The list is not dissimilar to that considered in connection with the prohibited methods relating to birds. The list of prohibited methods may be altered by ministerial order by adding further methods or omitting methods presently in it, and methods may be made to apply to particular kinds of animals.[367]

It is an offence to use, or to attempt to use, any of these methods.[368] Only two defences are available, one of which is restricted to a particular method. The defences are:

1. In the case of item i. in Appendix G, that the defendant can show that the article was set in position by him for the purpose of killing or taking, in the interests of public health, agriculture,[369] forestry, fisheries or nature conservation, any wild animals which could be lawfully killed or taken by the means described in item i., and that he took all reasonable precautions to prevent injury by those means to the wild animals listed in Schedule 6 set out in Appendix F;[370]

2. In the case of all methods, that the method was used under and in accordance with the terms of a licence issued to the defendant.[371]

---

[366] Wildlife and Countryside Act 1981, s. 11(1)(2), Sch. 6.

[367] Wildlife and Countryside Act 1981, s. 11(4).

[368] Wildlife and Countryside Act 1981, ss. 11(1)(2), 18(1).

[369] Though not defined in this context, the word "agriculture" is defined in Agricultural Holdings Act 1986, s. 98(1) and Agricultural Tenancies Act 1995, s. 38(1) as including horticulture, fruit growing, seed growing, dairy farming and livestock breeding and keeping, the use of land as grazing land, meadow land, osier land, market gardens and nursery grounds, and the use of land for woodlands where that use is ancillary to the farming of land for other purposes. This serves as a guide, but no more, to its meaning in its present context.

[370] Wildlife and Countryside Act 1981, s. 11(6). Put another way, this means that the defendant may use the methods in item 4, against any wild animals except those in Part III, if used in the interests described and if the precautions described are taken.

[371] Wildlife and Countryside Act 1981, s. 16(3).

Introduction of New Species into the Wild

A person commits an offence if he releases or allows to escape into the wild any animal or wild bird[372] which

a. is of a kind which is not ordinarily resident in, and is not a regular visitor to, Great Britain[373] in a wild state; or

b. is included in the list of animals at Schedule 9 in Appendix F[374] at the end of the book.[375]

The defences available in this instance are:

1. That the defendant can prove that he took all reasonable steps and exercised all due diligence to avoid committing the offence;[376]

2. That the act was done under and in accordance with the terms of a licence issued to the defendant.[377]

A person with the written authority (to be produced if required) of the Minister[378] may enter any land,[379] except a dwelling, to find out whether this offence is being, or has been, committed on that land.[380] The intentional obstruction of such a person is an offence.[381]

Other Offences relating to the Protection of Wild Animals

In the case of the specially protected animals whose names appear in Schedule 5 set out in Appendix F, the following further offences

---

[372] I.e. domestic or wild. See p. 185 for the wide meaning of the word "animal".

[373] For the meaning of "Great Britain" see note 276 on p. 174.

[374] The Appendix is reproduced from Wildlife and Countryside Act 1981, Sch. 9 Pt. I. The list may be varied by ministerial order: Wildlife and Countryside Act 1981, s. 22(5)(a).

[375] Wildlife and Countryside Act 1981, s. 14(1). It is also an offence to attempt to commit either of the offences mentioned: Wildlife and Countryside Act 1981, s. 18(1).

[376] Wildlife and Countryside Act 1981, s. 14(3). If this defence relies on an allegation that another person was responsible for the offence, certain procedural requirements must be followed: Wildlife and Countryside Act 1981, s. 14(4).

[377] Wildlife and Countryside Act 1981, s. 16(4)(c).

[378] I.e. the Minister for the Department for Environment, Food and Rural Affairs.

[379] For the definition of "land" see note 197 on p. 159.

[380] Wildlife and Countryside Act 1981, s. 14(5).

[381] Wildlife and Countryside Act 1981, s. 14(6).

are created. Attempts to commit them are also offences.[382] The defences available are listed after the description of each offence or group of offences. The offences are:

1. Intentionally to damage or destroy, or obstruct access to, any structure or place which a specially protected animal uses for shelter or protection;

2. Intentionally or recklessly[383] to disturb such an animal while it is occupying a structure or place so used.[384]

Defences for items 1. and 2. are:

    a. that the act was done in a dwelling-house but this is qualified in the case of a bat as stated in item 5. on page 186;[385]

    b. the defences stated at items 1., 2., 5., 7. and 8. on pages 186 to 187.[386]

3. Intentionally or recklessly to disturb any wild animal included in Schedule 5 as (a) dolphin or whale (*cetacea*), or (b) a basking shark (*cetorhinus maximus*).[387]

Defences for item 3 are those stated at items 1., 2., 5., 7. and 8. on pages 186 to 187.[388]

4. To sell,[389] offer or expose for sale, or to have in one's possession[390] or to transport for the purpose of sale:

    i. any live or dead animal in Schedule 5 of Appendix F; or

    ii. any part of such an animal; or

---

[382] Wildlife and Countryside Act 1981, s. 18(1).
[383] Inserted by the Countryside and Rights of Way Act 2000, Sch. 12, para. 5.
[384] Wildlife and Countryside Act 1981, s. 9(4).
[385] Wildlife and Countryside Act 1981, s. 10(2)(5).
[386] Wildlife and Countryside Act 1981, ss. 10(1)(3)(c), 16(3).
[387] Wildlife and Countryside Act 1981, s. 4A, inserted by the Countryside and Rights of Way Act 2000, Sch. 12, para. 5.
[388] Wildlife and Countryside Act 1981, ss. 10(1)(3)(c), 16(3).
[389] The word "sale" includes hire, barter and exchange and cognate expressions are interpreted accordingly: Wildlife and Countryside Act 1981, s. 27(1).
[390] For some notes on the meaning of "possession", see p. 68.

iii. anything derived from such an animal;[391]

5. To publish, or cause to be published, any advertisement[392] likely to be understood as conveying that the advertiser buys or sells, or intends to buy or sell, any of the things mentioned in item 3. above;[393]

The only defence for items 4. and 5. is that the act was done under and in accordance with the terms of a licence issued to the defendant.[394]

6. To have in one's possession or control any live or dead wild animal named in Schedule 5 of Appendix F, or any part of, or anything derived from, such an animal.[395]

Defences available in this case are:

a. That the defendant is able to show that:

i. the animal had not been killed or taken;[396] or

ii. the animal had been killed or taken otherwise than in contravention of any of the provisions in the Wildlife and Countryside Act 1981 for the protection of wildlife;[397] or

iii. the animal or other thing in the defendant's possession or control had been sold[398] (either to the defendant or any other person) otherwise than in contravention of the provisions of the Acts mentioned at ii. above;[399]

---

[391] Wildlife and Countryside Act 1981, s. 9(5)(a). Note 349 on p. 185 applies to this offence.

[392] "Advertise" includes a catalogue, a circular and a price list: Wildlife and Countryside Act 1981, s. 27(1).

[393] Wildlife and Countryside Act 1981, s. 9(5)(b).

[394] Wildlife and Countryside Act 1981, s. 16(4)(b).

[395] Wildlife and Countryside Act 1981, s. 9(2). Note 349 on p. 185 applies to this offence.

[396] This defence refers to any killing or taking by any person, from which the apparent conclusion is that the defence is restricted to the case of possession or control of a dead animal which died from natural causes. For an interpretation of take, see p. 115.

[397] This would include any of the provisions relating to wild birds.

[398] See note 389 on p. 190.

[399] Wildlife and Countryside Act 1981, s. 9(3).

    b. the defences stated at items 1. to 7. on pages 186 to 187.[400]

And lastly, it is made an offence if any person, for the purpose of committing any of the offences described in this section, has in his possession[401] anything capable of being used to commit one of those offences.[402]

Licences

In the case of all the offences against wild birds and wild animals, the possession of a licence authorising an act which would otherwise be an offence will exculpate the licence-holder, if the act is done under and in accordance with the terms of the licence.

Licences are issued, either for specified purposes or to cover acts which would otherwise be offences,[403] by the Nature Conservancy Council,[404] or the Minister, according to the subject matter of the licence and the location of the activity to be licensed.[405]

A licence may be: general or specific; granted to persons of a class[406] or to a particular person; subject to compliance with specified conditions; and modified or revoked at any time by the issuing authority. It will be valid for the period stated in it unless previously modified or revoked, and a reasonable charge may be made for it.[407]

---

[400] Wildlife and Countryside Act 1981, ss. 10, 16(3). Items 1.– 7., as set out on the pages mentioned, provide defences to what are otherwise offences of killing, taking or injuring the animals listed in Schedule 5 of Appendix F. It appears that the intention of the Wildlife and Countryside Act 1981, s. 10 is to make the same defences available for possession or control of an animal subsequent to its killing, taking or injuring in circumstances which are exonerated by items 1.–7.

[401] For some notes on the meaning of "possession", see p. 68.

[402] Wildlife and Countryside Act 1981, s. 18(2). The comment at note 178 on p. 156 will apply to this offence.

[403] Wildlife and Countryside Act 1981, ss. 16(3), 4(b)(c).

[404] I.e. English Nature or the Countryside Commission for Wales. Note that the functions of English Nature have now been transferred to the Department for Environment, Food and Rural Affairs.

[405] Wildlife and Countryside Act 1981, ss. 16(9)(b)–(e).

[406] The definition of class of persons may be framed by reference to any circumstances whatever, including persons being authorised by any other person: Wildlife and Countryside Act 1981, s. 16(8).

[407] Wildlife and Countryside Act 1981, s. 16(5).

A licence authorising the killing of wild animals for specified purposes will lay down the area within which, and the methods by which, the animals may be killed, and it cannot be granted for more than two years.[408]

A person commits an offence if, for the purpose of obtaining (for himself or another person) the grant of a licence, he:

a. makes a statement or representation, or furnishes a document or information, which he knows to be false in a material particular; or

b. recklessly makes a statement or representation, or furnishes a document or information, which is false in a material particular.[409]

Powers of the Court and of the Police

A substantial fine may be imposed on conviction of the offences which have been described, varying with the type of offence.[410] If the offence relates to more than one bird, animal or other thing, the maximum fine is determined as if there had been a separate offence for each bird, animal or thing.[411]

On conviction of any of the offences described, the court:

a. shall order the forfeiture of any bird, animal or other thing in respect of which the offence was committed;

b. may order the forfeiture of any vehicle, aircraft, hovercraft, boat, animal, weapon or other thing which was used to commit the offence;

c. in the case of the offences of releasing certain birds or animals into the wild or allowing them to escape there,[412] may order the forfeiture of any animal which is of the same kind as that in

---

[408] Wildlife and Countryside Act 1981, s. 16(6). It can be modified or revoked during its currency.
[409] Wildlife and Countryside Act 1981, s. 17. Attempts to commit any of the acts described are also offences: Wildlife and Countryside Act 1981, s. 18(1).
[410] Wildlife and Countryside Act 1981, s. 21(2)–(4).
[411] Wildlife and Countryside Act 1981, s. 21(5).
[412] For these offences, see p. 189.

respect of which the offence was committed and which was found in the possession of the accused.[413]

Constables[414] and wildlife inspectors are given wide powers, exercisable without a warrant, to stop and search persons suspected of committing offences, to search or examine anything which a suspect may then be using or have, to arrest a suspect if he fails satisfactorily to give his particulars, and to seize and detain things which may be evidence of an offence or which may be forfeited by the court as described above.[415] For these purposes constables may enter any land[416] except a dwelling house,[417] for the entry of which a warrant may be granted on certain grounds.[418]

G. KILLING OR INJURING OTHER PERSONS' ANIMALS

The destruction or damage by one person of another's property is a criminal offence governed by rules in the Criminal Damage Act of 1971. Domestic animals, since they are capable of ownership,[419] are always treated as property for this purpose; wild animals are so treated only if:

a. they have been tamed; or

b. they are ordinarily kept in captivity; or

c. they or their carcases have been reduced into possession[420] which has not been lost or abandoned; or

d. they are in course of being reduced into possession.[421]

The offence is committed if a person without lawful excuse

---

[413] Wildlife and Countryside Act 1981, ss. 21(6), 27(1).

[414] As well as police constables, including special police constables, the word "constables" including others holding that office, e.g. harbour constables. The hallmark of a constable is his attestation as such before, usually, a JP.

[415] Wildlife and Countryside Act 1981, ss19(1), 19ZA , 19ZB.

[416] For the definition of "land", see note 197 on p. 159.

[417] Wildlife and Countryside Act 1981, s. 19(2).

[418] Wildlife and Countryside Act 1981, s. 19(3).

[419] See pp. 1-3.

[420] No definition is given of the phrase "reduced into possession", but see note 23 on p. 3.

[421] Criminal Damage Act 1971, s. 10(1)(a).

destroys or damages any property belonging to[422] another, intending to destroy or damage any such property,[423] or being reckless as to whether any such property would be destroyed or damaged.[424] A person is treated as having a lawful excuse:

a. if at the time of the offence he believed[425] that the person or persons whom he believed to be entitled to consent to the destruction or damage:

    i. had so consented;

    ii. would have so consented if he or they had known of the destruction or damage and its circumstances; or

b. if he destroyed or damaged the property in question in order to protect property belonging to himself or another or a right or interest in property which was or which he believed to be vested in himself or another, and at the time of the offence he believed:

    i. that the property, right or interest was in immediate need of protection; and

    ii. that the means of protection adopted or proposed to be adopted were or would be reasonable having regard to all the circumstances.[426]

A number of allied offences is also created. It is made a more serious offence if, when destroying or damaging any property (including the offender's), there is an intention to endanger another's life or recklessness in that regard.[427] It is an offence without lawful excuse[428] to make a threat to another, intending that the other

---

[422] Property is treated as belonging to any person (a) having the custody or control of it; or (b) having in it any proprietary right or interest (not being an equitable interest arising only from an agreement to transfer or grant an interest); or (c) having a charge (i.e. a mortgage) on it: Criminal Damage Act 1971, s. 1(1).

[423] I.e. any property belonging to any other person, not necessarily the property destroyed or damaged.

[424] Criminal Damage Act 1971, s. 1(1).

[425] It is immaterial whether the belief is justified or not if it is honestly held: Criminal Damage Act 1971, s. 5(3).

[426] Criminal Damage Act 1971, s. 5(1), (2).

[427] Criminal Damage Act 1971, s. 1(2).

[428] "Lawful excuse" has the meaning discussed in the text above.

would fear it would be carried out:

a. to destroy or damage any property belonging to that other or a third person; or

b. to destroy or damage his own property in a way which he knows is likely to endanger the life of the other or a third person.[429]

A person commits an offence if he has anything in his custody or control intending without lawful excuse to use it, or cause or permit another to use it, to destroy or damage another's property or his own or the user's property in a way which he knows is likely to endanger another's life.[430]

The killing or injuring of one's own animal is not by itself an offence.[431]

A person convicted of killing or injuring an animal belonging to another person may be ordered by the court to pay compensation to that person.[432] A person who kills[433] a tame or domestic animal belonging to another makes himself liable to be sued for its value unless he can show that he had no other means of protecting his property.[434] To kill or take[435] wild animals on another's land which are not reduced into the possession of that other person is a trespass for which the trespasser can be sued.[436] If the animals are game,[437] he may be prosecuted.

The particular rules about killing or injuring dogs are discussed on pages 80 to 81.

---

[429] Criminal Damage Act 1971, s. 2.

[430] Criminal Damage Act 1971, s. 3.

[431] But it could be an offence if, for example, accompanied by cruelty (for which see earlier passages in this chapter).

[432] See further p. 151.

[433] Injury to the animal would presumably also justify a claim if thereby loss to its owner could be proved.

[434] *Cresswell v Sirl* [1947] 2 All ER 730; *Hamps v Darby* [1948] 2 All ER 474.

[435] For an interpretation of "take" see p. 115.

[436] See pp. 2-3 for theft of wild animals.

[437] Hares, rabbits and deer are the only four-legged game animals.

Chapter 9

ANIMAL DISEASES

Modern times have seen the introduction of a large volume of legislation aimed at the eradication and prevention of diseases in animals, and for these purposes statutory controls have been established over the whole field of animal movement, treatment and slaughter. The main provisions are found in the Animal Health Act 1981 and in a host of regulations made under that Act and its predecessors. This legislation confers wide powers on the Minister for DEFRA[1] and on local authorities.[2]

The expression "animals" in the 1981 Act means cattle,[3] sheep and goats and all other ruminating animals and swine.[4] The word may be further extended in meaning by orders of the Minister.[5] The expression "disease" in the Act, so far as applying to animals, means cattle plague[6], pleuro-pneumonia,[7] foot-and-mouth disease, sheep-pox, sheep scab or swine fever [8] and equine viral arteritis.[9]

---

[1] The functions of the Minister, so far as exercisable in relation to Wales, were transferred to the National Assembly for Wales, by the National Assembly for Wales (Transfer of Functions) Order 1999, SI 1999/672. "Minister" should be read and construed accordingly.

[2] These authorities are generally: the Common Council in the City of London for its area and, as regards imported animals, for the whole of Greater London; the London borough councils for their areas, except for imported animals; county councils for the remainder of England and in Wales county councils and county borough councils (Animal Health Act 1981, s. 50(1), (2), (5) (s. 50(2)(bb) inserted by Local Government (Wales) Act 1994 Sch. 16, para. 61).

[3] "Cattle" means bulls, cows, steers, heifers, and calves (Animal Health Act 1981, s. 89(1)).

[4] Animal Health Act 1981, s. 87(1).

[5] Animal Health Act 1981, s. 87(2), (3). See further *Halsbury's Laws of England*, 4th Ed., Vol. 2 (Reissue), para. 483, note 4 for a list of the orders.

[6] "Cattle plague" means rinderpest or the disease commonly called cattle plague (Animal Health Act 1981, s. 89(1)).

[7] "Pleuro-pneumonia" means contagious pleuro-pneumonia of cattle (Animal Health Act 1981, s. 89(1)).

[8] Animal Health Act 1981, s. 88(1). "Swine fever" means the disease known as typhoid fever of swine, soldier purples, red disease, hog cholera or swine plague (Animal Health Act 1981, s. 89(1)).

[9] Added to the definition of "disease" by Equine Viral Arteritis Order 1995, SI 1995/1755, Art. 2.

197

Other diseases may be included by the Minister's order,[10] and those so added for all or certain purposes are:

African horse sickness
African swine fever
Anthrax
Aujeszky's disease
Blue tongue
Bovine spongiform encephalopathy
Brucella abortus
Brucellosis
Classical swine fever
Contagious agalactia
Contagious equine metritis
Dourine
Enzootic bovine leukosis
Epizootic lymphangitis
Epizootic viral haemorrhagic disease
Equine infectious anaemia
Equine viral encephalomyelitis
Glanders, including farcy
Goat pox
Lumpy skin disease
Newcastle disease and Avian influenza
Paramyxovirus in pigeons
Peste des petits ruminants
Rabies
Rift Valley fever
Sheep and goat spongiform encephalopathy
Sheep pox
Swine vesicular disease
Teschen disease
Tuberculosis
Vesticular stomatitis
Viral haemorrhagic disease
Warble fly

---

10 Animal Health Act 1981, s. 88(2).

The control of animal diseases necessarily implies restrictions on the import, export and movement of animals, and these are dealt with in Chapter 3. Further provisions relating to diseased animals may be found on other pages as follows: owner's liability for diseased animals (pages 8 to 9); selling diseased animals (pages 9, 29 to 30); police powers to deal with them (page 151); and diseased deer (page 154).

The total volume of animal diseases legislation is such that a large volume on its own would be needed to cover the topic fully. This chapter can hope to do no more than broadly indicate the range of the subject.

Powers of Ministry's Vets

To obtain information necessary to eradicate animal diseases,[11] the Minister may authorise in writing any vet or other Ministry officer to inspect cattle, sheep, goats, all other ruminating animals, swine and horses.[12] A person so authorised may at all reasonable times enter on any land or premises to make his inspection, and may apply such tests and take such samples as he considers necessary; he must produce his written authority on demand.[13] Anyone who obstructs or impedes an authorised person is liable to prosecution.[14]

When a vet suspects certain diseases he is empowered to make enquiries and to examine animals, animal products and carcases on the premises concerned. He has powers of entry for this purpose, and those concerned must afford him the necessary facilities.[15]

To prevent disease spreading, the Minister may cause to be treated with serum or vaccine or both any animals which have been in

---

[11] "Disease" is not restricted by its definition above (Animal Health Act 1981, ss. 3(1), 87(4)).

[12] Animal Health Act 1981, s. 3(2), 87(1). "Horses" include asses and mules (Animal Health Act 1981, s. 89(1)).

[13] Animal Health Act 1981, s. 3(3).

[14] Animal Health Act 1981, s. 4(2).

[15] These powers, contained in the respective regulations, apply in the case of the following diseases: anthrax, cattle plague, bovine spongiform encephalopathy, lymphangitis, foot-and-mouth disease, glanders or farcy, parasitic mange, pleuropneumonia, rabies, sheep-pox, sheep scab, swine fever, swine vesicular disease, Teschen disease and infectious diseases of horses. The particular powers in relation to rabies are discussed on pp. 208-211.

contact with a diseased animal or bird, or which appear to him to be or to have been exposed to the infection of disease, or which are in an infected area.[16] These powers include the taking of any action necessary for the treatment to be administered or otherwise required in connection with the treatment. An authorised officer of the Ministry may for the purpose enter any land[17] or premises and take with him any other persons he requires. He must produce his written authority on demand.[18]

Powers to Destroy Wild Life

The Minister may make orders providing for the destruction of wild members of any species[19] of mammal (except man) in an area when he is satisfied that: there is a disease[20] which has been or is being transmitted from that species to any kind of animals[21] or poultry in that area; and that destruction of the species is necessary to eliminate, or substantially reduce the incidence of, that disease in such animals or poultry.[22] Methods of destruction otherwise unlawful may be used if the Minister is satisfied on certain matters.[23]

Orders so made may provide for: ensuring that the destruction is properly and effectively carried out; preventing persons from taking into captivity, harbouring, concealing or otherwise protecting wild life with intent to prevent its destruction, or obstructing or interfering with the processes of destruction; and regulating the ownership and disposal of carcases.[24]

Before beginning destruction on any land, the Minister must take all reasonable steps to inform the occupier and anyone else who

---

[16] For infected areas, see pp. 204-206.

[17] For the definition of "land", see note 197 on p. 159.

[18] Animal Health Act 1981, s. 16.

[19] References to wild members of any species in an area means members of the species in the area that are neither domesticated nor held in captivity (Animal Health Act 1981, s. 21(9)).

[20] I.e. one of the kinds of diseases listed on p. 198. But rabies, for which there are special provisions (see pp. 208-211), is excluded (Animal Health Act 1981, ss. 1(a), 21(1)(a)).

[21] "Animals" includes horses (Animal Health Act 1981, s. 21(9)).

[22] Animal Health Act 1981, s. 21(2).

[23] Animal Health Act 1981, s. 21(4).

[24] Animal Health Act 1981, s. 21(5).

may be there of his intention and the proposed methods of destruction which must be carried out as safely as possible.[25] When an order is in force, the Minister may "take such measures" (including the erection of fences or other obstacles) as he considers appropriate for preventing: the movement of living creatures[26] into or out of the destruction area, or any part of it, while destruction is being carried out; or the recolonisation of an area of destruction by the species being destroyed.[27] When, in the Minister's opinion, these measures are no longer necessary, he must remove anything erected or placed on the land and carry out any reasonably practicable reinstatement of the land.[28]

To implement these destruction orders "authorised officers"[29] are given powers of entry to any land:[30]

a. to take samples of wild life, their excreta and materials they may have been in contact with;

b. to carry out other investigations;

c. to destroy wild life which is the subject of an order;

d. to take any of the measures described in the last paragraph;

e. to ascertain whether destruction has been effectively carried out.[31]

If required by the owner, occupier or person in charge of the land, an authorised officer must produce a duly authenticated document showing his authority and state in writing his reasons for entering.[32]

---

25 Animal Health Act 1981, s. 21(6).
26 I.e. living creatures of any kind, domestic or wild, and whether of the species to be destroyed or not.
27 Animal Health Act 1981, s. 21(7).
28 Animal Health Act 1981, s. 21(8).
29 An authorised officer is an officer of the Minister, a veterinary inspector, or another person authorised by the Minister to exercise the powers described in the text (Animal Health Act 1981, s. 22(1)).
30 For the definition of "land", see note 197 on p. 159. There is no power of entry to a dwelling (Animal Health Act 1981, s. 22(5)).
31 Animal Health Act 1981, s. 22(2), (3), (4). The purposes for which these powers of entry may be exercised are much abbreviated in the text. Some powers are exercisable before an order is made and others up to 2 years after its revocation.
32 Animal Health Act 1981, s. 22(6).

His powers of entry to certain nature reserves are subject to conditions.[33]

Giving Notice of Disease and Separating Diseased Animals

Every person having in his possession or under his charge an animal[34] affected with disease[35] shall:

a.　as far as practicable keep that animal separate from animals not so affected; and

b.　with all practicable speed give notice[36] to a local police constable that he has an affected animal.[37]

Failure so to act in either case is an offence.[38] A person prosecuted is presumed to have known of the existence of the disease unless and until he shows to the satisfaction of the court that he had no knowledge of it and could not with reasonable diligence have obtained that knowledge.[39]

The following persons, if required in writing by the Ministry, the local authority or an inspector, must give all information in their possession about diseased animals, their movements and the persons into or through whose hands the animals have passed. Those required to give this information[40] are:

1.　Every person who has or has had in his possession[41] or under his charge any animal[42] affected with or suspected of disease or

---

[33]　Animal Health Act 1981, s. 22(7).

[34]　For the definition of "animal", see p. 197.

[35]　For the definition of "disease", see p. 197.

[36]　The notice must be in writing and delivered to the police constable personally or left at his house: Animal Health Act 1981, s. 83(3). Although the Act allows the notice to be sent through the post, it is suggested that this would be quite unsatisfactory in the circumstances. It will be advisable to have a copy of the notice receipted by the constable and endorsed by him with the time and date of receipt; the onus of proving that the notice was given rests upon the person giving it (*Huggins v Ward* (1873) LR 8 QB 521).

[37]　Animal Health Act 1981, s. 15(1).

[38]　Animal Health Act 1981, s. 15(7).

[39]　Animal Health Act 1981, s. 79(2).

[40]　Failure to give it or to give false information is an offence (Animals (Miscellaneous Provisions) Order 1927, SR & O 1927/290, Art. 12(1)).

[41]　For some notes on the meaning of "possession", see p. 68.

[42]　"Animal" in this context means cattle, sheep, goats, all other ruminating animals, swine, horses, asses, mules, dogs and other canine animals (Animals (Miscellaneous Provisions) Order 1927, SR & O 1927/290, Art. 1).

any animal which has been in any way in contact with such an animal; and

2. Any auctioneer who has sold or offered for sale any animal as described in 1.[43]

Infected Places

When a local authority or Ministry inspector has been told or suspects that an animal disease exists or has existed within a limited time on premises, he may serve notice on the occupier of the premises, and they become an infected place until the notice is withdrawn.[44] Movement and activity in infected places are governed by rules which vary according to the disease. For example, the rules may prohibit: the movement of animals except under licence; the removal of carcases,[45] fodder,[46] litter,[47] dung and other things except under licence or with permission; the removal of milk; the removal of fleeces without permission; and the tending without permission of unaffected animals by a person who has attended diseased or affected animals. The rules may require persons leaving infected premises to disinfect their clothing in disinfectant provided and to wash their hands; and may require liquid manure to be disinfected before being drained away. Places where animals affected with disease have been kept must or may be required by the rules to be disinfected and cleansed in the ways described in the rules.[48]

A person owning or having charge of any animals in an infected place may put up a notice, at or near the entrance to a building or enclosure in which the animals are, forbidding entry without

---

[43]   Animals (Miscellaneous Provisions) Order 1927, SR & O 1927/290, Art. 12(1).

[44]   Ministerial orders giving authority for individual diseases to be dealt with in this way are made under Animal Heath Act 1981, s. 17(1). For a list of relevant diseases see p. 198.

[45]   "Carcase" means the carcase of an animal and includes parts of a carcase, and the meat, bines, hide, skin, hooves, offal or other part of an animal, separately or otherwise, or any portion thereof (Animal Heath Act 1981, s. 89(1)).

[46]   "Fodder" means hay or other substance commonly used for food of animals (Animal Heath Act 1981, s. 89(1)).

[47]   "Litter" means straw or other substance commonly used for bedding or otherwise for or about animals (Animal Heath Act 1981, s. 89(1)).

[48]   See generally s. 7(1) and the orders made or having effect wholly or in part under the provisions of the subsection (cf *Halsbury's Laws of England*, 4th Ed., Vol. 2 (Reissue), para 490, note 2).

permission. It then becomes an offence for anyone to enter those places without permission unless he has by law a right of entry.[49]

Infected and Controlled Areas

An infected area is an area surrounding an infected place with defined boundaries a certain number of miles from the infected place. A controlled area, which operates only in cases of foot-and-mouth disease and, exceptionally, swine vesicular disease, is normally much larger than an infected area.[50] It is imposed (usually, but not always, around an infected area) when there is a risk of widespread dissemination of disease, for instance when disease is believed to have been present in animals in a market which have been moved over a wide area from it. Both types of area are declared as such by special order of the Minister. The following are the main provisions which operate in these areas.

In cases of swine vesicular disease[51] no animal may be moved out of an infected area at all, or out of a controlled area except under licence into a contiguous infected area. No animal may be moved into an infected or controlled area, except under licence direct to a farm (where it must be detained for 14 days) or to a slaughterhouse (where it must be slaughtered) not less than 3 km from an infected place. No animal may be moved by road, rail or water within an infected or controlled area except under licence, which will not be granted for movement to an unlicensed market or sale, or to farm premises for sale there, or from a licensed market or sale except to a slaughterhouse in the same area, or by road or water within two miles of an infected place. Animals may however be moved directly through an infected or controlled area provided they are not untrucked within the area.

In cases of foot-and-mouth disease no animal[52] may be moved out

---

49 Animal Health Act 1981, ss. 27, 72(6). A person having such a right would be an inspector of the Ministry or local authority.
50 For example, at the time of publication, the whole of Great Britain is a "control area" for the purposes of the current outbreak of foot and mouth disease.
51 Swine Vesicular Disease Order 1972, SI 1972/1980 (amended by SI 1973/101, SI 177/944 and SI 1993/3119).
52 "Animal" means cattle, sheep, goats, all other ruminating animals, swine and elephants (Foot and Mouth Disease Order 1983, SI 1983/1950, Pt. I, Art. 3, as amended by SIs 2001/1078, 2001/1407, 2001/1509, 2001/1514, 2001/1862, 2001/1874).

of the area lying within an 8 km radius of the place of suspected outbreak.[53] No animal may be moved through the infected area, except to a slaughterhouse (where it must be slaughtered) not less than 3 km from an infected place, nor may animals pass through the infected area by road or water, but animals may be transported through the infected area provided that they were not loaded within the infected area and are transported by rail or, subject to a licence granted by an inspector of the Minister, by motorway.[54] The Order also regulates the movement of imported animals in infected and controlled areas, the holding of markets for such animals there, the disposal of slaughterhouse manure there, and the prohibition of hunting. In an infected area cattle, sheep, goats, pigs and elephants must not be allowed to stray on roads; persons clipping or dipping sheep or using vehicles to transport animals must take special disinfection precautions; inspectors may prohibit entry to footpaths, fields, sheds and other places except under licence or with permission; all dogs within the infected area must at all times be confined, chained up or under effectual personal control except when in a house; and an inspector may require the occupier of premises in an infected area in which dogs or poultry are kept to control them in particular ways.[55] Milk originating in a controlled area, and whey or other liquid derived from it, may not be fed to animals on other premises unless the milk has been pasteurised or boiled.[56]

In the case of swine fever, no person may move swine into or out of an infected area, or within an infected area by road or water, except under licence or by rail through the area provided they are not untrucked within it; and no one may cause or permit swine to stray on a road within the area. A licence may permit the movement of swine through an infected area provided they are transported in a mechanically-propelled vehicle, are not unloaded during the journey, and are being taken to a slaughterhouse or bacon factory,

---

[53] Foot and Mouth Disease Order 1983, SI 1983/1950, Pt. I, Art. 8(1), as amended.
[54] Foot and Mouth Disease Order 1983, SI 1983/1950, Pt. III, Art. 18, as amended.
[55] See generally Foot and Mouth Disease Order 1983, SI 1983/1950, Pt. III & Pt. IV, Arts. 34A–37, as amended.
[56] Foot and Mouth Disease Order 1983, SI 1983/1950, Pt. III, Art. 22 & Pt. IV, Art. 34, as amended.

to premises used for keeping swine other than in connection with their sale, or to a vessel on which they are to be shipped abroad.[57]

In the case of sheep scab, there are restrictions on movement of sheep out of an infected area (sometimes known as "a movement area" or "dipping area") and on the marketing of sheep in the area. All sheep in the area may be required to be dipped in a stated period unless slaughtered during the period. Infected areas may be of any size up to the whole of Great Britain.[58]

Movement of Animals

The Minister is given very wide powers[59] to make orders prohibiting and regulating the movement of animals in almost all circumstances in which they are not in an enclosed field, e.g. when being driven, transported, sold or awaiting sale, awaiting slaughter, or grazing on unenclosed land.[60] The main purposes of the orders are to prevent the spread of disease and unnecessary suffering.

By way of example, a local authority inspector finding a diseased animal, or one suspected of being affected, may seize it with other animals in the same place, and may detain and isolate them where they are or move them to an isolated place for detention. They can then only be moved under the Minister's direction or licence. It is an offence for a person to expose an animal affected or suspected of being affected with certain diseases[61] in a market or other place where animals are commonly exposed for sale or exhibited, to move it by road, rail or water, to place it or allow it to stray on common, unenclosed or insufficiently fenced land, or to graze it on roadside verges.[62]

---

[57] Swine Fever (Infected Area Restrictions) Order 1956, SI 1956/1750, Arts. 5, 6, 7.
[58] See generally Sheep Scab Order 1986, SI 1986/862 (amended by SI 1987/836).
[59] By Animal Health Act 1981, ss. 7(1)(a)(b), 8(1), 25, 26, 37.
[60] For example, Foot and Mouth Disease Order 1983, SI 1983/1950, Art. 34A, inserted by SI 1993/1847.
[61] The diseases are: cattle plague, epizootic lymphangitis, foot-and-mouth disease, glanders or farcy, parasitic mange, pleuro-pneumonia, sheep-pox, sheep scab, swine fever and swine vesicular disease.
[62] See the the diseases listed on p. 198 and Animal Health Act 1981, s. 25.

Slaughter of Animals

The Minister has power to slaughter diseased animals and those suspected of disease or exposed to infection. In some cases slaughter is compulsory, and in others there is a discretion.[63]

Except in some cases,[64] compensation will be paid for animals slaughtered. The rate varies according to the disease for which the animal was slaughtered and according to whether the animal was actually affected with the disease or not. In the case of some diseases the amount of compensation is regulated by the Act of 1981[65] or orders made under it. Where it is not, the procedure is for the Minister to give a notice of value to the owner and that becomes the compensation payable unless the owner within 14 days serves a counter-notice disputing it. In that event the sum is settled by arbitration.[66]

The carcase of an animal belongs to the Minister when he orders its slaughter, and will be buried, sold or otherwise disposed of at his direction.[67] If the sum received on sale of the carcase exceeds the compensation paid, the excess is due to the animal's owner after deducting reasonable expenses.[68] The Minister is entitled to bury the carcase in any suitable ground in the possession or occupation of the animal's owner or in any common or unenclosed land.[69] It is an offence to dig up the carcase except with a licence from the Minister.[70]

Insurers of animals slaughtered on the Minister's orders may

---

[63] Animal Health Act 1981, ss. 31, 32, Sch. 3.
[64] These are briefly: a diseased or suspect animal slaughtered in an export quarantine station (Animal Health Act 1981, s. 12(2)); cases provided for by orders which the Minister may make under Animal Health Act 1981, s. 10(2)(d) and Sch. 2, para. 12; and where the animal, being imported, was diseased on landing or, coming from an EC Member State, had been exposed to infection, when the Minister may withhold compensation wholly or partly (Animal Health Act 1981, s. 34(6)).
[65] Animal Health Act 1981, ss. 31, 32(2), Sch. 3, paras. 1(4), 2(3), 3(2), 4(2).
[66] Diseases of Animals (Ascertainment of Compensation) Order 1959, SI 1959/ 1335, Art. 3.
[67] Animal Health Act 1981, s. 34(2).
[68] Animal Health Act 1981, s. 34(3).
[69] Animal Health Act 1981, s. 34(4).
[70] Animal Health Act 1981, s. 35(3)(c); Animals (Miscellaneous Provisions) Order 1927, SR & O 1927/290, Art. 16.

deduct compensation paid by the Minister from payments to the owner for which they are liable.[71]

Rabies

Concern with the increasing risk of rabies[72] spreading to animals[73] within Great Britain led to the passing of the Rabies Act[74] in 1974 to strengthen the powers relating to animal diseases then contained in the Disease of Animals Act 1950. The extra powers so given merit particular attention.

Where the Minister[75] has declared an area to be infected[76] for rabies purposes, he may take steps to secure the destruction of foxes in the area, except those held in captivity. Officers of the Ministry and persons authorised in writing by the Minister may enter any land[77] (other than a dwelling-house) to destroy foxes or to decide whether to destroy them. Methods of destruction otherwise unlawful may be used. The occupier and anyone else on the land must be warned beforehand by the Minister that he proposes to destroy foxes and the methods to be used. The warning will be by service of a written notice or "such other method as may be appropriate in the circumstances". The Minister may erect fences or other obstacles on the land, as part of the destruction operation, to restrict the movement of animals into and out of the infected area. The Minister also has power to forbid the movement of animals into or out of an infected area, to control their movements within the area, to seize, detain and destroy uncontrolled animals,

---

71 Animal Health Act 1981, s. 34(5).
72 "Rabies virus" means of the genus lyssavirus of the family Rhabdoviridae.
73 "Animals" to which the Rabies (Control) Order 1974, SI 1974/2212, applies means those animals within the following orders, save for man: artiodactyla, carnivora, chiroptera, dermoptera, edentata, hyracoidean, insectivora, lagamorpha, marsupialia, monotremata, perissodactyla, pholidota, primates, proboscidea, rodentia, and tubulidentata (Rabies (Control) Order 1974, SI 1974/2212, Art. 2(1), Sch. 1).
74 Now repealed and re-enacted by Animal Health Act 1981.
75 The functions of the Minister, so far as exercisable in relation to Wales, were transferred to the National Assembly for Wales, by the National Assembly for Wales (Transfer of Functions) Order 1999, SI 1999/672. "Minister" should be read and construed accordingly.
76 For infected areas, generally, see pp. 204-206. See also Rabies (Control) Order 1974, SI 1974/2212, Art. 9(1) and Animal Health Act 1981, s. 20.
77 "Land" includes buildings (Rabies (Control) Order 1974, SI 1974/2212, Art. 2(2)).

and to introduce compulsory vaccination. The carcase of every fox destroyed belongs to the Minister and is to be disposed of as he determines.[78]

By further order the powers described in the last paragraph may be extended to apply to any wild animal in an infected area not held in captivity.[79]

The holding of sporting and recreational activities on land in an infected area may be prohibited by serving a written notice on the person responsible for holding the activity. A veterinary inspector of the Minister may serve such notices when in his opinion the activity might cause the spread of rabies.[80]

A person who knows or suspects that an animal (whether in captivity or not) is affected with rabies, or was so affected at its death, must with all practicable speed give notice[81] of the fact to an inspector[82] or a police constable, unless he reasonably believes that someone else has done so. Further, a person who knows or suspects that an animal in his possession or under his charge is, or was at the time of death, affected with rabies must as far as practicable keep that animal or the carcase separate from any other animal.[83]

When a veterinary manager[84] suspects that rabies exists, or has within the previous 56 days existed, at any premises[85] or that there is an animal there who has been or may have been exposed to the infection of that disease, he has to make enquiries about the correctness of his information and examine any animal or carcase found at the premises. For these two purposes the inspector may:

---

[78] Rabies (Control) Order 1974, SI 1974/2212, Arts. 9, 10 and Sch. 3.

[79] Animal Health Act 1981, s. 19(1).

[80] Rabies (Control) Order 1974, SI 1974/2212, Art. 11.

[81] Written notice is required: Animal Health Act 1981, s. 83(1).

[82] This is a diseases of animals inspector of the Ministry or local authority: Rabies (Control) Order 1974, SI 1974/2212, Art. 2(1).

[83] Rabies (Control) Order 1974, SI 1974/2212, Art. 4(1), (2). These provisions do not apply in cases prescribed by order for the purpose of regulating the keeping, import or use of rabies virus (Rabies (Control) Order 1974, SI 1974/2212, Art. 4(4)).

[84] References to "veterinary inspector" or "veterinary officer" within the Order should read "veterinary manager" (SI 1995/2922).

[85] "Premises" includes land, with or without buildings (Rabies (Control) Order 1974, SI 1974/2212, Art. 2(1)).

a. enter on any part of the premises; and

b. remove from the premises any animal affected, or suspected of being affected, with rabies, or another animal which has been in contact with such an animal, or the carcase of any of these kinds of animals, to a place for veterinary observation or diagnostic tests; and

c. take samples for diagnosis from any animal on the premises, whether or not it is one of the kinds of animals described in b. above.

The occupier of the premises and his employees must give the inspector such reasonable assistance as may be required in performing these tasks. If there is or has been on premises an animal or carcase as described in b. above, the following people must give all reasonable facilities for the inspector's inquiries, for the removal of any animal or carcase and for the taking of samples:

1. The occupier of those premises;

2. The vet (if any) who has been attending or has been consulted about the animal or carcase;

3. Any person who has been in charge of the animal or carcase or in any manner in contact with it.

Further, the persons described above must, if required to do so by an officer of the Ministry, give such information as they possess about the animal or carcase, about the location or movements of any other animal in their possession or under their charge, or about any other animal with which any animal described in b. above may have been in contact.[86]

The extent of the powers described shows the serious view taken of the dangers of rabies. A little thought will show how wide these powers are. By way of illustration, a veterinary manager need only suspect (though he must have grounds for his suspicion) that there is on premises an animal which may have been exposed to rabies

---

[86] Rabies (Control) Order 1974, SI 1974/2212, Art. 6.

to give him the right – without notice or warning – to enter those premises (which includes houses and other buildings as well as bare land). Having entered, he has the right to remove an animal (which includes pet dogs and cats) which has been in contact with another animal suspected of rabies. There is no right of redress or appeal. Indeed, those involved must give the inspector every assistance in doing these and the other things described, and will be liable to prosecution if they do not comply in any way.[87] Further, an animal affected, suspected of being affected or exposed to the infection of rabies may be slaughtered by Ministry officials. Prior written notice may be served requiring the animal to be surrendered for slaughter or detained pending slaughter. Compensation is payable.[88]

The restrictions aimed at preventing the introduction of rabies into the country through imported animals are discussed on pages 55 to 58.

---

[87]   Rabies (Control) Order 1974, SI 1974/2212, Art. 13.
[88]   Animal Health Act 1981, s. 32(1)–(3); Rabies (Control) Order 1974, SI 1974/ 2212, Art. 3, 8. If the animal was affected with rabies when slaughtered, compensation is payable at a rate of 50% of its market value immediately before it contracted the disease. In all other cases, the full market value immediately before slaughter is payable (Rabies (Compensation) Order 1976, SI 1976/2195, Art. 3).

Chapter 10

EXHIBITIONS, PUBLIC PERFORMANCES AND ZOOS

Exhibition and Training of Performing Animals

With the exceptions later mentioned, it is an offence for anyone to exhibit[1] or train[2] any performing animal[3] unless he is registered with the county council[4] in whose area he lives.[5] Applications for registration must contain particulars of the animals and of the general nature of the performances for which they are to be exhibited or trained. Unless the applicant is prohibited from being registered,[6] he will receive a certificate of registration on payment of a fee of such amount as the council may charge.[7] There appears to be no discretion for the council to refuse registration if the applicant is not prohibited from being registered and the application correctly made out and the fee paid.

The particulars on the application form are entered in the council's register (which is open to inspection)[8] and recorded in the certificate

---

[1]   "Exhibit" means exhibit at any entertainment to which the public are admitted whether on payment of money or otherwise (Performing Animals (Regulation) Act 1925, s. 5(1)).

[2]   "Train" means train for the purpose of such an exhibition as is defined by reference to the meaning of "exhibit" above (Performing Animals (Regulation) Act 1925, s. 5(1)).

[3]   The only restriction on the meaning of "animal" is that it is not to include invertebrates (Performing Animals (Regulation) Act 1925, s.5 (1)). Thus, all mammals, birds, fishes, reptiles and amphibians are included in the meaning.

[4]   In the City of London, the registration authority is the Common Council of the City and, in a London borough, the London borough council (Performing Animals (Regulation) Act 1925, s. 5(1); Local Government Act 1963, s. 4(2)(b)).

[5]   A person having no fixed place of residence in Great Britain may apply for registration to the council of such one of the following districts as he may choose: the City of London, Birmingham, Bristol, Cardiff, Kingston-upon-Hull, Leeds, Liverpool, Manchester, Newcastle upon Tyne, Plymouth and Southampton in England and Wales; and Aberdeen, Dundee, Edinburgh and Glasgow in Scotland (Performing Animals (Regulation) Act 1925, s. 1(2); Performing Animals Rules 1925 (S R & O 1925/1219, amended by SI 1968/1464)).

[6]   As to such prohibition, or disqualification as it is there called, see p. 214.

[7]   Performing Animals (Regulation) Act 1925, s. 1(2).

[8]   Subject to the payment of a fee.

issued. An applicant may apply to have the particulars varied, when the council will cancel the existing certificate and issue a new one.[9]

There is no need to register for the training of animals for *bona fide* military, police, agricultural or sporting purposes, or for the exhibition of animals so trained.[10]

If a magistrates' court is satisfied on complaint made by the police or a council officer that the training or exhibition of any performing animal has been accompanied by cruelty and should be prohibited or allowed only subject to conditions, the court may make an order accordingly.[11] There is a right of appeal to the Crown Court.[12] The order comes into force seven days after it is made or, if an appeal is lodged within that time, when the appeal is determined. Particulars of the order will be endorsed on the issued certificate and entered in the council's register.[13]

Where such performing animals are trained, exhibited or kept, a police officer or an authorised officer of the council[14] has power to enter premises to inspect the them and the animals, and to request the production of a registration certificate, but may not get on or behind the stage during a public performance.[15]

Offences punishable with a fine have been created if a person does any of the following things:

1. Exhibits or trains a performing animal without being registered;

2. Exhibits or trains such an animal outside the terms of registration;

3. Fails to comply with an order of the magistrates' court;

---

[9] Performing Animals (Regulation) Act 1925, s. 1. No fee is payable for a certificate in this case.
[10] Performing Animals (Regulation) Act 1925, s 7.
[11] A copy of any order must be sent by the court to the local authority and to the Secretary of State.
[12] Performing Animals (Regulation) Act 1925, ss. 2(2), 4(2) (s. 2(2) amended by the Courts Act 1971, s. 56(2), Sch. 9, Pt. I).
[13] Performing Animals (Regulation) Act 1925, s. 2.
[14] I.e. the council who has registration powers in the area (see p. 212).
[15] Performing Animals (Regulation) Act 1925, s. 3.

4. Obstructs or wilfully[16] delays an officer when exercising his powers of entry and inspection;

5. Conceals any animal to avoid its inspection;

6. Fails to produce his certificate to the court for endorsement;

7. Applies to be registered when prohibited from being registered by a court.[17]

When a person is convicted of any of these offences, or of offences against the Protection of Animals Act 1911,[18] the convicting court may, as well as or instead of fining the offender:

a. if he is registered under the Act, order that his name be removed from the register; and

b. order him to be disqualified from being registered, either permanently or for such time as the order may stipulate.

The same provisions of appeal, the effective date of the order and the recording of the order as apply to an order made after complaint to the court[19] will apply to the orders described above.[20]

Public exhibitions of experiments on living animals are dealt with on page 255.

Performances Involving Bulls or Horses

No person shall promote, or cause or knowingly permit to take place, any public performance[21] which includes any episode consisting of or involving the following:

---

[16] This means deliberately and intentionally, and not by accident or inadvertence (*R v Senior* [1899] 1 Q B 282 at pp. 290-291).

[17] Performing Animals (Regulation) Act 1925, s. 4(1).

[18] For offences, see pp. 132-150.

[19] See p. 213.

[20] Performing Animals (Regulation) Act 1925, s. 4(2).

[21] Unlike the provisions described in the last section and in the next, there is no definition in this case of what constitutes a public performance. It is suggested that it is enough if the performance is available to the public with or without payment. It does not include a public cinema performance (Performing Animals (Regulation) Act 1925, s. 1(3)), for which see the next section.

1. Throwing or casting, with ropes or other appliances, any unbroken horse[22] or untrained bull;[23] or

2. Wrestling, fighting or struggling with any untrained bull; or

3. Riding, or attempting to ride, any horse or bull which by the use of any appliance or treatment involving cruelty is, or has been, stimulated with the intention of making it buck during the performance.

No person shall take part in any of the episodes described in a public performance.[24]

The foregoing are offences punishable by fine or imprisonment or both.[25] In cases 1. and 2. if an animal appears to be, or is represented to spectators to be, unbroken or untrained, it is for the person prosecuted to prove[26] to the court that it is in fact broken or trained. In case 3. the defendant will be entitled to be acquitted if he is able to prove to the court that he did not know, or could not reasonably be expected to know, that an appliance or treatment was to be or was used on the horse before or during the performance. No such defence is available if the animal is a bull.[27]

Films

No person is to exhibit to the public,[28] or supply to another person for public exhibition (whether by the person supplied or someone else), any film, wherever produced, if in connection with its production any scene represented in the film was organised or directed in such a way as to involve the cruel infliction of pain or

---

[22] "Horse" includes any mare, gelding, pony, foal, colt, filly or stallion (Protection of Animals Act 1911, s. 15(d); Protection of Animals Act 1934, s. 1(3)).

[23] "Bull" includes any cow, bullock, heifer, calf, steer, or ox (Protection of Animals Act 1911, s. 5(d); Protection of Animals Act 1934, s. 1(3)).

[24] Protection of Animals Act 1934, s. 1(1).

[25] Protection of Animals Act 1934, s. 2.

[26] The onus is discharged on a balance of probability. See *R v Carr-Briant* [1943] 2 All ER 156.

[27] Protection of Animals Act 1934, s. 1(2).

[28] A film is deemed to be exhibited to the public when, and only when, it is exhibited in a place to which for the time being members of the general public as such have access, whether on payment of money or otherwise (Cinematograph Films (Animals) Act 1937, s. 1(4)(a)).

terror on any animal[29] or the cruel goading of any animal to fury.[30] Contravention is an offence punishable with a fine or imprisonment or both.[31] These provisions are in addition to protection afforded under section 1 of the Protection of Animals Act 1911 and section 1 of the Wild Mammals (Protection) Act 1996.

In any proceedings the court may (without prejudice to any other mode of proof) infer from the film as exhibited or supplied that a scene represented in it was organised or directed in such a way as to involve the cruel infliction of pain or terror on an animal or the cruel goading of it to fury. Whether or not the court draws such an inference, the defendant will be entitled to be acquitted if he proves to the court that he believed, and had reasonable cause to believe, that no scene represented in the film was organised or directed as described above.[32]

Zoos

It is unlawful to operate a zoo[33] except under the authority of a licence issued by the local authority[34] for the area within which the whole or the major part of the zoo is situated. Animals covered by the Zoo Licensing Act[35] are of the classes Mammalia, Aves, Reptilia, Amphibia, Pisces and Insecta and any other multi-cellular organism that is not a plant or fungus.[36]

---

29   The long definition of "animal" is to be found in Appendix E at the end of the book (Protection of Animals Act 1911, s. 15; Cinematograph Films (Animals) Act 1937, s. 1(4)(b)).

30   Cinematograph Films (Animals) Act 1937, s. 1(1).

31   Cinematograph Films (Animals) Act 1937, s. 1(3).

32   Cinematograph Films (Animals) Act 1937, s. 1(2).

33   "Zoo" means an establishment where animals are kept for exhibition to the public otherwise than for the purposes of a circus and otherwise as a pet shop. The Act applies to any zoo to which members of the public have access, with or without charge for admission, on more than seven days in any period of 12 consecutive months (Zoo Licensing Act 1981, s. 1(2)).

34   "Local authority" means the district councils, the councils of London boroughs and the Common Council of the City of London: Zoo Licensing Act 1981, s. 3.

35   The functions of the Secretary of State in relation to the Zoo Licensing Act, so far as exercisable in relation to Wales, transferred to the National Assembly for Wales (The National Assembly for Wales (Transfer of Functions) Order 1999, SI 1999/672). References to "Secretary of State" hereafter should be read and construed accordingly.

36   Zoo Licensing Act 1981, s. 21(1). Note that "wild animals" means animals not normally domesticated in Great Britain.

An application to the local authority[37] for a licence for a zoo cannot be entertained unless written notice of it has been given at least two months beforehand containing the following information:

1. The situation of the zoo for which the application is being made;

2. The kinds of animals listed in taxonomic category of Order and approximate numbers of each group kept or to be kept for exhibition on the premises and the arrangements for their accommodation, maintenance and well-being;

3. The approximate numbers and categories of staff employed or to be employed in the zoo;

4. The approximate number of visitors and motor vehicles for which accommodation is or is to be provided;

5. The approximate number and position of the means of access provided or to be provided to the premises.[38]

The applicant must, within the same time constraints, have published in one local newspaper circulating in the locality and one national newspaper details of the situation of the zoo for which the application is being made, and similarly exhibit a copy of the notice at the site.[39]

The licensing authority must take into account representations made by or on behalf of a variety of specified persons including, amongst others,[40] the applicant, the police, any governing body of any national institution concerned with the operation of zoos. In addition, before granting or refusing to grant a licence for a zoo, the local authority must also consider inspectors' reports or consult such persons nominated by the Secretary of State.[41]

---

[37] "Local authority" means, in England, the district councils, the councils of London boroughs and the Common Council of the City of London; and in Wales, the councils of counties and county boroughs.

[38] Zoo Licensing Act 1981, s. 2(b).

[39] The notice so exhibited must state that the notice to the local authority may be inspected at the offices of the local authority free of charge and during reasonable hours: Zoo Licensing Act 1981, ss. 2(2), 3.

[40] For a full list of those persons to whom the local authority may receive representations, see Zoo Licensing Act 1981, s. 3(2).

[41] Zoo Licensing Act 1981, s. 4(1). Note that, at the time of publication, the functions of the Secreatary of State were being transferred to the Minister for DEFRA.

The local authority must refuse to grant a licence if they are satisfied that the establishment or continuance of the zoo would injuriously affect the health or safety of persons living in the neighbourhood of the zoo, or seriously affect the preservation of law and order.[42] They may refuse a licence if they are not satisfied that the standards of accommodation, staffing or management are adequate for the proper care and well-being of the animals or any of them or otherwise for the proper conduct of the zoo,[43] or if the applicant, and (where the applicant is a body corporate) a director, manager or similar officer or a keeper in the zoo has been convicted of certain offences involving ill-treatment of animals.[44] They may also refuse a licence if planning permission has not been granted. Other than the forgoing grounds for refusal the local authority is obliged to grant a licence and if they do refuse to grant it they must send to the applicant by post a written statement of the grounds of their refusal.[45]

An original licence is for four years, and a fresh licence granted to an existing licence holder is for six years from the expiry of the existing one.[46] The local authority may grant a licence subject to such conditions as they think necessary or desirable for ensuring the proper conduct of the zoo during the period of the licence. In addition to those conditions contained in section 5(3) of the Act, the local authority must have regard to any standards specified by the Secretary of State under section 9 and sent by him to the authority. The licence may be similarly transferred to another person or surrendered.[47]

---

[42] Zoo Licensing Act 1981, s. 4(2).

[43] Zoo Licensing Act 1981, s. 4(3).

[44] The conviction must arise from any of the following enactments: the Zoo Licensing Act 1981; the Protection of Animals Acts 1911–1964; the Protection of Animals (Scotland) Act 1912–1964; the Pet Animals Act 1951; the Animal Boarding Establishments Act 1963; the Riding Establishments Acts 1964–1970; the Breeding of Dogs Act 1973; the Dangerous Wild Animals Act 1976; the Endangered Species (Import and Export) Act 1976; and Part I of the Wildlife and Countryside Act 1981.

[45] Zoo Licensing Act 1981, s. 4(7). When a licence is granted the local authority must send it by post and the licence or a copy of it has to be publicly displayed at each public entrance to the zoo (Zoo Licensing Act 1981, s. 4(8)).

[46] Zoo Licensing Act 1981, s. 5(1). There are provisions for charging fees for the grant, renewal or transfer of a licence and for the applications for the same and for expenses of inspectors (Zoo Licensing Act 1981, s. 15).

[47] Zoo Licensing Act 1981, s. 7.

Following consultation,[48] the Secretary of State must compile a list consisting of two parts.[49] In part one must be kept the names of veterinary surgeons and veterinary practitioners who have experience of animals of kinds kept in zoos. In part two must be kept the names of persons who in the Secretary of State's opinion are competent to inspect zoos, advise on keeping them, the welfare of the animals and the management of zoos generally. These persons may charge for their services and expenses as the Secretary of State may from time to time determine.

The local authority must carry out periodic inspections, on giving not less than 28 days' notice to the operator of the zoo of the date on which such inspection is proposed to be undertaken. Such inspections must be carried out during the first year of the grant of an original licence, and thereafter during every three years, but not later than six months before the end of the fourth year (or sixth year if it is renewed in the third year).[50] The local authority is required to carry out informal investigations in each year in which no formal inspection is made.[51]

Special investigations of a zoo may at any time be carried out if, having regard to the criteria laid down in section 11(1)(a) – (d), the local authority consider it appropriate to do so. The inspection must be carried out by persons competent to conduct such an inspection.[52]

Where the local authority is the owner of a zoo, the local authority must, as soon as practicable after granting a licence, send to the Secretary of State a copy of the licence and the inspector's report (and any comments they may have on it). The Secretary of State may then decide[53] whether or not to revoke the licence.

---

[48] The Secretary of State must consult with the presidents of the British Veterinary Association, the National Federation of Zoological Gardens and the National Zoological Association, and with such other persons as he thinks fit (Zoo Licensing Act 1981, s. 8(1)).

[49] Zoo Licensing Act 1981, s. 8(1)–(3).

[50] Zoo Licensing Act 1981, s. 10(3).

[51] Zoo Licensing Act 1981, s. 12.

[52] Zoo Licensing Act 1981, s. 11(2)–(3).

[53] In arriving at such a decision, the Secretary of State must have regard to the grounds contained in s. 17(1)(a)–(d) of the Act.

The Secretary of State may exempt a zoo from the whole or part of the Zoo Licensing Act 1981 if a local authority informs him that in its opinion such a dispensation should be made because of the small size of the zoo or the small number of the kinds of animals kept there.[54]

At any time after the grant of a licence, it may be altered by the local authority if in their opinion it is necessary or desirable to do so for ensuring the proper conduct of the zoo during the period of the licence.[55] Before making such a variation, cancellation, or applying additional conditions to the licence,[56] the local authority must give the licence holder an opportunity to make representations.[57] Similarly, the Secretary of State may direct a local authority to alter a licence.[58]

An aggrieved person has a right of appeal to a magistrate for the area concerned against a refusal to grant a licence, any variation or cancellation of a condition or the revocation of a licence.[59] Such an appeal must be brought within 21 days from receipt of the local authority's written decision.[60] The court is given a wide discretion and may confirm, vary or reverse the local authority's decision and may give such directions as it thinks fit.[61] Where a licence is revoked under section 17 of the Act, it remains in force until six months after the revocation, or until the determination or abandonment of an appeal. If the decision of the court confirms the revocation, then the licence expires six months from the date of the confirmation.[62]

---

[54] *Halsbury's Laws of England*, 4th Ed., Vol. 2 (Reissue), para. 401.
[55] Zoo Licensing Act 1981, s. 16(1).
[56] Zoo Licensing Act 1981, s. 16(4). Such conditions must be consistent with the terms of a condition attached or varied in pursuance of a direction by the Secretary of State: Zoo Licensing Act 1981, s. 16(5).
[57] Zoo Licensing Act 1981, s. 16(2).
[58] The authority must give effect to such a direction within a reasonable time: Zoo Licensing Act 1981, s. 16(3).
[59] Zoo Licensing Act 1981, s. 18(1).
[60] Zoo Licensing Act 1981, s. 18(2).
[61] Zoo Licensing Act 1981, s. 18(3).
[62] Zoo Licensing Act 1981, s. 18(9).

Chapter 11

PESTS

Destructive Animals Generally

By operating the procedure described below the Minister for the Department for Environment, Food and Rural Affairs[1] can take steps to clear land of destructive animals.

The Minister may serve a written notice[2] if it appears to him that it is expedient to do so for the purpose of preventing damage to crops, pasture,[3] animal or human foodstuffs, livestock,[4] trees, hedges, banks or any works on land.[5] The notice will require the person served to take such steps (including any steps specified in the notice) as may be necessary for the killing, taking[6] or destruction on the land described in the notice of such of the following animals as the notice may detail: rabbits,[7] hares and other rodents,[8] deer, foxes, moles,[9]

---

[1] The functions of the Minister in relation to the relevant sections dealing with pests of the Agriculture Act 1947 and the Prevention of Damage by Pests Act 1949, the Pests Act 1954 and the Forestry Act 1967 are, so far as exercisable in relation to Wales, transferred to the National Assembly of Wales (The National Assembly for Wales (Transfer of Functions) Order 1999, SI 1999/672). References to Minister hereafter should be read and construed accordingly.

[2] Notice must be served by delivering it personally to the person to be served, by leaving it at his last known address, or by posting it to him by registered letter or recorded delivery service. If an incorporated company or other body is to be served, notice must be given by one of the means described to its secretary or clerk at its registered or principal office (Agriculture Act 1947, s. 107(1)–(3)).

[3] "Pasture" includes meadow (Agriculture Act 1947, s. 109(3)).

[4] "Livestock" includes any creature kept for the production of food, wool, skins or fur, or for the purpose of its use in the farming of land (Agriculture Act 1947, s. 109(3)).

[5] Agriculture Act 1947, s. 98(1).

[6] For an interpretation of the meaning of taking an animal see p. 115.

[7] For the particular provisions dealing with the destruction of rabbits see pp. 226-229. The making of a rabbit clearance order under the Pests Act 1954, s. 1(6) does not prevent the issue of notices under the Agriculture Act 1947, s. 98(4) in relation to the area designated by the order.

[8] Rodents, being animals of the order *Rodentia*, will include rats, mice and squirrels. Other measures against rats and mice are dealt with on pp. 229-233.

[9] Agriculture Act 1947, s. 98(1), (4). Other animals may be added to the list by Ministerial regulation. See also generally the Prevention of Damage by Pests Act 1949 and the Forestry Act 1967, s. 7.

221

and wild birds.[10] The land in question may be land of any kind.

The person to be served with the notice is the person who has the right to kill, take or destroy the kind of animal described in the notice on the land identified by it.[11] This will generally be the occupier of it, but the rights will sometimes belong to someone else, e.g. a shooting tenant or a landlord who has reserved the game rights.[12] So far as rabbits are concerned, the notice may be served on the occupier whether or not he has the right to kill them.[13]

The notice may require that the steps to be taken shall be taken within the time stipulated in it.[14]

The Minister may assist in complying with the notice by providing such services and equipment, appliances and other materials as he thinks may be required. A charge may be made for this assistance and recovered from the person requesting it.[15] He may also make financial contributions towards the cost of complying with a notice. Both forms of aid may extend to destroying or reducing breeding places or cover for rabbits or excluding rabbits from them, and preventing rabbits living in any place from spreading to or doing damage in another place.[16]

With the three exceptions mentioned below, the notice cannot require any killing, taking or destruction which would otherwise be prohibited by law.[17] The exceptions are:

1. Game may be killed out of season, and the person served with

---

[10] The general provisions of the Wildlife and Countryside Act 1981 are relaxed to allow for the death or injury or damage to their eggs in relation to wild birds other than those listed in Schedule 1 to the 1981 Act: Wildlife and Countryside Act 1981, s. 4(1). See further pp. 176-178. Whilst the Agriculture Act 1947, s. 98(1) refers to the Protection of Birds Act 1954, it is submitted that by virtue of the Interpretation Act 1978, s. (2)(a), the Wildlife and Countryside Act 1981 is the effective Act. See also the Wildlife and Countryside Act 1981, ss. 1, 6, 19 and 22 and generally pp. 174-184.

[11] Agriculture Act 1947, s.98(1).

[12] See pp. 124-128 for details of these rights.

[13] Pests Act 1954, s. 1(6). He will anyhow have the right under the Ground Game Act 1880, for which see pp. 121-124.

[14] Agriculture Act 1947, s. 98(1).

[15] Agriculture Act 1947, s. 101.

[16] Pests Act 1954, ss. 2(2), 3(1).

[17] Agriculture Act 1947, s. 98(2).

a notice may not use the excuse for non-compliance with it that the game he is required to kill is out of season;[18]

2. A game licence need not be held when complying with a notice, and a person who has had a notice may sell game destroyed in the course of complying with it as if he had held a game licence;[19]

3. The use of poisonous gas and substances generating it in the holes, burrows or earths of the animals to be destroyed is permitted.[20]

If the Minister considers it expedient, for the purpose of preventing damage to crops, pasture, animal or human foodstuffs, livestock, trees, hedges, banks or any works on land, to prevent the escape of any animals[21] from any land, he may serve[22] written notice on the occupier requiring him, within the time given in the notice, to take such steps as may be necessary to prevent the animals' escape, including any steps which may be detailed in the notice.[23]

There is no right of appeal against either of the two kinds of notice which have been considered. Failure to comply with their requirements is an offence punishable by fine.[24] Additionally, on

---

[18] Agriculture Act 1947, s. 98(2), proviso. As to close seasons for game see pp. 115-116.

[19] Agriculture Act 1947, s. 100(4) (amended by the Local Government Act 1966, s. 43(2)). As to game licences and the selling of game see pp. 116-121.

[20] Agriculture Act 1947, s. 98(3). Apart from this provision, the use of these methods is permitted only for the extermination of rabbits. The methods may not be used on any animals added to those listed, for which see note 9 and the text thereto on p. 221 (Agriculture Act 1947, s. 98(4), proviso). A person is not guilty of an offence under the Protection of Animals Act 1911, s. 8 by reason only that he uses poisonous gas in a rabbit hole, or places in a rabbit hole a substance which, by evaporation or in contact with moisture, generates poisonous gas (Prevention of Damage by Rabbits Act 1939, s. 4).

[21] The Act puts no restriction on the meaning of "animals", but for the meaning in law generally, see p. 1.

[22] As to the means of serving notice, see note 2 on p. 221. In this case, if the land is used for agriculture, the notice may be served on the agent or employee of the occupier who is responsible for the control of the farming of the land, instead of on the occupier himself (Agriculture Act 1947, s. 100(6)).

[23] Agriculture Act 1947, s.99.

[24] Agriculture Act 1947, s.100(1). This includes a daily fine while the default continues.

failure to comply, a person authorised by the Minister may enter[25] the land and take such steps as the Minister may direct to secure compliance with the notice. The reasonable cost of taking these steps is recoverable by the Minister from the person served with the notice.[26]

If a person incurs expense in complying with either kind of notice or if the Minister recovers money from him as just described, and he considers that the expense should be borne wholly or partly by someone else having an interest in the land, he may apply to the County Court for a full or partial indemnity from the other person.[27] No other grounds are given upon which the application to the court may be made. It would seem to be justified if for any reason a person, other than the recipient of the Minister's notice, was partly or wholly responsible for the state of affairs giving rise to the notice. Thus, an occupier, receiving notice about the escape of animals and not having the right under the terms of his tenancy to destroy them, might justifiably claim that the cost of measures to prevent their escape should be borne by the person having that right.

The Minister may give such directions "as appear to him to be expedient" authorising the keeping of animals killed or taken under these provisions (except those dealing with escape) and their disposal for use for food or otherwise.[28] This appears to give the Minister unfettered control over the animals' carcasses, some of which will have appreciable value as food; there is no provision for compensation.

The Forestry Commissioners[29] have separate powers to prevent damage to trees by pests. These powers may be operated if they are satisfied that trees or tree plants are being, or are likely to be,

---

[25] The person must, if required, produce authentication of his authority and, if the land is used for residential purposes, give 24 hours' notice of intended entry (Agriculture Act 1947, s. 106 (2),(3)). He need hold no game licence and may sell game as if he had a licence (Agriculture Act 1947, s. 100(4)).

[26] Agriculture Act 1947, s. 100(2). Any dispute over the amount of the cost is settled by arbitration.

[27] Agriculture Act 1947, s. 100(5).

[28] Agriculture Act 1947, s. 100(3).

[29] See note 1 on p. 221.

damaged by rabbits, hares or vermin[30] owing to the failure of an occupier[31] of land to destroy sufficiently those animals on his land, or otherwise to take steps for the prevention of damage by them.[32] In such a case the Commissioners may authorise in writing any competent person to enter on the land and kill or take the animals described. But, before doing so, they must give the occupier and owner of the land such opportunity[33] as the Commissioners think reasonable of destroying the animals or taking steps to prevent the damage.[34]

The net cost of the action so taken by the Commissioners is recoverable from the occupier[35] of the land as a civil debt.[36] The person authorised to enter the land must produce his written authority if required; obstruction of him is an offence punishable with a fine.[37]

The Commissioners' officers and others authorised by them may at any time enter land for any purpose connected with the exercise of these powers, e.g. to assess the quantity of vermin on it. Written authority must again be produced if asked for, and obstruction is similarly punishable.[38]

Local authorities may seize, destroy, sell or otherwise dispose of any house doves and pigeons, starlings and sparrows[39] which in its

---

[30] The expression "vermin" includes squirrels (Forestry Act 1967, s. 7(5)(b)) but does not include the red squirrel which is protected under the Wildlife and Countryside Act 1981, Sch. 5. It is suggested that the general meaning of the word "vermin" is sufficiently wide as to embrace in this context any creature capable of damaging trees, although no exception is allowed against protected animals under these provisions. This is in contrast to the exceptions allowed for agricultural pest control (see Wildlife and Countryside Act 1981, s. 10(1)).

[31] The person entitled to kill rabbits, hares or vermin on common land is deemed to be the occupier of that land (Forestry Act 1967, s. 7(5)(a)). For a definition of "common land" see note 100 on p. 14, though this is not expressly applied to the 1967 Act.

[32] Forestry Act 1967, s. 7(1).

[33] Neither the kind of opportunity nor the means of giving it are detailed, thus leaving both to the Commissioners' discretion.

[34] Forestry Act 1967, s. 7(2).

[35] There is no right of recovery from the owner, if he is not the occupier, or other sanction available against him..

[36] Forestry Act 1967, s. 7(3).

[37] Forestry Act 1967, s. 7(4).

[38] Forestry Act 1967, s. 48(1), (3).

[39] Licences granted under the Wildlife and Countryside Act 1981 cover the destruction and disposal of the four species.

belief have no owner and which constitute a nuisance or annoyance[40] or are causing damage.[41] The authority must take reasonable precautions to ensure that the seizure and destruction is undertaken humanely and not in contravention of the Wildlife and Countryside Act 1981.[42]

Rabbits

The Minister may make orders known as "rabbit clearance orders". They designate areas as rabbit clearance areas to be freed, so far as practicable, of wild rabbits, and may provide for and regulate the steps to be taken to that end.[43]

By Rabbit Clearance Order No. 148, the Minister has designated the whole of England and Wales (excluding the City of London, the Scilly Isles and Skokholm Island) as a rabbit clearance area.

An occupier of land[44] in a rabbit clearance area must take the necessary steps to kill or take[45] wild rabbits on his land. Where it is not reasonably practicable to destroy them, he must take steps to prevent them causing damage. In particular, he must comply with any directions in the order about the steps to be taken towards these ends and about the time in which they are to be taken.[46]

No additional right is given to the occupier to authorise others to kill rabbits on his land with firearms,[47] but the Minister may on the occupier's request permit the occupier to authorise more persons to kill rabbits in this way than is otherwise permitted[48] if the Minister is satisfied:

---

40 Public Health Act 1961, s. 74(1), (2).
41 Public Health Act 1961, s. 74(1).
42 Public Health Act 1961, s. 74(3)(4) (amended by the Wildlife and Countryside Act 1981, s. 72(6)). See also generally Wildlife and Countryside Act 1981, ss. 1–27.
43 Pests Act 1954, s. 1(1) (amended by the Transfer of Functions (Ministry of Food) Order 1955, SI 1955/554). The orders may be varied or revoked by later orders of the Minister.
44 The expression "occupier" in relation to unoccupied land means the person entitled to occupy it (Pests Act 1954, s. 1(13)).
45 For an interpretation of the word "take", see p. 115.
46 Pests Act 1954, s. 1(2).
47 Pests Act 1954, s. 1(3).
48 Under the Ground Game Act 1880 the occupier may authorise only one other person to kill rabbits by shooting on his land – see p. 122.

a. that the circumstances necessitate a greater use of firearms than the occupier has the right to authorise; and

b. that the occupier has tried to obtain the sanction of the persons who, apart from the Ground Game Act 1880, have the right to take rabbits on his lands;[49] and

c. that their sanction has been unreasonably withheld.[50]

This sanction will not be treated as unreasonably withheld if, so far as the use of firearms is required, the persons asked for it are themselves taking or proposing to take adequate steps to destroy the rabbits.[51]

Persons authorised by the occupier to take rabbits in order to comply with a rabbit clearance order cannot be prosecuted for the unlawful destruction or pursuit of game[52] whilst acting in accordance with their authorisations.[53]

There is no right of appeal or other action which can be taken against a rabbit clearance order or its requirements except, as mentioned below, to object to the proposal to make the order. The following provisions dealt with earlier in this chapter when considering notices by the Minister to deal with pests apply to rabbit clearance orders:

1. Game licences and selling of game (page 223);

2. The results of failure to comply with requirements (pages 223 to 224);

3. Obtaining indemnity from another person (page 224);

---

49 I.e. the persons to whom the shooting is let, or the landlord if the shooting is held by him.
50 Pests Act 1954, s. 1(4) (amended by the Transfer of Functions (Ministry of Food) Order 1955, SI 1955/554). Additional persons so authorised are subject to the same provisions (for which see p. 123) about production of their authorisations given by the occupier as the person authorised under the Ground Game Act 1880.
51 Pests Act 1954, s. 1(5).
52 This is a reference to the poaching offences such as are created by the Night Poaching Act 1828, ss. 1 and 9, and the Game Act 1931, ss. 30 and 32.
53 Pests Act 1954, s. 1(7).

4. Disposal of animals by the Minister (page 224).[54]

Authorised officers of the Minister may enter land at all reasonable times to see whether a rabbit clearance order should be made or to check whether the order's requirements are being met.[55]

The Minister must give notice of a proposal to make a rabbit clearance order so as to inform persons interested in land in the area and, when it is made, publish it in such manner as he thinks fit,[56] take steps to bring it to the notice of persons likely to be affected, and enable them to buy copies of it.[57] The notice of a proposal must allow at least 14 days for representations to be made to the Minister; when making the order the Minister may, but need not, give effect to the representations[58] and may issue the order either modified or unmodified.

The Minister has further powers by which he can require an occupier to deal with rabbits. If the Minister thinks it expedient for the purpose of preventing damage by rabbits to crops, pasture,[59] trees, hedges, banks or any works on land, he may by written notice served[60] on the occupier of any land[61] require him to take the steps detailed in the notice within the time given to destroy or reduce the breeding places or cover for rabbits, or to exclude rabbits from them, or to prevent rabbits living in any place on the land from spreading to or doing damage in any other place. But this notice is provisional; the occupier and others interested in the land may make written objections to it which must be considered by the Minister before serving a final and effective notice on the occupier. If the occupier holds the land under a contract of tenancy, copies

---

54 Pests Act 1954, s. 1(9).
55 Pests Act 1954, s. 1(8) (amended by the Transfer of Functions (Ministry of Food) Order 1955, SI 1955/554).
56 For example, by notices on public boards and in the local press.
57 Pests Act 1954, ss. 1(10), (11)(b).
58 Pests Act 1954, s. 1(2).
59 "Pasture" includes meadow (Agriculture Act 1947, s. 109(3)).
60 As to the service of notices see note 2 on p. 221 and note 22 on p. 223.
61 If the land is unoccupied, notices may be served on the person entitled to occupy it. Agriculture Act 1947, s. 98(7) (amended by the Pests Act 1954 s. 2(1) and amended by the Transfer of Functions (Ministry of Food) Order 1955, SI 1955/554).

of both notices must be served also on the person to whom he pays rent.[62]

The provisions considered on pages 222 to 223 dealing with game licences, the selling of game, the results of failure to comply with requirements, the disposal of animals by the Minister, the steps for obtaining indemnity from another person, and with assistance from the Minister all apply to the situation created by the type of notice just considered.[63]

Rats and Mice

Local authorities[64] have a duty to keep their areas, so far as practicable, free from rats and mice[65] and in particular to carry out such inspections as may be necessary of their land and destroy such rats and mice so found. To that end they have been given certain powers.

The occupier of any land[66] must at once give written notice[67] to the local authority when he knows that rats or mice are living on or resorting to his land in substantial numbers,[68] but need not do so if:

a. his land is agricultural land;[69] or

---

[62] Agriculture Act 1947, s. 98(7) (amended by the Pests Act 1954, s. 2(1) and amended by the Transfer of Functions (Ministry of Food) Order 1955, SI 1955/554).

[63] Agriculture Act 1947, ss. 100 (s. 100(1) amended by virtue of the Criminal Justices Act 1982, s. 46), 100(4) (amended by the Local Government Act 1966, s. 43(2)(a), Sch. 6, Pt. 1)), 101, 106(1)–(3); Pests Act 1954, ss. 2 (amended by the Transfer of Functions (Ministry of Food) Order 1955, SI 1955/554) and 3.

[64] "Local authorities" means the Common Council of the City of London and the councils of London and county districts: Prevention of Damage by Pests Act 1949, s. 1(1) (amended by the London Government Act 1963, s. 83(1), Sch. 17, para. 10, and the Local Government Act 1972, s. 272(1), Sch. 30). A local authority's functions under these provisions may be conferred on a housing action trust: Housing Act 1988, s. 68.

[65] Prevention of Damage by Pests Act 1949, s. 2(1).

[66] "Land" includes land covered with water and any building or part of a building: Prevention of Damage by Pests Act 1949, s. 28(1).

[67] No particular form of notice is required.

[68] Prevention of Damage by Pests Act 1949, s. 3(1). Failure to give notice is punishable by a fine: Prevention of Damage by Pests Act 1949, s. 3(4).There appears to be no definition of "substantial numbers".

[69] "Agricultural land" means land used for agriculture as that word is defined in the Agriculture Act 1947, s. 109(1), (3): Prevention of Damage by Pests Act 1949, s. 28(1). The definition is given in note 369 on p. 188. The Minister may by regulations exempt other kinds of land from the requirement (Prevention of Damage by Pests Act 1949, s. 3(2)) but has not as yet done so.

b. a notice of infestation is given.[70]

Whether or not notice by an occupier is served on them, if the local authority consider that steps should be taken for the purpose of destroying rats or mice on land or keeping it free from them, they may serve written notice on the owner[71] or occupier requiring him to take, within such reasonable time as may be given by the notice, such reasonable steps for those purposes as may be detailed in the notice.[72] In particular, the notice may require a form of treatment to be applied to the land at particular times and the carrying out of structural repairs or other works.[73]

If the owner of the land is not the occupier, the local authority may serve a notice on both;[74] the owner is entitled to complain to a Magistrates' Court (if he considers that such is the case) that the occupier is preventing him from doing the work which the owner's notice requires, when the magistrates may order the occupier to permit the work to be done.[75]

An owner or occupier receiving a notice requiring structural works to be done may appeal to a Magistrates' Court, but only on particular grounds.[76] Those grounds and the appeal procedures relating to them are set out in full in Appendix I at the end of the book. An appeal must be made within 21 days from receiving the notice,[77] and there is a further right of appeal to the Crown Court.[78] It appears that there is no right of appeal against requirements in a notice which do not relate to structural works.

---

70 Prevention of Damage by Pests Act 1949, s. 3(2), (3).
71 "Owner" means, as respects England and Wales, the person for the time being receiving the rackrent of the premises, whether on his own account or as agent or trustee for another person, or who would so receive the rackrent if the premises were let at rackrent (the Clean Air Act 1993, s. 64 which consolidated the Public Heath Act 1936, s. 343(1)). Cf Prevention of Damage by Pests Act 1949, s. 28.
72 Prevention of Damage by Pests Act 1949, s. 4(1).
73 Prevention of Damage by Pests Act 1949, s. 4(2).
74 Prevention of Damage by Pests Act 1949, s. 4(1).
75 Prevention of Damage by Pests Act 1949, s. 4(4).
76 Public Health Act 1936, s. 290(3)–(5); Prevention of Damage by Pests Act 1949, s. 4(5).
77 The notice itself must state the right of appeal and the time limit (Public Health Act 1936, s. 300(3); Prevention of Damage by Pests Act 1949, s. 4(5)).
78 Public Health Act 1936, ss. 300(2), 301.

If an owner or occupier served with a notice fails to take the steps which it requires at the time or within the period given in the notice, the local authority may take those steps themselves and recover their reasonable expenses from the person in default.[79] Also, the person defaulting commits an offence punishable by fine.[80]

Where land affected by rats or mice[81] is in multiple occupation and the council consider that it should be dealt with as one unit, the council may enter the land and take the necessary steps (except structural works) to deal with the vermin without serving the notices just considered. At least 7 days' notice of entry must be given, and this must show the steps proposed to be taken. The council's expenses in this are recoverable from the occupiers in proportion to the expenditure on their individual properties.[82]

Powers similar to those just described are given to the Minister for the Department for Environment, Food and Rural Affairs[83] to deal with cases of infestation[84] of food[85] and things associated with it. With the exceptions mentioned below, every person whose business consists of or includes the manufacture,[86] storage, transport or sale of food must at once give written notice to the Minister when he knows that infestation is present:

a. in any premises or vehicle, or any equipment belonging to either, used or likely to be used in the course of that business for the manufacture, storage, transport or sale of food; or

---

[79] Prevention of Damage by Pests Act 1949, ss. 5(1) and 7(1).

[80] Prevention of Damage by Pests Act 1949, s. 5(2).

[81] I.e. land on which rats or mice are living or resorting to in substantial numbers.

[82] Prevention of Damage by Pests Act 1949, ss. 6 and 7(1). Unoccupied land is treated as being occupied by the owner.

[83] Prevention of Damage by Pests Act 1949, s. 28 (1) (amended by SI 1955/554). See also note 1 on p. 221.

[84] "Infestation" means the presence of rats, mice, insects or mites in numbers or under conditions which involve an immediate or potential risk of substantial loss of or damage to food (Prevention of Damage by Pests Act 1949, s. 28(1)).

[85] "Food" includes any substance ordinarily used in the composition or preparation of food, the seeds of any cereal or vegetable, and any feeding stuffs for animals, but does not include growing crops (Prevention of Damage by Pests Act 1949, s. 28(1)).

[86] "Manufacture" includes processing (Prevention of Damage by Pests Act 1949, s. 28(1)).

b. in any food manufactured, stored, transported or sold in the course of that business, or in any other goods for the time being in his possession[87] which are in contact or likely to come into contact with any such food.[88]

Similarly, but again with exceptions, as mentioned below, every person whose business consists of or includes the manufacture, sale, repair or cleaning of containers must at once give written notice to the Minister when he knows that there is any infestation in any container[89] in his possession which is to be used for the reception of food in the course of any business of the kind mentioned in the last paragraph.[90]

The exceptions referred to earlier are exceptions which may be made by the Minister in regulations.[91] Regulations so made relax the requirements to give notice when, briefly:[92] named types of food or premises are infested with insects or mites only; a carrier in certain circumstances is involved; or the Minister decides on an application to him to relax or exclude the requirements.[93] The Minister is empowered[94] to prohibit or restrict the delivery of food or other goods for which notice is to be given as described above and has done so in the same regulations.[95]

Whether or not such notices are given, the Minister may give directions, for preventing or mitigating damage to food, to persons whose business is involved with it or with food containers. If he thinks the infestation cannot be remedied by any treatment, his directions may require the destruction of the food or containers involved.[96]

---

87 As to the meaning of "possession", see p. 68.
88 Prevention of Damage by Pests Act 1949, s. 13(1).
89 "Container" includes sacks, boxes, tins and other similar articles: Prevention of Damage by Pests Act 1949, s. 28(1).
90 Prevention of Damage by Pests Act 1949, s. 13(2).
91 Prevention of Damage by Pests Act 1949, s. 13(3)(a).
92 For full details, the text of the regulations must be referred to.
93 Prevention of Damage by Pests (Infestation of Food) Regulations 1950, SI 1950/416.
94 Prevention of Damage by Pests Act 1949, s. 13(3)(b).
95 Prevention of Damage by Pests (Infestation of Food) Regulations 1950, SI 1950/416, Arts. 5 and 8.
96 Prevention of Damage by Pests Act 1949, s. 14.

When the directions require any structural work to be done or any food or container to be destroyed, any person aggrieved may appeal to the magistrates[97] and thence, in a case of structural works only, to the Crown Court.[98]

In default of compliance with a notice, the Minister may by order authorise the person named in it to take the steps necessary for compliance. The expenses of this are recoverable from the person in default who also commits an offence by non-compliance.[99]

The Minister may make regulations for controlling the methods for keeping down or destroying rats, mice, insects or mites which may be used by persons carrying on business in pest destruction and control.[100]

The application of the earlier provisions in this section for dealing with rats and mice has been extended so as to apply the provisions, wholly or partly, to ships, vessels and hovercraft and places connected with them.[101]

Destructive Foreign Animals

The Destructive Imported Animals Act of 1932 is designed to prohibit or control the import into, and the keeping in, Great Britain[102] of destructive non-indigenous mammals. The controls which the Act gives are exercised by the Minister[103] through the making of regulations and the granting of licences.

The only animals which the Act names are musk rats (*Fiber*

---

[97] Within 21 days from receipt of the directions in the case of structural work, or 7 days in the other case (Prevention of Damage by Pests Act 1949, s. 15(1)).

[98] Prevention of Damage by Pests Act 1949, s. 15. The directions must state the right of appeal and the time limits.

[99] Prevention of Damage by Pests Act 1949, ss. 16(1), (2), 17.

[100] Prevention of Damage by Pests Act 1949, s. 19(1). No such regulations have yet been made.

[101] Prevention of Damage by Pests (Application to Shipping) Order 1951, SI 1951/967.

[102] Any reference to importation into Great Britain does not include a reference to importation from a Member State (Destructive Imported Animals Act 1932 (Amendment) Regulations 1992, SI 1992/3302).

[103] Except that the functions under ss. 1, 2 and 10, so far as they relate to the importation of the types of animals to which this Act relates, are transferred to the National Assembly of Wales so far as they have been transferred to the Secretary of State by the Transfer of Functions (Wales) Order 1969 (The National Assembly of Wales (Transfer of Functions) Order 1999, SI 1999/672).

zibethicus) and musquash (*Ondatra zibethica*),[104] but it allows the Minister to make orders bringing other animals into its orbit; these further animals can only be drawn from species of mammals which on 17th March 1932 were not established in a wild state in Great Britain, or had only become so established within the preceding 50 years, but excluding species which on that date were commonly kept in Great Britain in a domesticated state.[105] To date, the animals added in this way are mink, grey squirrels, rabbits other than the European rabbit, and coypus. The Minister's orders may prohibit absolutely the importing[106] and keeping[107] of the animals or allow their import and keeping under licence.

The present position is that the keeping of musk rats, musquash, grey squirrels (*Sciurus carolinensis*) and rabbits other than the European rabbit (*Oryctolagus cuniculus*) is absolutely prohibited,[108] i.e. no licence can be granted. To keep them is an offence punishable by fine, and on conviction the court may order the animals to be forfeited and destroyed.[109] Mink (*Mustela vison*) and coypus (*Myocastor coypus*) may only be kept if a licence to do so is issued by the Minister.[110] Keeping without a licence, or contravention or

---

[104] Destructive Imported Animals Act 1932, s. 1(1).

[105] Destructive Imported Animals Act 1932, s. 10(1). Also, the Minister is required to be satisfied that because of their destructive habitats it is desirable to prohibit or control these mammals' import or keeping and to destroy any which may be at large.

[106] For the importing of these kinds of animals see pp. 47-48.

[107] There is no definition of "keeping" in the Act but its wording and that of the regulations indicates that the word signifies a deliberate maintaining of the animals as distinct from merely letting them exist at large. The measures which can be taken against them when they do so exist are described on p. 236.

[108] Musk-Rats (Prohibition of Importation and Keeping) Order 1933 (SR & O 1933/106) made under Destructive Imported Animals Act 1932, s.1; Grey Squirrels (Prohibition of Importation and Keeping) Order 1937 (SR & O 1937/478); Destructive Imported Animals Act 1932, s. 10; Non-Indigenous Rabbits (Prohibition of Importation and Keeping) Order 1954 (SR & O 1954/927); Destructive Imported Animals Act 1932, s. 10.

[109] Destructive Imported Animals Act 1932, ss. 1(1), 6(1) and 10(1), together with the Orders cited in note 108.

[110] Mink Keeping (England) Order, SI 2000/3402 and Mink Keeping (Wales) Order, SI 2000/3340 made under Destructive Imported Animals Act 1932, s. 10(1) which prohibits the keeping of any mink on certain off-shore islands of England and Wales. These orders took effect on the 1st January 2001 and cease to have effect on 1st January 2004; the Coypus (Prohibition on Keeping) Order 1987, SI 1987/2195 prohibits absolutely the keeping of coypus other than under special licence (Coypus (Special Licence) (Fees) Regulations 1997, SI 1997/2751). All previous regulations have been revoked by the Coypus (Keeping) (Revocation) Regulations 1987.

failing to comply with the terms of a licence or with any regulation made under the Act,[111] are offences with a liability to a fine and a court order as before.[112]

A licence to keep coypus or mink will be issued on payment of the fee laid down,[113] will be in force for 12 months and may be renewed, but may be revoked if the licence holder fails to comply with any of its terms or the regulations dealing with keeping, or if he commits an offence under the Act.[114] The terms of the licence will require the licensee:

a. in the case of coypus, to inform the Minister of the name and address of any person to whom he disposes of the coypus;

b. in the case of mink, to inform persons to whom he disposes of them of their obligation to obtain a licence to keep them;

c. in the case of mink, to inform the Minister of any alteration, at the place where they are kept, to a guard fence or to a baffle attached to it at least 14 days before he proposes to make the alteration;

d. in both cases, to inform the Minister of any change of occupancy of the premises where the animals are kept or if they cease to be kept there;

e. in both cases, to make returns to the Minister when required stating the number of each sex of animal kept;

f. in both cases, to give immediate notice to the Minister if any animal escapes;

g. in both cases, to permit persons authorised by the Minister at

---

[111] I.e. the regulations about keeping the animals cited in note 113 below.

[112] Destructive Imported Animals Act 1932, ss. 1(1), 6(1), 10(1); the Orders cited in note 110 on p. 234.

[113] The fees currently payable are: £185 for mink kept for exhibition and scientific purposes and £630 for a licence granted under Destructive Imported Animals Act 1932, s. 3 (Mink (Keeping) (Amendment) Regulations 1997, SI 1997/2750) and £185 for coypus (Coypus (Special Licence) (Fees) Regulations 1997, SI 1997/2751).

[114] Destructive Imported Animals Act 1932, ss. 2 and 3.

reasonable times to enter and inspect the premises where the animals are kept.[115]

The licensee will also be required to comply with the regulations about the manner in which the animals are to be kept. Coypus, when not being transported, must be confined in enclosures[116] constructed so as to prevent their escape. They must only be transported in closed cages or other containers similarly constructed. The requirements for mink are much lengthier and more detailed; briefly, they must be kept in escape-proof cages or other containers which in turn must be kept in enclosures or buildings constructed in accordance with the regulations' specifications.[117]

The occupier of any land[118] who knows that musk rats (or musquash), grey squirrels, rabbits other than the European rabbit, mink or coypus (other than those which may be and are kept under licence) are to be found[119] on his land must give notice[120] at once to the Minister. As soon as the Minister becomes aware of this situation[121] he may take the steps he considers necessary for the animals' destruction, and it is the occupier's duty to afford all such facilities as he can to persons employed by the Minister for destroying the animals.[122]

A special licence may be given by the Minister to anyone who wants to keep the animals described in the last paragraph for

---

[115] See regulations in respect of mink and coypus previously cited.

[116] I.e. cages, hutches, pens, stockades, buildings and parts of buildings.

[117] Destructive Imported Animals Act 1932, ss. 1(1), 8(1), 10(1), 11; Mink (Keeping) Regulations 1975, SI 1975/2223.

[118] "Land" includes land covered with water and any buildings and any other erection on land and any cellar, sewer, drain or culvert in or under land: Destructive Imported Animals Act 1932, s. 11.

[119] Note that there is no indication of the numbers necessary to require a notice to be given, unlike the case for rats and mice where "substantial numbers" are mentioned: see p. 229.

[120] Written notice is not required, but it is advisable since failure to give it is an offence.

[121] This may happen either through the notice given to the Minister by the occupier or through other sources of information.

[122] Destructive Imported Animals Act 1932, ss. 1(1), 5(1)–(3), 10(1), 11; the Orders cited in notes 108 and 110 on p. 234.

The occupier is not required to pay for or towards the cost of destruction. There can be no action for damages for the killing or wounding of any of these animals found at large (Destructive Imported Animals Act 1932, s. 5(5)).

exhibition or scientific research or other exceptional purposes. The licence, which is revocable at any time, will require the animals to be kept in such manner and upon such conditions as it may specify.[123]

As mentioned earlier,[124] other animals may be brought into the orbit of the Act by Ministerial orders. If this happens, any person who on the date of the relevant order is keeping animals described in it for profit in Great Britain[125] is entitled to receive compensation from the Minister for his losses which will ensue as a result of the order being made.[126]

In addition to the offences described on pages 233 to 236, the following offences, all punishable by fines, are created by the Act:

1. Turning loose any musk rat (or musquash), grey squirrels, non-European rabbits, mink or coypus, or wilfully[127] allowing them to escape;[128]

2. Obstructing any officer of, or person authorised or employed by, the Minister in the execution of his duty under the Act;

3. An occupier failing to give the required notice that the animals described in 1. above are to be found on his land.[129]

---

[123] Destructive Imported Animals Act 1932, ss. 1(1), 8(1), 10(1), 11.

[124] On p. 234.

[125] I.e. England, Wales and Scotland.

[126] Destructive Imported Animals Act 1932, ss. 1(1), 7(1), 10(1), 11.

[127] This means deliberately and intentionally, and not by accident or inadvertence (*R v Senior* (1899) 1 QB 283 at 290–291).

[128] From what the animals are to escape in order for an offence to occur is not clear. It is perhaps intended to refer to the enclosures, containers, cages, etc. in which licensed mink and coypus must be kept (see p. 236) and to the similar requirements under a special licence (see text above).

[129] Destructive Imported Animals Act 1932, ss. 1(1), 6(1), 10(1), 11; the Orders cited in notes 108 and 110 on p. 234.

Chapter 12

EXPERIMENTS

Regulated Procedures

The Animal (Scientific Procedures) Act 1986 regulates the procedures performed on protected animals. A "protected animal" is any living[1] vertebrate[2] other than man. The protection afforded by the Act extends to any such vertebrate in its foetal, larval or embryonic form from the stage of its development when (1) in the case of a mammal, bird or reptile, half the gestation or incubation period for the relevant species has elapsed; or (2) in any other case, it becomes capable of independent feeding.[3]

A "regulated procedure" means any experiment or other scientific procedure applied to a protected animal which may have the effect of causing that animal, pain, suffering, distress or lasting harm.[4] In determining whether any procedure may have the foregoing effect, the use of an anaesthetic or analgesic, decerebration and any other procedure for the rendering an animal insentient shall be disregarded.[5] Also regulated are experimental or other scientific procedures where:

a. part of a series or combination of such procedures (whether the same or different) applied to the same animal;

b. a series or combination of such procedures which have the

---

[1] An animal is regarded as living until the permanent cessation of circulation or the destruction of the brain: Animals (Scientific Procedures) Act 1986, s. 1(4).

[2] "Vertebrate" means any animal of the Sub-phylum Vertebrata of the Phylum Chordata and "invertebrate" means any animal not of that Sub-phylum (Animals (Scientific Procedures) Act 1986, s. 1(5)). The Secretary of State may extend the definition of protected animal so as to include invertebrates of any description (Animals (Scientific Procedures) Act 1986, s. 1(3)(a)).

[3] Animals (Scientific Procedures) Act 1986, s. 1(2). The Secretary of State may alter the stage of development (Animals (Scientific Procedures) Act 1986, s. 1(3)(b)).

[4] Animals (Scientific Procedures) Act 1986, s. 2(1).

[5] Animals (Scientific Procedures) Act 1986, s. 2(4). The administration of an anaesthetic or analgesic to a protected animal, or decerebration or any other such procedure applied to such an animal, for the purpose of any experimental or other scientific procedure shall itself be a regulated procedure (Animals (Scientific Procedures) Act 1986, s. 2(4)).

effect of causing the animal pain, suffering, distress or lasting harm;

c. throughout the series or combination of procedures the animal is a protected animal or it attains the status of a protected animal in its development.[6]

If the birth or hatching of a protected animal results in, or is liable to result in, pain, suffering, distress or lasting harm then such practice is also a protected procedure for the purpose of the Act.[7]

In any event the use of neuromuscular blocking agents is prohibited[8] as is their use instead of an anaesthetic.[9]

Excluded from the definition of regulated procedure are the following:

1. The ringing, tagging or marking of an animal or the application of any other humane procedure for the sole purpose of enabling it to be identified if it causes only momentary pain or distress and no lasting harm;[10]

2. The administration of any substance or article to an animal for the purposes of a medical test of a substance or an article in accordance with the Medicines Act 1968;[11]

3. Killing an animal unless it is killed for experimentation or other scientific use in a designated establishment[12] and the method used is not appropriate to the animal;[13]

---

[6] Animals (Scientific Procedures) Act 1986, s. 2(2).
[7] Animals (Scientific Procedures) Act 1986, s. 2(3).
[8] The use of such blocking agents is permitted if so authorised by the personal and project licences (Animals (Scientific Procedures) Act 1986, s. 17(1), proviso).
[9] Animals (Scientific Procedures) Act 1986, s. 17(2).
[10] Animals (Scientific Procedures) Act 1986, s. 2(5).
[11] Animals (Scientific Procedures) Act 1986, s. 2(6); i.e. a test within the meaning of the Medicines Act 1968, s. 36(6).
[12] See Animals (Scientific Procedures) Act 1986, ss. 6 and 7 and pp. 247-248.
[13] Animals (Scientific Procedures) Act 1986, s. 2(7). "Appropriate" means appropriate under Sch. 1, which prescribes standard methods of humane killing for (1) animals other than foetal, larval and embryonic forms, and (2) foetal, larval and embryonic forms. The Schedule may be amended by order of the Secretary of State (Animals (Scientific Procedures) Act 1986, s. 2(9)).

4. Recognised veterinary, agricultural or animal husbandry practice.[14]

Licences

Scientific procedures performed on protected animals must be authorised by two types of licence: a *personal licence* qualifying the licencee to apply a regulated procedure which is part of a programme of work specified in a *project licence*. Each licence must specify the place where the procedure is to be carried out.[15]

To perform a regulated procedure without such licences is punishable by a fine, imprisonment or both.[16]

Before granting a licence or issuing a certificate,[17] the Secretary of State[18] must consult one of the inspectors appointed under the Act[19] and may also consult an independent assessor[20] or the Animals Procedure Committee established under the Act.[21]

A licence or certificate may be varied or revoked by the Secretary of State either on the ground of breach of a condition[22] or in any other case in which it appears to him appropriate to do so,[23] or at the request of the holder.[24] The applicant has rights to make written or oral representations to the Secretary of State before he refuses a licence or certificate or varies or revokes it.[25]

It is an offence[26] if, for the purpose of obtaining or assisting another

---

[14] Animals (Scientific Procedures) Act 1986, s. 2(8).
[15] Animals (Scientific Procedures) Act 1986, s. 3.
[16] Animals (Scientific Procedures) Act 1986, s. 22(1).
[17] I.e. a certificate of designation: see pp. 248-250.
[18] Note that, at the time of publication, the functions of the Secretary of State were in the process of being transferred to the Minister for DEFRA.
[19] I.e. under s. 18, Animals (Scientific Procedures) Act 1986.
[20] If the Secretary of State proposes to consult an independent assessor he must notify the applicant, and in selecting the assessor he must have regard to any representations made by the applicant (Animals (Scientific Procedures) Act, s. 9(2)).
[21] Animals (Scientific Procedures) Act, s. 9(1).
[22] The conditions on which a licence or certificate is issued are dealt with separately on pp. 242-243 and 245-247.
[23] The Secretary of State has powers to suspend the licence or certificate for a period not exceeding three months where it is necessary for the welfare of any protected animals (Animals (Scientific Procedures) Act, s. 13).
[24] Animals (Scientific Procedures) Act, s. 11.
[25] Animals (Scientific Procedures) Act, s. 12.
[26] Subject to a fine, imprisonment or both.

to obtain a licence or certificate, he furnishes information which he knows to be false or misleading in a material particular or recklessly furnishes information which is false or misleading in a material particular.[27]

Personal Licence

A personal licence is a licence granted by the Secretary of State qualifying the holder to apply specified regulated procedures to animals of specified descriptions at a specified place[28] or specified places.[29]

An application for a personal licence is made to the Secretary of State in a prescribed form and supported by such information as may be reasonably required. Unless otherwise dispensed with by the Secretary of State, the application must be endorsed by a person who is himself a holder of a personal licence or a licensee by virtue of Schedule 4 of the Act, and who has knowledge of the biological or other relevant qualifications and of the training experience and character of the applicant.[30] The person endorsing an application should, if practicable, be a person occupying a position of authority at a place where the applicant is to be authorised by the licence to carry out the procedures specified in it.[31] No person may be granted a licence if under the age of 18.[32]

The Secretary of State must be satisfied that the person has appropriate education and training (including instruction in a relevant scientific discipline) for the purpose of applying the relevant procedures to be specified in the licence and is competent to apply those procedures in accordance with the conditions which are to be included in the licence and to handle and take care of laboratory animals.[33]

---

[27] Animals (Scientific Procedures) Act 1986, s. 23.
[28] Animals (Scientific Procedures) Act 1986, s. 30(2) defines "place" as any place within the seaward limits of the territorial waters of the United Kingdom, including any vessel other than a ship which is not a British ship.
[29] Animals (Scientific Procedures) Act 1986, s. 4.
[30] Animals (Scientific Procedures) Act 1986, s. 4(3)(b).
[31] Animals (Scientific Procedures) Act 1986, s. 4(3)(b), proviso.
[32] Animals (Scientific Procedures) Act 1986, s. 4(4).
[33] Animals (Scientific Procedures) Act 1986, s. 4(4A), inserted by the Animals (Scientific Procedures) Act 1986 (Amendment) Regulations 1998, SI 1998/1974.

A personal licence continues in force until revoked, but such licence is to be reviewed by the Secretary of State at intervals not exceeding five years and may for that purpose require the holder to supply him with such information as he may reasonably require.[34]

Before applying for a licence, the applicant is advised to refer to the Guidance on the Operation of the Animals (Scientific Procedures) Act 1986.[35]

Conditions Attached to the Personal Licence

A personal licence must include the following conditions:

1. That the holder shall take precautions to prevent or reduce to the minimum consistent with the purposes of the authorised procedures any pain, distress or discomfort to the animals to which those procedures may be applied;

2. An invoidable termination, that is one specifying circumstances in which a protected animal which is being or has been subjected to a regulated procedure must in every case be immediately killed by a method appropriate[36] to the animal or by such other method as may be authorised by the licence;[37]

3. Such other conditions as the Secretary of State considers appropriate to ensure that the authorised procedures are carried it in accordance with the conditions contained in Schedule 2A of the Animals (Scientific Procedures) Act 1986.[38]

In addition to the compulsory conditions, the Secretary of State may add such conditions as he thinks fit.[39]

A breach of a condition in a licence does not invalidate it but is a

---

[34] Animals (Scientific Procedures) Act 1986, s. 4(5).

[35] HMSO 1990: HC 182, ISBN 0102182906.

[36] As for the appropriate methods of killing see Animals (Scientific Procedures) Act 1986, Sch. 1.

[37] Animals (Scientific Procedures) Act 1986, s. 10(2).

[38] Animals (Scientific Procedures) Act 1986, s. 5(a) as substituted by the Animals (Scientific Procedures) Act 1986 (Amendment) Regulations 1998, SI 1998/1974, Reg. 2, paras. 1, 4(1), (2). The full text of Schedule 2A is set out in Appendix J of this book.

[39] Animals (Scientific Procedures) Act 1986, s. 10(1).

ground for variation or revocation.[40]

Project Licences

The project licence, granted by the Secretary of State, is held by a senior researcher who takes overall responsibility for the programme,[41] and specifies the regulated procedures[42] to animals of specified descriptions at a specified place[43] or specified places.[44]

The Secretary of State cannot grant a licence for any programme unless he is satisfied that it is undertaken for one or more of the following purposes:

1. The prevention (whether by the testing of any product or otherwise) or the diagnosis or treatment of disease, ill-health or abnormality, or their effects, in man, animals or plants;

2. The assessment, detection, regulation or modification of physiological conditions in man, animals or plants;

3. The protection of the natural environment in the interests of the health or welfare of man or animals;

4. The advancement of knowledge in biological or behavioural sciences;

5. Education or training otherwise than in primary or secondary schools;

6. Forensic enquiries;

7. The breeding of animals for experimental or other scientific use.[45]

Additionally, the Secretary of State cannot grant a licence for any of the above programmes unless he:

a. has weighed the likely adverse effects on the animals concerned

---

[40] Animals (Scientific Procedures) Act 1986, s. 10(7).
[41] Animals (Scientific Procedures) Act 1986, s. 5(2).
[42] See p. 238 as to the meaning of "regulated procedure".
[43] See footnote 28 on p. 241 as to the meaning of "place".
[44] Animals (Scientific Procedures) Act 1986, s. 5(1).
[45] Animals (Scientific Procedures) Act 1986, s. 5(3).

against the benefit likely to accrue as a result of the programme to be specified in the licence;[46]

b. is satisfied that the purpose of the programme to be specified in the licence cannot be achieved satisfactorily by any other reasonably practicable method not entailing the use of protected animals;[47]

c. that the regulated procedures to be used are those which use the minimum number of animals, involve animals with the lowest degree of neurophysiological sensitivity, cause the least pain, suffering, distress or lasting harm, and are most likely to produce satisfactory results;[48]

d. is satisfied that where the use of cats, dogs, primates or equidae is intended that:

   i. no other species are suitable for the purposes of the programme; or

   ii. that it is not practicable to obtain animals of any other species that are suitable for those purposes.[49]

A project licence may continue in force for such period as is specified in the licence and may be renewed for further periods (without prejudice to the grant of a new licence in respect of the programme in question) unless (a) it is revoked,[50] (b) more than five years have passed since the original grant,[51] or (c) the holder of the licence dies.[52]

---

[46] Animals (Scientific Procedures) Act 1986, s. 5(4).

[47] Animals (Scientific Procedures) Act 1986, s. 5(a) as substituted by the Animals (Scientific Procedures) Act 1986 (Amendment) Regulations 1998, SI 1998/1974, Reg 2, Sch. 1, 3.

[48] Animals (Scientific Procedures) Act 1986, s. 5(a) as substituted by the Animals (Scientific Procedures) Act 1986 (Amendment) Regulations 1998, SI 1998/1974, Reg 2, Sch. 1, 3.

[49] Animals (Scientific Procedures) Act 1986, s. 5(6).

[50] Animals (Scientific Procedures) Act 1986, s. 5(7).

[51] Animals (Scientific Procedures) Act 1986, s. 5(7).

[52] Animals (Scientific Procedures) Act 1986, s. 5(8). The sub-section also contains provisions regarding notification of the Secretary of State of death of the holder.

Conditions Attached to the Project Licence

Unless the Secretary of State considers that an exception is justified, a project licence must contain the following conditions:[53]

1. That no cat or dog shall be used under the licence unless it has been bred at and obtained from a designated breeding establishment;[54] and

2. That no other protected animal of a specified[55] description shall be used under the licence unless it has been bred at a designated breeding establishment or obtained from a designated supplying establishment;[56] and

3. That no vertebrate of an endangered species shall be used under the licence;[57] and

4. That no protected animal taken from the wild shall be used under the licence.[58]

No exception may be made from the condition required by paragraph 3. above unless the Secretary of State is satisfied that the use of the species in question will be in conformity with the Council Regulation[59] and that the purposes of the programme of work specified in the licence are either research aimed at preservation of

---

[53] Animals (Scientific Procedures) Act 1986, s. 10(3).
[54] No exception shall be made unless the Secretary of State is satisfied that no animal suitable for the purpose of the programme specified in the licence can be obtained in accordance with the condition (Animals (Scientific Procedures) Act 1986, s. 10(3), proviso).
[55] See Animals (Scientific Procedures) Act 1986, Sch. 2.
[56] See p. 251 for the meaning of "designated supplying establishment".
[57] Animals (Scientific Procedures) Act 1986, s. 10(3)(c) as added by the Animals (Scientific Procedures) Act 1986 (Amendment) Regulations 1993, SI 1993/2102, Reg. 2(1), 2(a).
[58] Animals (Scientific Procedures) Act 1986, s. 10(3)(d) added by the Animals (Scientific Procedures) Act 1986 (Amendment) Regulations 1998, SI 1998/1974, Reg. 2, Sch., paras. 1, 4(1), 5.
[59] "Council Regulation" means Council Regulation (EEC) No. 3626/82 as amended by Commission Regulation (EEC) No. 869/88 and Commission Regulation (EEC) No. 1970/92 (Animals (Scientific Procedures) Act 1986, s. 10(3A) as added to by the Animals (Scientific Procedures) Act 1986 (Amendment) Regulations 1993, SI 1993/2102, Reg. 2(1), (3).

the species[60] in question or essential bio-medical purposes[61] where the species in question exceptionally proves to be the only one suitable for those purposes.[62]

The Secretary of State may make such conditions as he considers appropriate to ensure that:

a. where a protected animal has been subjected to a series of regulated procedures for a particular purpose, at the conclusion of the series a veterinary surgeon, or, if none is available, another suitably qualified person determines whether the animal should be kept alive;[63]

b. if that person considers that it is likely to remain in lasting pain or distress, the animal is killed by an appropriate method,[64] or by such other method as may be authorised by the personal licence of the person by whom the animal is killed;[65] and

c. that where the animal is to be kept alive, it is kept at a designated establishment[66] under the supervision of a veterinary surgeon or other suitably qualified person unless it is moved to another designated establishment or a veterinary surgeon certifies that

---

[60] "Species" means "endangered species" which in turn means a species listed in Appendix 1 of the Convention on International Trade in Endangered Species of Fauna and Flora (which is set out in Annex A to the Council Regulation) or in Annex C.1 to the Council Regulation: Animals (Scientific Procedures) Act 1986, s.10(3A) as added to by the Animals (Scientific Procedures) Act 1986 (Amendment) Regulations 1993, SI 1993/2102, Reg. 2(1), 3.

[61] "Essential bio-medical purposes" has the same meaning as in Council Directive No. 86/609/EEC: Animals (Scientific Procedures) Act 1986, s. 10(3) as added to by the Animals (Scientific Procedures) Act 1986 (Amendment) Regulations 1993, SI 1993/2102, Reg 2(1), 3. It is effectively where the species is the only one suitably available.

[62] Animals (Scientific Procedures) Act 1986, s. 10(3), proviso as added to by the Animals (Scientific Procedures) Act 1986 (Amendment) Regulations 1993, SI 1993/2102, Reg. 2(1), 2(b).

[63] Animals (Scientific Procedures) Act 1986, s. 10(3D)(a) added by the Animals (Scientific Procedures) Act 1986 (Amendment) Regulations 1998, SI 1998/1974, Reg. 2, Sch., paras. 1, 4(1), (4)–(6).

[64] I.e. appropriate under Animals (Scientific Procedures) Act 1986, Sch. 1.

[65] Animals (Scientific Procedures) Act 1986, s. 10(3D)(b) added by the Animals (Scientific Procedures) Act 1986 (Amendment) Regulations 1998, SI 1998/1974, Reg. 2, Sch., paras. 1, 4(1), (4)–(6).

[66] Animals (Scientific Procedures) Act 1986, s. 10(3D)(c) added by the Animals (Scientific Procedures) Act 1986 (Amendment) Regulations 1998, SI 1998/1974, Reg. 2, Sch., paras. 1, 4(1), (4)–(6).

it will not suffer if it ceases to be kept at a designated establishment.[67]

Where a project licence authorises the setting free of a protected animal in the course of a series of regulated procedures, the licence must include a condition requiring the prior consent of the Secretary of State to setting free the animal.[68] Such consent cannot be given unless he is satisfied that:

a. the maximum possible care has been given to safeguard the animal's well-being;

b. that the animal's state of health allows it to be set free; and

c. that the setting free of the animal poses no danger to public health or the environment.[69]

A breach of a condition in a licence does not invalidate it but is a ground for variation or revocation.[70]

Designated Establishments

Regulated procedures performed on protected animals[71] may not be undertaken other than at a place designated by the Secretary of State as a scientific procedure establishment.[72] Following submission of an application on a prescribed form and with such supporting information as the Secretary of State may reasonably require,[73] the Secretary of State may issue a certificate of designation with such conditions as are described further below. The certificate

---

[67] Animals (Scientific Procedures) Act 1986, s. 10(6D) added by the Animals (Scientific Procedures) Act 1986 (Amendment) Regulations 1998, SI 1998/1974, Reg. 2, Sch., paras. 1, 4(1), (4)–(6).

[68] Animals (Scientific Procedures) Act 1986, s. 10(3B) added by the Animals (Scientific Procedures) Act 1986 (Amendment) Regulations 1998, SI 1998/1974, Reg. 2, Sch., paras. 1, 4(1), (4)–(6).

[69] Animals (Scientific Procedures) Act 1986, s. 10(3C) added by the Animals (Scientific Procedures) Act 1986 (Amendment) Regulations 1998, SI 1998/1974, Reg. 2, Sch., paras. 1, 4(1), (4)–(6).

[70] Animals (Scientific Procedures) Act, s. 10(7).

[71] Dangerous wild animals kept in establishments designated by the Secretary of State are exempt from the Dangerous Wild Animals Act 1976 by s. 5(4) of that Act.

[72] Animals (Scientific Procedures) Act 1986, s. 6.

[73] Animals (Scientific Procedures) Act 1986, s. 6(3).

cannot be issued except to a person occupying a position of authority at the establishment in question;[74] and the applicant nominates both a person responsible for the day-to-day care of the protected animals kept there for experimental or other scientific purposes at the establishment, and a veterinary surgeon or other suitably qualified person to provide advice on their health and welfare.[75] The standard conditions under which the certificate of designation is issued can be found in Appendix II (Scientific Procedure Establishments) and Appendix III (Breeding and Supply Establishments) of the DEFRA guidance notes.[76]

If it appears to any person so specified in a certificate that the health or welfare of any protected animal gives rise to concern, he must notify the holder of the personal licence in charge of the animal, or, if there is no such person or it is not practicable to notify him, take steps to ensure that the animal is cared for and, if such is necessary, that it is killed by an appropriate[77] or approved method.[78]

A certificate of designation shall continue until revoked.[79]

Conditions Attached to the Certificate of Designation

The conditions must include a condition:

a. prohibiting the killing of protected animals, other than by an appropriate method or one approved by the Secretary of State, kept at the establishment for experiment or other scientific purposes but not subjected to a regulated procedure or required to be killed;[80]

b. to secure the availability of a person competent to kill animals in an appropriate[81] and approved method;[82]

c. for the keeping of records as respects the source and disposal of

---

74 Animals (Scientific Procedures) Act 1986, s. 6(4).
75 Animals (Scientific Procedures) Act 1986, s. 6(5).
76 See further note 35 on p. 242.
77 I.e. appropriate under Animals (Scientific Procedures) Act 1986, Sch. 1.
78 Animals (Scientific Procedures) Act 1986, s. 6(6).
79 Animals (Scientific Procedures) Act 1986, s. 6(7).
80 Animals (Scientific Procedures) Act 1986, s.10(5).
81 I.e. appropriate under Animals (Scientific Procedures) Act 1986, Sch. 1.
82 Animals (Scientific Procedures) Act 1986, s. 10(6)(a).

animals kept at the establishment;[83]

d. to ensure sufficient trained staff are provided at the establishment and that the persons who take care of protected animals at the establishment, and those who supervise such persons, have appropriate education and training;[84]

e. relating to the care and accommodation of protected animals kept or used at the establishment as the Secretary of State considers appropriate to ensure that:

   i. the environment, housing, freedom of movement, food, water and care provided for each such animal are appropriate for the animal's health and well-being;[85]

   ii. that any restrictions on the extent to which each such animal can satisfy its physiological and ethological needs are kept to the absolute minimum;[86]

   iii. that the environmental conditions in which such animals are kept or used are checked daily;

   iv. that the well-being and state of health of such animals are monitored by a suitably qualified person in order to prevent pain or avoidable suffering, distress or lasting harm; and

   v. that arrangements are made to ensure that any defect or suffering discovered is eliminated as quickly as possible;[87]

---

[83] Animals (Scientific Procedures) Act 1986, s. 10(6)(b).

[84] Animals (Scientific Procedures) Act 1986, s. 10(5A) added by the Animals (Scientific Procedures) Act 1986 (Amendment) Regulations 1998, SI 1998/1974, Reg. 2, Sch., paras. 1, 4(1), (4)–(6).

[85] When considering what conditions are appropriate to ensure these conditions are satisfied, the Secretary of State shall have regard to the guidance in Annex II to Council Directive No. 86/609/EEC: Animals (Scientific Procedures) Act 1986, s. 10(6C) added by the Animals (Scientific Procedures) Act 1986 (Amendment) Regulations 1998, SI 1998/1974, Reg. 2, Sch., paras. 1, 4(1), (4)–(6).

[86] When considering what conditions are appropriate to ensure these conditions are satisfied, the Secretary of State shall have regard to the guidance in Annex II to Council Directive No. 86/609/EEC: Animals (Scientific Procedures) Act 1986, s. 10(6C) added by the Animals (Scientific Procedures) Act 1986 (Amendment) Regulations 1998, SI 1998/1974, Reg. 2, Sch., paras. 1, 4(1), (4)–(6).

[87] Animals (Scientific Procedures) Act 1986, s. 10(6B) added by the Animals (Scientific Procedures) Act 1986 (Amendment) Regulations 1998, SI 1998/1974, Reg. 2, Sch., paras. 1, 4(1), (4)–(6).

f. that where the animal is to be kept alive, following a series of
    regulated procedures, it is kept at a designated establishment[88]
    under the supervision of a veterinary surgeon or other suitably
    qualified person unless it is moved to another designated
    establishment or a veterinary surgeon certifies that it will not
    suffer if it ceases to be kept at a designated establishment.[89]

Where the certificate permits dogs, cats or primates to be kept at the
establishment in question, the certificate must include conditions
requiring the holder of the certificate to ensure that:

a. particulars of the identity and origin of each dog, cat or primate
    kept at the establishment are entered in the records referred to
    in c. above;

b. before it is weaned, every dog, cat or primate in the establishment
    not falling within c. below is provided with an individual
    identification mark in the least painful manner possible;

c. that where a dog, cat or primate is transferred from one
    establishment to another before it is weaned and it is not
    practicable to mark it beforehand, the records kept by the
    establishment receiving the animal identify that animal's mother
    until the animal is provided with an individual identification
    mark; and

d. that any unmarked dog, cat or primate which is taken into the
    establishment after being weaned is provided as soon as possible
    thereafter with an individual identification mark.[90]

A breach of a condition in a licence does not invalidate it but is a
ground for variation or revocation.[91]

---

[88] Animals (Scientific Procedures) Act 1986, s. 10(3D)(c) added by the Animals
      (Scientific Procedures) Act 1986 (Amendment) Regulations 1998, SI 1998/1974,
      Reg. 2, Sch., paras. 1, 4(1), (4)–(6).
[89] Animals (Scientific Procedures) Act 1986, s. 10(6D) added by the Animals
      (Scientific Procedures) Act 1986 (Amendment) Regulations 1998, SI 1998/1974,
      Reg. 2, Sch., paras. 1, 4(1), (4)–(6).
[90] Animals (Scientific Procedures) Act 1986, s. 10(5A) added by the Animals
      (Scientific Procedures) Act 1986 (Amendment) Regulations 1998, SI 1998/1974,
      Reg. 2, Sch., paras. 1, 4(1), (4)–(6).
[91] Animals (Scientific Procedures) Act 1986, s. 10(7).

Breeding and Supplying Establishments

A person must not at any place breed for use in regulated procedures (whether there or elsewhere) protected animals of a specified description[92] unless that place is designated by a certificate issued by the Secretary of State as a breeding establishment.[93] A person must not keep at any establishment any such protected animals which have not been bred there but are to be supplied for use elsewhere in regulated procedures, unless that place is designated by the Secretary of State as a supplying establishment.[94]

Following submission of an application on a prescribed form and with such supporting information as the Secretary of State may reasonably require,[95] the Secretary of State may issue a certificate of designation with such conditions as are described further below.

The certificate cannot be issued unless the applicant nominates both a person responsible for the day-to-day care of the animals kept there for breeding at the establishment, or, as the case may be, kept for the purpose of being supplied for use in regulated procedures, and a veterinary surgeon or other suitably qualified person to provide advice on their health and welfare.[96]

If it appears to any person so specified in a certificate that the health or welfare of any protected animal gives rise to concern, he must notify the holder of the personal licence in charge of the animal, or, if there is no such person or it is not practicable to notify him, take steps to ensure that the animal is cared for and, if such is necessary, that it is killed by an appropriate[97] or approved method.[98]

A certificate of designation shall continue until revoked.[99]

---

92 I.e. those specified in Animals (Scientific Procedures) Act 1986, Sch. 2.
93 Animals (Scientific Procedures) Act 1986, s. 7(1).
94 Animals (Scientific Procedures) Act 1986, s. 7(2)
95 Animals (Scientific Procedures) Act 1986, s. 7(3).
96 Animals (Scientific Procedures) Act 1986, s. 7(5).
97 I.e. appropriate under Animals (Scientific Procedures) Act 1986, Sch. 1.
98 Animals (Scientific Procedures) Act 1986, s. 7(6).
99 Animals (Scientific Procedures) Act 1986, s. 7(8).

Re-use of Protected Animals

Where a protected animal has been subjected to a series of regulated procedures for a particular purpose and any of those procedures has caused severe pain or distress to the animal then that animal cannot be used for any other further regulated procedures which will entail severe pain or distress,[100] except with the consent[101] of the Secretary of State.[102]

Where a protected animal has been subjected to a series of regulated procedures for a particular purpose and has been given a general anaesthetic for any of those procedures and been allowed to recover consciousness , that animal cannot be used for any other further regulated procedures which will entail severe pain or distress, except when the Secretary has given his consent[103] and:

a. the procedure, or each procedure, for which the anaesthetic was given consisted only of surgical preparation essential for a subsequent procedure; or

b. the anaesthetic was administered solely to immobilise the animal; or

c. the animal will be under general anaesthetic throughout the further procedures and will not be allowed to recover consciousness.[104]

---

[100] Animals (Scientific Procedures) Act 1986, s. 14(1) substituted by the Animals (Scientific Procedures) Act 1986 (Amendment) Regulations 1998, SI 1998/1974, Reg. 2, Sch., paras. 1, 5.

[101] Such consent may relate to a specified animal or to animals used in specified procedures or specified circumstances: Animals (Scientific Procedures) Act 1986, s. 14(4) substituted by the Animals (Scientific Procedures) Act 1986 (Amendment) Regulations 1998, SI 1998/1974, Reg. 2, Sch., paras. 1, 5.

[102] Animals (Scientific Procedures) Act 1986, s. 14(3) substituted by the Animals (Scientific Procedures) Act 1986 (Amendment) Regulations 1998, SI 1998/1974, Reg. 2, Sch. paras. 1, 5.

[103] Such consent may relate to a specified animal or to animals used in specified procedures or specified circumstances: Animals (Scientific Procedures) Act 1986, s. 14(4) substituted by the Animals (Scientific Procedures) Act 1986 (Amendment) Regulations 1998, SI 1998/1974, Reg. 2, Sch., paras. 1, 5.

[104] Animals (Scientific Procedures) Act 1986, s. 14(2) substituted by the Animals (Scientific Procedures) Act 1986 (Amendment) Regulations 1998, SI 1998/1974, Reg. 2, Sch., paras. 1, 5.

A person who contravenes these provisions is liable to a fine, imprisonment or both.[105]

Killing Animals at the Conclusion of Regulated Procedures

A protected animal which has been subjected to a series of regulated procedures for a particular purpose and at the conclusion of the series is suffering or likely to suffer adverse effects must be killed by an appropriate method[106] by the person who applied those procedures or the last of them[107] unless an alternative method is authorised by the conditions of the personal licence of the person by whom it is killed.[108]

A person who contravenes these provisions is liable to a fine, imprisonment or both.[109]

Prohibition of Public Displays

No person may carry out any regulated procedure as an exhibition to the general public or carry out such procedure which is shown live on television for general reception.[110] Similarly, no person may publish a notice or advertisement announcing the carrying out of any regulated procedure in the foregoing manner.[111]

A person who contravenes these provisions is liable to a fine, imprisonment or both.[112]

Inspection, Search and Prosecutions

Inspectors, whom he thinks have the requisite medical and veterinary qualifications, may be appointed by the Secretary of State.[113] An

---

[105] Animals (Scientific Procedures) Act 1986, s. 22(3).
[106] I.e. appropriate under Animals (Scientific Procedures) Act 1986, Sch. 1.
[107] Animals (Scientific Procedures) Act 1986, s. 15(1).
[108] Animals (Scientific Procedures) Act 1986, s. 15(2).
[109] Animals (Scientific Procedures) Act 1986, s. 22(3).
[110] Animals (Scientific Procedures) Act 1986, s. 16(1).
[111] Animals (Scientific Procedures) Act 1986, s. 16(2).
[112] Animals (Scientific Procedures) Act 1986, s. 22(3).
[113] Animals (Scientific Procedures) Act 1986, s. 18(1).

inspector has a number of duties[114] and may require a protected animal to be killed immediately by an appropriate method if he considers that it is undergoing excessive suffering.[115]

If a justice of the peace is satisfied by information on oath that there are reasonable grounds for believing that an offence under the Animals (Scientific Procedures) Act 1986 has been or is being committed at any place, he may issue a warrant authorising a constable (if necessary accompanied by an inspector)[116] to enter that place, if need be by such force as is reasonably necessary, to search it and to require any person found there to give him their name and address.[117]

An offence is committed if the person intentionally obstructs[118] a constable or inspector in the exercise of his warrant, or refuses to give his name and address.[119]

Prosecution for an offence committed under the Animals (Scientific Procedures) Act 1986[120] or under section 1 of the Protection of

---

[114] The duties are:
  (1) to advise the Secretary of State on applications for personal and project licences, on request for their variation or revocation and on their periodical review;
  (2) to advise the Secretary of State on applications for certificates of designation and on requests for their variation and revocation;
  (3) to visit places where regulated procedures are carried out for the purpose of determining whether those procedures are authorised by the requisite licences and whether the conditions of those licences are being complied with;
  (4) to visit designated establishments for the purpose of determining whether the conditions of the certificates in respect of those establishments are being complied with;
  (5) to report to the Secretary of State any case in which any provision of the Animals (Scientific Procedures) Act 1986 or any condition of a licence or certificate under the said Act has not been or is not being complied with and to advise him on the action to be taken in any such case.
  (Animals (Scientific Procedures) Act 1986, s. 18(2).)
[115] Animals (Scientific Procedures) Act 1986, s. 18(3).
[116] Animals (Scientific Procedures) Act 1986, s. 25(2).
[117] Animals (Scientific Procedures) Act 1986, s. 25(1).
[118] Obstruction need not involve physical violence, and there is authority that anything which makes it more difficult for a person to perform his duties amounts to obstruction (*Hinchcliffe v Sheldon* [1955] 3 All ER 406).
[119] Animals (Scientific Procedures) Act 1986, s. 25(3).
[120] Summary proceedings for an offence under the Act may be taken against any person at any place at which he is for the time being: Animals (Scientific Procedures) Act 1986, s. 26(2). An information triable summarily in England and

Animals Act 1911 which is alleged to have been committed in respect of an animal at a designated establishment, may not be brought in England and Wales except by the Director of Public Prosecutions unless he gives his consent.[121]

Protection of Confidential Information

A person is guilty of an offence if, other than for the purpose of discharging his functions under the Animals (Scientific Procedures) Act 1986, he discloses any information which has been obtained by him in the exercise of those functions and which he knows or has reasonable grounds for believing to have been given in confidence.[122]

A person who contravenes these provisions is liable to a fine, imprisonment or both.[123]

The Animals Procedures Committee, Guidance, Codes of Practice and Statistics

The Secretary of State is advised by the Animal Procedures Committee (APC), which consists of a chairman and twelve other members,[124] each appointed by the Secretary of State. The function of the committee is to advise (and report[125] to) the Secretary of State on such matters concerned with the Animals (Scientific Procedures) Act 1986, and his functions under it, as the APC may

---

Wales may be so tried if it is laid at any time within three years after the commission of the offence and within six months after the date on which evidence sufficient in the opinion of the Director of Public Prosecutions to justify the proceedings comes to his knowledge (Animals (Scientific Procedures) Act 1986, s. 26(3)).

[121] Animals (Scientific Procedures) Act 1986, s. 26.

[122] Animals (Scientific Procedures) Act 1986, s. 24(1).

[123] Animals (Scientific Procedures) Act 1986, s. 24(2).

[124] The Secretary of State shall have regard to the desirability of ensuring that the interests of animal welfare are adequately represented. At least two-thirds of the committee shall consist of persons having full registration qualifications as a medical practitioner or veterinary surgeon or qualifications or experience in a biological subject approved by the Secretary of State as relevant to the work of the committee. At least one member shall be a barrister, solicitor or advocate. Not more than one half of those persons mentioned must either hold or have held in the previous six years any licence under the Animals (Scientific Procedures) Act 1986 or under the Cruelty to Animals Act 1876 (Animals (Scientific Procedures) Act 1986, s. 19(3), (4)).

[125] Animals (Scientific Procedures) Act 1986, s. 20(5).

determine or as may be referred to it by the Secretary of State.[126]

The APC studies all applications for procedures involving substantial severity on primates and any work on wild caught primates. It may also promote research relevant to it functions and may obtain advice or assistance from other persons with knowledge or experience appearing to the APC to be relevant to its functions.[127] Such functions may be performed by sub-committees.[128]

Additionally, the APC is consulted[129] before the Secretary of State publishes or alters any information to serve as guidance with respect to the manner in which he proposes to exercise his power to grant licences and certificates under the Animals (Scientific Procedures) Act 1986 and with respect to the conditions which he proposes to include in such licences and certificates.[130] As well as the guidance issued in respect of licences and certificates, the Secretary of State must publish, and consult the APC on, such codes of practice[131] as to the care of protected animals and their use for regulated procedures and may approve such codes issued by other persons.[132]

The Secretary of State must in each year publish and lay before Parliament such information as he considers appropriate with respect to the use of protected animals in the previous year for experimental or other scientific purposes.[133]

---

[126] Animals (Scientific Procedures) Act 1986, s. 20(1).
[127] Animals (Scientific Procedures) Act 1986, s. 20(4).
[128] Animals (Scientific Procedures) Act 1986, s. 20(3).
[129] Animals (Scientific Procedures) Act 1986, s. 21(3).
[130] Animals (Scientific Procedures) Act 1986, s. 21(1).
[131] A revised code of practice entitled "The Humane Killing of Animals under Schedule 1 to the Animals (Scientific Procedures) Act 1986" was issued on 13th January 1997.
[132] Animals (Scientific Procedures) Act 1986, s. 21(2).
[133] Animals (Scientific Procedures) Act 1986, s. 21(7).

APPENDICES

Appendix A

CALCULATION TABLES FOR THE TRANSPORTATION OF ANIMALS[1]

The Welfare of Animals (Transport) Order 1997, SI 1997/1480

TABLE A
Vehicle Standards and Journey Times
Farmed Livestock and Horses (other than Registered Horses)

Journeys on "basic" vehicles[2]	
All journeys	8 hours followed by 24 hours' rest
Journeys on "higher standard" vehicles[3]	
Unweaned calves, lambs, kids and foals which are still on a milk diet and unweaned piglets	A maximum of 9 hours, a mid-journey rest of at least one hour, then a further maximum of 9 hours
Other cattle, sheep and goats	A maximum of 14 hours, a mid-journey rest of at least one hour, then a further maximum of 14 hours
Pigs	A maximum of 24 hours with continuous access to liquid
Other horses (excluding registered horses)	A maximum of 24 hours with liquid and, if necessary, food every 8 hours

---

[1]   These tables and the footnotes below have been taken from the DEFRA guidance on the Welfare of Animals (Transport) Order 1997, SI 1997/1480 which may be located at the Ministry's web-site: www.defra.gov.uk.

[2]   "Basic vehicles" means all vehicles used to transport animals must comply with the "basic" standards set out in Schedules 1 and 2 of the Order (and the additional requirements in Schedules 3 to 5 as appropriate to the species). For farm livestock and horses, vehicles which meet only this minimum standard must be regarded as basic standard vehicles.

[3]   "Higher standard vehicles" means vehicles used to transport farm livestock and horses (except registered horses) for journeys longer than 8 hours must comply with the additional requirements set out in paragraph 2 of Schedule 7 to the Order.

TABLE B
Journeys Involving Travel by Sea or Air
Farmed Livestock and Horses (other than Registered Horses)

"Calculation" of maximum journey times
For all journeys by **road** the journey time is the time between the loading of the first animal and the unloading of the last animal at the final destination.
Where journeys include the transport of a road vehicle on a ferry, during which time the animals are not unloaded, the time spent on board the vessel counts towards the total journey time. If the maximum permitted journey time is reached during the sea journey, the animals must be unloaded, rested, fed and watered for 12 hours at or near the port of unloading before the journey may continue. This rest may only be taken on the lorry if facilities are available to feed and water the animals and the animals have sufficient space to lie down to rest simultaneously.
Time spent by animals in pens on board a vessel fitted for the transport of unloaded livestock does *not* count towards the total journey time.
In principle, time spent on an aircraft does not count towards the total journey time when animals are carried in accordance with the standards set by the International Air Transport Association and adequate provision can be made to feed and water the animals in flight.

LEGISLATION ON INTRA-COMMUNITY TRADE

Animals and Animals Products (Import and Export) (England and Wales) Regulations 2000,[1] Schedule 3, Part 1
(Applicable to Regulations 4, 5(1), 6, 7(4), 8(4), 10, 12(7)(a), 29(2)(b) and 34)

BOVINE ANIMALS AND SWINE

1. Council Directive 64/432/EEC on health problems affecting intra-Community trade in bovine animals and swine as replaced by the Annex to Council Directive 97/12/EC (OJ No. L109, 25.4.97, p. 1).

Council Directive 97/12/EC and Council Directive 64/432/EEC have been amended by:

Commission Decision 90/208/EEC (OJ No. L108, 28.4.90, p. 102);
Commission Decision 90/425/EC (OJ No. L224, 18.8.90, p. 29);
Commission Decision 91/52/EEC (OJ No. L34, 6.2.91, p. 12);
Commission Decision 95/108/EC (OJ No. L79, 7.4.95, p. 29);
Commission Decision 95/109/EC (OJ No. L79, 7.4.95, p. 32);
Council Directive 98/46/EC (OJ No. L198, 15.7.98, p. 22);
Council Directive 98/99/EC (OJ No. L358, 31.12.98, p. 107);
Commission Decision 98/362/EC (OJ No. L163, 6.6.98, p. 48);
Commission Decision 98/548/EC (OJ No. L263, 26.9.98, p. 35);
Commission Decision 98/621/EC (OJ No. L296, 5.11.98, p. 15)
Commission Decision 99/384/EC (OJ No. L146, 11.6.99, p. 52);
Commission Decision 99/399/EC (OJ No. L150, 17.6.99, p. 32);
Commission Decision 99/579/EC (OJ No. L219, 19.8.99, p. 53);
and as read with the European international instruments.

Relevant provisions: Articles 3.2, 4.1, 5.1, 5.2, 5.5, 6.1, 6.2, 6.3, 7 (in the case of imports) and 12.3.

(a) The official health certificate accompanying all cattle imported into England or Wales from Spain must contain the statement: "Live cattle in accordance with Commission Decision 90/208/EEC on contagious bovine pleuro-pneumonia".

(b) The official health certificate accompanying all cattle imported into England or Wales from Portugal must contain the statement "Live

---

[1] The Animals and Animals Products (Import and Export) (England and Wales) Regulations 2000, SI 2000/1673, as amended by SI 2000/2524 and SI 2000/2900.

cattle in accordance with Commission Decision 91/52/EEC on contagious bovine pleuro-pneumonia".

(c) The official health certificate accompanying all swine imported into England or Wales from any other member State except Austria, Denmark, Finland and Sweden and those regions of France and Germany specified in Commission Decisions amending Decision 93/24/EEC must contain the statement: "Pigs in accordance with Commission Decision 93/24/EEC of 11 December 1992 concerning Aujeszky's disease. In the case of pigs for breeding, the test used was the whole virus ELISA/ELISA for g1 antibodies (delete where applicable)".

(d) In the event of the prohibition on the export of cattle from England or Wales imposed by Commission Decision 98/256/EC on emergency measures to protect against Bovine Spongiform Encephalopathy (OJ No. L113, 15.4.98, p. 32) being revoked so as to allow the despatch of cattle from Great Britain to another member State or a third country, the official health certificate accompanying all cattle exported from England or Wales to Denmark or Finland must contain the statement: "Bovines in accordance with Commission Decision 93/42/EEC of 21 December 1992 concerning IBR for bovines being sent to member States or Regions listed in the Annex to the said Decision".

(e) In the event of the prohibition on the export of cattle from Great Britain imposed by Commission Decision 98/256/EC on emergency measures to protect against Bovine Spongiform Encephalopathy (OJ No. L113. 15.4.98, p. 32) being revoked so as to allow the despatch of cattle from England or Wales to another member State or a third country, the official health certificate accompanying all cattle exported from England or Wales to Austria and Sweden must contain the statement "Bovines in accordance with Commission Decision 95/109/EC".

(f) In accordance with Commission Decision 95/108/EC, the importation into England or Wales from the Italian region of Sardinia of animals of the suidae family is prohibited.

BOVINE SEMEN

2. Council Directive 88/407/EEC laying down the animal health requirements applicable to intra-Community trade in, and imports of, semen of domestic animals of the bovine species (OJ No. L194, 22.7.88, p. 10), as amended by:

Council Directive 90/120/EEC (OJ No. L71, 17.3.90, p. 37);
Council Directive 90/425/EEC (OJ No. L224, 18.8.90, p. 29);
Council Directive 93/60/EEC (OJ No. L186, 28.7.93, p. 28);
and as read with the European international instruments.

Relevant provisions: Articles 3, 4.1, and 6.

BOVINE EMBRYOS

3. Council Directive 89/556/EEC on animal health conditions concerning intra-Community trade in and importation from third countries of embryos of domestic animals of the bovine species (OJ No. L302, 19.10.89, p.1), as amended by, and as read with:

> Council Directive 90/425/EEC (OJ No. L224, 18.8.90, p. 29);
> Commission Decision 92/290/EEC (OJ No. L152, 4.6.92, p. 37);
> Council Directive 93/52/EEC (OJ No. L175, 19.7.93, p. 21);
> Commission Decision 94/113/EC (OJ No. L53, 24.2.94, p. 23);
> and as read with the European international instruments.

Relevant provisions: Articles 3 and 6.

EQUIDAE

4. Council Directive 90/426/EEC on health conditions governing the movement of equidae and their import from third countries (OJ No. L224, 18.8.90, p. 42), as amended by, and as read with:

> Council Directive 90/425/EEC (OJ No. L224, 18.8.90, p. 29);
> Council Directive 91/496/EEC (OJ No. L268, 24.9.91, p. 56);
> Council Directive 92/36/EEC (OJ No. L157, 10.6.92, p. 28);
> Commission Decision 92/130/EEC (OJ No. L47, 22.2.92, p. 26);
> and as read with the European international instruments.

Relevant provisions: Articles 4, 5, 7.1, and 8.

(a) The requirements of Articles 4.1, 4.2 and 8 shall not apply in respect of the export to or the import from the Republic of Ireland of any equidae, or the export to or the import from France of registered horses accompanied by an identification document provided for in Council Directive 90/427/EEC (OJ No. L224, 18.8.90, p. 55).

(b) The derogation permitted under Article 7.2 shall not apply in relation to equidae brought into England or Wales.

PORCINE SEMEN

5. Council Directive 90/429/EEC laying down the animal health requirements applicable to intra-Community trade in and imports of semen of domestic animals of the porcine species (OJ No. L224, 18.8.90, p. 62) and Commission Decision 99/608/EC (OJ No. L242, 14.9.99, p. 20);

and as read with the European international instruments.

Relevant provisions: Articles 3, 4.1, 4.2 and 6.1.

The official health certification accompanying all porcine semen imported into England or Wales from any other member State must state that the semen was collected from boars "on a collection centre which only contains animals that have not been vaccinated against Aujeszky's disease and which have reacted negatively to the serum neutralisation test or to the ELISA test for Aujeszky's disease, in accordance with the provisions of Council Directive 90/429/EEC" and paragraph 13(b)(ii) of the model health certificate provided in Annex D of Council Directive 90/429/EEC must be deleted in all cases.

POULTRY AND HATCHING EGGS

6. Council Directive 90/539/EEC on animal health conditions governing intra-Community trade in, and imports from, third countries of poultry and hatching eggs (OJ No. L303, 30.10.90, p. 6), as amended by, and as read with:

> Council Directive 90/425/EEC (OJ No. L224, 18.8.90, p. 29);
> Council Directive 91/494/EEC (OJ No. L268, 24.9.91, p. 35);
> Council Directive 91/496/EEC (OJ No. L268, 24.9.91, p. 56);
> Council Directive 92/65/EEC (OJ No. L268, 14.9.92, p. 54);
> Commission Decision 92/340/EEC (OJ No. L188, 8.7.92, p. 34);
> Commission Decision 92/369/EEC (OJ No. L195, 14.7.92, p. 25);
> Council Directive 93/120/EEC (OJ No. L340, 31.12.93, p. 35);
> Commission Decision 95/160/EC (OJ No. L105, 9.5.95, p. 40);
> Commission Decision 95/161/EC (OJ No. L105, 9.5.95, p. 44);
> Council Directive 95/410/EC (OJ No. L243, 11.10.95, p. 25);
> Commission Decision 97/278/EC (OJ No. L110, 26.4.97, p. 77);
> Council Directive 99/90/EC (OJ No. L300, 23.11.1999, p. 19);
> and as read with the European international instruments.

Relevant provisions: Articles 6 to 11, 12.1, and 15 to 17.

(a) The official health certification accompanying breeding poultry exported from England or Wales to Finland or Sweden must contain the statement that they have been tested for salmonella with negative results in accordance with Commission Decision 95/160/EC of 21 April 1995.

(b) The official health certification accompanying day-old chicks exported from England or Wales to Finland or Sweden must contain the statement that they come from flocks which have been tested for salmonella with negative results in accordance with Commission Decision 95/160/EC of 21 April 1995.

(c) The official health certification accompanying laying hens exported from England or Wales to Finland or Sweden must contain the statement that they have been tested for salmonella with negative results in accordance with Commission Decision 95/161/EC of 21 April 1995.

(d) The official health certification accompanying poultry for slaughter exported from England or Wales to Finland or Sweden must contain the statement that they have undergone microbiological testing with negative results in accordance with Council Decision 95/410/EC of 22 June 1995.

ANIMAL WASTE

7. Council Directive 90/667/EEC laying down the veterinary rules for the disposal and processing of animal waste, for its placing on the market and for the prevention of pathogens in feeding stuffs of animal or fish origin (OJ No. L363, 27.12.90, p. 51), as amended by, and as read with:

> Council Directive 92/118/EEC (OJ No. L62, 15.3.93, p. 49);
> Commission Decision 92/562/EEC (OJ No. L359, 9.12.92, p. 23);
> Commission Decision 97/735/EC ((OJ No. L294, 28.10.97, p. 7);
> Commission Decision 99/534/EC (OJ No. L204, 4.8.99, p. 37);
> and as read with the European international instruments.

Relevant provisions: Articles 3, 5 and 15

FISH
Farmed fish

8. – (1) Council Directive 91/67/EEC concerning the animal health conditions governing the placing on the market of aquaculture animals and products (OJ No. L46, 19.2.91, p. 1), as amended by, and as read with:

> Commission Decision 92/528/EEC (OJ No. L332, 18.11.92, p. 25);
> Commission Decision 92/538/EEC (OJ No. L347, 28.11.92, p. 67) (as amended by Commission Decision 94/817/EC (OJ No. L337, 24.12.94, p. 88));
> Commission Decision 93/22/EEC (OJ No. L16, 25.1.93, p. 8);
> Commission Decision 93/39/EEC (OJ No. L16, 25.1.93, p. 46);
> Commission Decision 93/40/EEC (OJ No. L16, 25.1.93, p. 47);
> Commission Decision 93/44/EEC (OJ No. L16, 25.1.93, p. 53) (as amended by Commission Decision 94/865/EC (OJ No. L352, 31.12.94, p. 75));
> Council Directive 93/54/EEC (OJ No. L175, 19.7.93, p. 34) insofar as it applies to exports;
> Commission Decision 93/55/EEC (OJ No, L14, 22.1.93, p. 24) (as amended by Commission Decision 93/169/EC (OJ No. L71, 24.3.93, p. 16));
> Commission Decision 93/56/EEC (OJ No. L14, 22.1.93, p. 25);
> Commission Decision 93/57/EEC (OJ No. L14, 22.1.93, p. 26);
> Commission Decision 93/58/EEC (OJ No. L14, 22.1.93, p. 27);
> Commission Decision 93/73/EEC (OJ No. L27, 4.2.93, p. 34) (as amended by Commission Decision 97/804/EC (OJ No. L329,

29.11.97, p. 70));

Commission Decision 93/74/EEC (OJ No. L27, 4.2.93, p. 35) (as amended by Commission Decision 94/450/EC (OJ No. L187, 22.7.94, p. 8) and Commission Decision 96/218/EC (OJ No. L72, 21.3.96, p. 39) and Commission Decision 99/489/EC (OJ No. L190, 23.7.99, p. 41));

Commission Decision 94/862/EC (OJ No. L352, 31.12.94, p. 72);

Commission Decision 94/863/EC (OJ No. L352, 31.12.94, p. 73);

Commission Decision 94/864/EC (OJ No. L352, 31.12.94, p. 74);

Commission Decision 95/336/EC (OJ No. L195, 18.8.95, p. 26);

Commission Decision 95/352/EC (OJ No. L204, 30.8.95, p. 13);

Commission Decision 95/124/EC (OJ No. L84, 14.4.95, p. 6) (as amended by Commission Decision 96/265/EC (OJ No. L91, 12.4.96, p. 72), Commission Decision 97/228/EC (OJ No. L91, 5.4.97, p. 35), Commission Decision 99/521/EC (OJ No. L199, 30.7.99, p. 73), Commission Decision 2000/173/EC (OJ No. L55, 29.2.2000, p. 74) and Commission Decision 2000/312/EC (OJ No. L104, 29.4.2000, p. 80));

Commission Decision 95/125/EC (OJ No. L84, 14.4.95, p. 8) (as amended by Commission Decision 95/481/EC (OJ No. L275, 18.11.95, p. 26) and Commission Decision 99/550/EC (OJ No. L209, 7.8.99, p. 39));

Commission Decision 95/470/EC (OJ No. L269, 11.11.95, p. 28);

Commission Decision 95/473/EC (OJ No. L269, 11.11.95, p. 31) (as amended by Commission Decision 96/289/EC (OJ No. L109, 3.5.96, p. 23), Commission Decision 97/227/EC (OJ No. L91, 5.4.97, p. 33), Commission Decision 99/556/EC (OJ No. L211, 11.8.99, p. 50) and Commission Decision 2000/172/EC OJ No. L55, 29.2.2000, p. 71));

Commission Decision 95/479/EC (OJ No. L275, 18.1.95, p. 23);

Commission Decision 96/94/EC (OJ No. L21, 27.1.96, p. 73);

Commission Decision 96/221/EC (OJ No. L74, 22.3.96, p. 42);

Commission Decision 96/233/EC (OJ No. L77, 27.3.96, p. 33) (as amended by Commission Decision 97/234/EC (OJ No. L94, 9.4.97, p. 15) and Commission Decision 99/512/EC (OJ No. L195, 28.7.99, p. 37));

Commission Decision 96/490/EC (OJ No. L202, 10.8.96, p. 21);

Council Directive 97/79/EC (OJ No. L24, 30.1.98, p. 31);

Commission Decision 97/185/EC (OJ No. L77, 19.3.97, p. 31);

Commission Decision 98/357/EEC (OJ No. L162, 5.6.98, p. 42);

Commission Decision 98/359/EC (OJ No. L163, 6.6.98, p. 43);

Commission Decision 98/361/EC (OJ No. L163, 6.6.98, p. 46) (as amended by Commission Decision 99/513/EC (OJ No. L195, 28.7.99, p. 39), Commission Decision 2000/187/EC (OJ No. L59, 4.3.2000, p. 14) and Commission Decision 2000/311/EC (OJ No. L104, 29.4.2000, p. 77));

Commission Decision 98/395/EC (OJ No. L176, 20.6.98, p. 30);
Council Directive 98/45/EC (OJ No. L189, 3.7.98, p. 12);
Commission Decision 99/567/EC (OJ No. 216, 14.8.99, p. 13);
Commission Decision 2000/171/EC (OJ No. L55, 29.2.2000, p. 70);
Commission Decision 2000/173/EC (OJ No. L55, 29.2.2000, p. 74);
Commission Decision 2000/174/EC (OJ No. L55, 29.2.2000, p. 77);
Commission Decision 2000/188/EC (OJ No. L59, 4.3.2000, p. 17);
Commission Decision 2000/310/EC (OJ No. L104, 29.4.2000, p. 76);
Commission Decision 2000/312/EC (OJ No. L104, 29.4.2000, p. 80);
and as read with the European international instruments.

Relevant provisions: The following provisions in so far as they apply to
live fish, eggs and gametes – Articles 3, 4, 7 to 11, and 14 and 16.

(a) Aquaculture animals and products from Iceland and Norway to which
Directive 91/67/EEC applies must be imported at a border inspection
post.

(b) In accordance with the derogation in paragraph 8 of Annex 1 of the
Decision on the conclusion of the Agreement on the European
Economic Area between the European Communities, their Member
States and the Republic of Austria, the Republic of Finland, the
Republic of Iceland, the Principality of Liechtenstein, the Kingdom
of Norway, the Kingdom of Sweden and the Swiss Confederation, the
provisions of Directive 91/67/EEC shall not apply to imports of live
fish and crustaceans as well as eggs and gametes of fish and crustaceans
for farming or restocking which come from Iceland or Norway. Great
Britain shall retain existing national measures in respect of imports of
these animals and animal products.

Fish other than farmed fish

8. – (2) Council Directive 91/493/EEC laying down the health conditions for
the production and placing on the market of fishery products (OJ No.
L268, 24.9.91, p. 15), as amended by, and as read with:

Council Directive 95/71/EC (OJ No. L332, 30.12.95, p. 40);
Council Directive 92/48/EEC (OJ No. L187, 7.7.92, p. 41), laying
down the minimum hygiene rules applicable to fishery products
caught on board certain vessels in accordance with Article 3(1)(a)(I)
of Council Directive 91/493/EEC.

Relevant provisions: Article 4 of Council Directive 91/493/EEC.

Live bivalve molluses

8. – (3) Council Directive 91/492/EEC laying down the health conditions for
the production and placing on the market of live shellfish (OJ No. L268,
24.9.91, p. 1), as amended by, and as read with, Council Directive 97/61/
EC (OJ No. L295, 29.10.97, p. 35).

Relevant provisions: Articles 3(1)(a)-(i), 3(2), 4, 7, 8, and 9.

OVINE AND CAPRINE ANIMALS

9. Council Directive 91/68/EEC on animal health conditions governing intra-Community trade in ovine and caprine animals (OJ No. L46, 19.2.91, p. 19) as read with:

> Council Directive 90/425/EC (OJ No. L224, 18.8.90, p. 29);
> Council Directive 92/102/EEC (OJ No. L355, 5.12.92, p. 32);
> Commission Decision 93/52/EEC (OJ No. L13, 21.1.93, p. 14);
> Commission Decision 94/164/EEC (OJ No. L74, 17.3.94, p. 42);
> Commission Decision 94/877/EC (OJ No. L352, 31.12.94, p. 102);
> Commission Decision 94/953/EEC (OJ No. L371, 31.12.94, p. 14);
> Commission Decision 94/965/EEC (OJ No. L371, 31.12.94, p. 31);
> Commission Decision 94/972/EEC (OJ No. L371, 31.12.94, p. 48);
> Commission Decision 97/315/EC (OJ No. L137, 28.5.97, p. 20);
> and as read with the European international instruments.

Relevant provisions: Articles 4, 5, 6 and 9.

(a) Only uncastrated rams for breeding with that have been tested for contagious epididimytis (Brucella ovis) in accordance with Article 6.c or Council Directive 91/68/EEC may be imported into England or Wales.

(b) The official health certification accompanying all sheep and goats for fattening and breeding imported into England or Wales must confirm that the animals are eligible for entry into an officially brucellosis free ovine or caprine holding in accordance with Annex A, Chapter 1, point D of Council Directive 91/68/EEC.

OTHER ANIMALS, SEMEN, OVA AND EMBRYOS

10. Council Directive 92/65/EEC laying down animal health requirements governing trade in and imports into the Community of animals, semen, ova and embryos not subject to animal health requirements laid down in specific Community rules referred to in Council Directive 90/425/EEC (OJ No. L268, 14.9.92, p. 54), as amended by, and as read with:

> Commission Decision 95/176/EC (OJ No. L117, 24.5.95, p. 23);
> Commission Decision 95/294/EC (OJ No. L182, 2.8.95, p. 27);
> Commission Decision 95/307/EC (OJ No. L185, 4.8.95, p. 58);
> Commission Decision 95/388/EC (OJ No. L234, 3.10.95, p. 30);
> Commission Decision 95/483/EC (OJ No. L275, 18.11.95, p. 30);
> and as read with the European international instruments and Joint Committee Decision 69/96 of 17 July 1998 amending Annex 1 (Veterinary and Phytosanitary matters) to the Agreement on the European Economic Area (OJ No. L158, 24.6.99).

Relevant provisions: Articles 3 to 9, 10.1, 10.2 (only insofar as it concerns exports), and 11 to 13.

(a) By way of derogation from the requirements of Article 5.1, the Minister (or in Wales the National Assembly for Wales) may authorise in writing the purchase by a body, institute or centre approved under Regulation 9 of these Regulations of apes belonging to an individual.

(b) The importation into England or Wales of lagomorphs which cannot be shown to have been born on the holding of origin and kept in captivity since birth is prohibited except in accordance with the provisions of the Rabies (Importation of Dogs, Cats and Other Mammals) Order 1974. Lagomorphs born on the holding of origin and kept in captivity since birth must be accompanied on importation by an official health certificate confirming that status and that the holding of origin has been free from rabies for at least one month.

(c) Animals (other than carnivores, primates, bats and lagomorphs) born on the holding of origin and kept in captivity since birth must be accompanied on importation by a certificate completed by the exporter confirming that status and that the animals do not show any obvious signs of disease at the time of export, and that the premises of origin are not subject to any animal health restrictions.

PATHOGENS

11. Council Directive 92/118/EEC laying down animal and public health requirements governing trade in and imports into the Community of products not subject to the said requirements laid down in specific Community rules referred to in Annex A(I) to Directive 89/662/EEC and, as regards pathogens, to Directive 90/425/EEC (OJ No. L62, 15.3.93, p. 49).

Relevant provisions: Articles 6 and 7.1.

PURE-BRED ANIMALS OF THE BOVINE SPECIES

12. Council Directive 77/504/EEC on pure-bred breeding animals of the bovine species (OJ No. L206, 12.8.1977, p. 8), as amended by, and as read with:

The Act concerning the conditions of accession of the Hellenic Republic to the European Communities (OJ No. L291, 19.11.79, p. 17);
Council Directive 79/268/EEC (OJ No. L62, 13.3.79, p. 5);
Council Regulation 3768/85/EEC (OJ No. L362, 31.12.85, p. 8);
Council Directive 85/586/EEC (OJ No. L372, 31.12.85, p. 44);
Commission Decision 86/404/EEC (OJ No. L233, 20.8.86, p. 19);
Commission Decision 88/124/EEC (OJ No. L62, 8.3.88, p. 32);

Council Directive 91/174/EEC (OJ No. L85, 5.4.91, p. 37);
Council Directive 94/28/EC (OJ No. L178, 12.7.94, p. 66);
Commission Decision 96/80/EC (OJ No. L19, 25.1.96, p. 50);
Commission Decision 96/510/EC (OJ No. L210, 20.8.96, p. 53);
and as read with the European international instruments.

Relevant provisions: Articles 5 and 7.

BREEDING ANIMALS OF THE PORCINE SPECIES

13. Council Directive 88/661/EEC on the zootechnical standards applicable to breeding animals of the porcine species (OJ No. L382, 31.12.1988, p. 36), as amended by, and as read with:

Commission Decision 89/503/EEC (OJ No. L247, 23.8.89, p. 22);
Commission Decision 89/506/EEC (OJ No. L247, 23.8.89, p. 34);
Council Directive 94/28/EC (OJ No. L178, 12.7.94, p. 66);
Commission Decision 96/510/EC (OJ No. L210, 20.08.96, p. 53);
and as read with the European international instruments.

Relevant provisions: Articles 2.2, 5, 7.2 and 9.

PURE-BRED BREEDING SHEEP AND GOATS

14. Council Directive 89/361/EEC concerning pure-bred breeding sheep and goats (OJ No. L153, 6.6.1989, p. 30), as amended by, and as read with:

Commission Decision 90/258/EEC (OJ No. L145, 8.6.90, p. 39);
Council Directive 94/28/EC (OJ No. L178, 12.7.94, p. 66);
Commission Decision 96/510/EC (OJ No. L210, 20.08.96, p. 53);
and as read with the European international instruments.

Relevant provisions: Articles 3.2 and 6.

EQUIDAE

15. Council Directive 90/427/EEC on the zootechnical and genealogical conditions governing intra-Community trade in equidae (OJ No. L224, 18.8.90, p. 55), as amended by, and as read with:

Commission Decision 92/353/EEC (OJ No. L192, 11.7.92, p. 63);
Commission Decision 92/354/EEC (OJ No. L192, 11.7.92, p. 66);
Commission Decision 93/623/EEC (OJ No. L298, 3.12.93, p. 45);
Council Directive 94/28/EC (OJ No. L178, 12.7.94, p. 66);
Commission Decision 96/78/EC (OJ No. L19, 25.1.96, p. 39);
Commission Decision 96/510/EC (OJ No. L210, 20.08.1996, p. 53);
and as read with the European international instruments.

Relevant provisions: Articles 6 and 8.

Appendix C

ANIMALS AFFECTED BY THE RABIES (IMPORTATION OF DOGS, CATS AND OTHER MAMMALS) ORDER 1974[1]

PART I
Animals Subject to Quarantine

Order		Common names of some species[2]
Chiroptera	Desmodontidae only	Vampire bats

PART II
Animals Subject to 6 Months' Quarantine

Order		Common names of some species
Carnivora	All families and species	Dogs, cats,[3] jackals, foxes, wolves, bears, racoons, coatis, pandas, otters, weasels, martens, polecats, badgers, skunks, mink, ratels, genets, civets, linsangs, mongooses, hyaenas, ocelets, panthers, pumas, cheetahs, lions, tigers, leopards
Chiroptera	All families except Desmodontidae	Bats, flying foxes

---

[1] Rabies (Importation of Dogs, Cats and Other Mammals) Order 1974, SI 1974/ 2211, Sch 1. This Order has been disapplied in relation to imports from another member State of the European Community or other specified countries, in certain circumstances: the Animals and Animal Products (Import and Export) (England and Wales) Regulations 2000, SI 2000/1673, Reg 34, Sch 6. The Order continues to apply to all carnivores, primates and bats. It continues to apply to the importation of all other animals unless such animals are imported by way of trade and can be shown to have been born on the holding of origin and kept in captivity since birth. See pp. 55-65.

[2] The names are for guidance only and do not forms part of the Order: Rabies (Importation of Dogs, Cats and Other Mammals) Order 1974, Sch 1, footnote. The effect is that the order will apply to any animal belonging to the orders of mammals listed in the first column (with the reservations made in the second column) whether or not its common name appears in the third column.

[3] The Pet Travel Scheme (Pilot Arrangements) (England) Order 1999, SI 1999/ 3443, as amended, creates, in limited circumstances, an exemption from the requirements for pet cats and dogs imported into England to be placed in quarantine under the Rabies (Importation of Dogs, Cats and Other Mammals) Order 1974, SI 1974/2211. See pp. 58-65.

271

Dermoptera		Flying lemurs
Edentata		Anteaters, sloths, armadillos
Hyracoidea		Hyraxes
Insectivora		Solenodons, tenrecs, otter shrews, golden moles, hedgehogs, elephant shrews, shrews, moles, desmans
Lagomorpha		Pikas, rabbits, hare
Marsupialia		Opossums, marsupial mice, dasyures, marsupial moles, marsupial anteaters, bandicoots, rat opossums, cuscuses, phalangers, koalas, wombats, wallabies, kangaroos
Primates	All families except Hominidae (Man)	Tree-shrews, lemurs, indrises, sifakas, aye-ayes, lorises, bushbabies, tarsiers, titis, uakaris, sakis, howlers, capuchins, squirrel monkeys, marmosets, tamarins, macaques, mangabeys, baboons, langurs, gibbons, great apes
Rodentia		Gophers, squirrels, chipmunks, marmots, scaly-tailed squirrels, pocket mice, kangaroo-rats, beavers, mountain beavers, springhaas, mice, rats, hamsters, lemmings, voles, gerbils, water rats, dormice, jumping mice, jerboas, porcupines, cavies (including guinea-pigs), capybaras, chinchillas, spiny rats, gundis

PART III
Additional Animals for Contact Purposes (Article 15)[4]

Order	*Common names of some species*
Artiodactyla	Pigs, peccaries, hippopotamuses, camels, llamas, chevrotains, deer, giraffes, pronghorns, cattle, antelopes, duikers, gazelles, goats, sheep

---

4   See p. 58.

Monotremata	Echidnas, duck-billed platypuses
Perissodactyla	Horses, asses, zebras, tapirs, rhinoceroses
Pholidota	Pangolins
Proboscidea	Elephants
Tubulidentata	Aardvarks

Appendix D

KINDS OF DANGEROUS WILD ANIMALS

Dangerous Wild Animals Act 1976
(as substituted by SI 1984/1111)

The second column of the Schedule to the Dangerous Wild Animals Act 1976 is included by way of explanation. In the event of any dispute or proceedings, only the first column is to be taken into account: Dangerous Wild Animals Act 1976, s. 7(5).

Scientific name of kind	*Common name or names*
MAMMALS	
Marsupials	
Dasyuridae of the species Sarcophilus harrisi	The Tasmanian devil
Macropodidae of the species Macropus fuliginosus, Macropus giganteus, Macropus robustus and Macropus rufus	Grey kangaroos, the euro, the wallaroo and the red kangaroo
Primates	
Callitrichidae of the species of the genera Leontophithecus and Saguinus	Tamarins
Cebidae	New-world monkeys (including capuchin, howler, saki, spider, squirrel, titi, uakari and woolly monkeys and the night monkey (otherwise known as the douroucouli))
Cercopithecidae	Old-world monkeys (including baboons, the drill, colobus monkeys, the gelada, guenons, langurs, leaf monkeys, macaques, the mandrill, mangabeys, the patas and proboscis monkeys and the talapoin)
Indriidae	Leaping lemurs (including the indri, sifakas and the woolly lemur)

Lemuridae, except the species of the genus Hapalemur	Large lemurs (the broad-nosed gentle lemur and the grey gentle lemur are excepted)
Pongidae	Anthropoid apes (including chimpanzees, gibbons, the gorilla and the orang-utan)

Edentates

Bradypodidae	Sloths
Dasypodidae of the species Priodontes giganteus (otherwise known as Priodontes maximus)	The giant armadillo
Myrmecophagidae of the species Myrmecophaga tridactyla	The giant anteater

Rodents

Erithizontidae of the species Erithizon dorsatum	The North American porcupine
Hydrochoeridae	The capybara
Hystricidae of the species of the genus Hystrix	Crested porcupines

Carnivores

Ailuropodidae (Ailuridae)	The giant panda and the red panda
Canidae, except the species of the genera Alopex, Dusicyon, Otocyon, Nyctereutes and Vulpes and the species Canis familiaris	Jackals, wild dogs, wolves and the coyote (foxes, the raccoon-dog and the domestic dog are excepted)
Felidae, except the species Felis catus	The bobcat, caracal, cheetah, cougar, jaguar, lion, leopard, lynx, ocelot, puma, serval, tiger and all other cats (the domestic cat is excepted)
Hyaenidae except the species Proteles cristatus	Hyaenas (except the aardwolf)
Mustelidae of the species of the genera Arctonyx, Aonyx, Enhdra, Lutra (except Lutra lutra), Melogale, Mydaus, Pteronura and Taxidea and of the species Eira barbara, Gulo gulo, Martes pennanti and Mellivora capensis	Badgers (except the Eurasian badger), otters (except the European otter), and the tayra, wolverine, fisher and ratel (otherwise known as the honey badger)

Procyonidae	Cacomistles, raccoons, coatis, olingos, the little coatimundi and the kinkajou
Ursidae	Bears
Viverridae of the species of the genus Viverra and of the species Arctictis binturong and Cryptoprocta ferox	The African, large-spotted, Malay and large Indian civets, the binturong and the fossa

Pinnipedes

Odobenidae, Otariidae and Phocidae, except Phoca vitulina and Halichoerus grypus	The walrus, eared seals, and sealions and earless seals (the common and grey seals are excepted)

Elephants

Elephantidae	Elephants

Odd-toed ungulates

Equidae, except the species Equus asinus, Equus caballus and Equus asinus x Equus caballus	Asses, horses and zebras (the donkey, domestic horse and domestic hybrids are excepted)
Rhinocerotidae	Rhinoceroses
Tapiridae	Tapirs

Hyraxes

Procaviidae	Tree and rock hyraxes (otherwise known as dassies)

Aardvark

Orycteropidae	The aardvark

Even-toed ungulates

Antilocapridae	The pronghorn
Bovidae, except any domestic form of the genera Bos and Bubalus, of the species Capra aegagrus (hircus) and the species Ovis aries	Antelopes, bison, buffalo, cattle, gazelles, goats and sheep (domestic cattle, goats and sheep are excepted)
Camelidae except the species Lama glama and Lama pacos	Camels, the guanaco and the vicugna (the domestic llama and alpaca are excepted)

Cervidae of the species Alces alces and Rangifer tarandus, except any domestic form of the species Rangifer tarandus	The moose or elk and the caribou or reindeer (the domestic reindeer is excepted)
Giraffidae	The giraffe and the okapi
Hippopotamidae	The hippopotamus and the pygmy hippopotamus
Suidae, except any domestic form of the species Sus scrofa	Old-world pigs (including the wild boar and the wart hog) (the domestic pig is excepted)
Tayassuidae	New-world pigs (otherwise known as peccaries)
Any hybrid of a kind of animal specified in the foregoing provisions of this column where one parent is, or both parents are, of a kind so specified	Mammalian hybrids with a parent (or parents) of a specified kind

BIRDS
Cassowaries and emu

Casuariidae	Cassowaries
Dromaiidae	The emu

Ostrich

Struthionidae	The ostrich

REPTILES
Crocodilians

Alligatoridae	Alligators and caimans
Crocodylidae	Crocodiles and the false gharial
Gavialidae	The gharial (otherwise known as the gavial)

Lizards and snakes

Colubridae of the species of the genera Atractaspis, Malpolon, Psammophis and Thelatornis and of the species Boiga dendrophila, Dispholidus typus, Rhabdophis subminiatus and Rhabdophis tigrinus	Mole vipers and certain rear-fanged venomous snakes (including the moila and montpellier snakes, sand snakes, twig snakes, the mangrove (otherwise known as the yellow-ringed catsnake), the boomslang,

	the red-necked keelback and the yamakagashi (otherwise known as the Japanese tiger-snake))
Elapidae	Certain front-fanged venomous snakes (including cobras, coral snakes, the desert black snake, kraits, mambas, sea snakes and all Australian poisonous snakes (including the death adders))
Helodermatidae	The gila monster and the (Mexican) beaded lizard
Viperidae	Certain front-fanged venomous snakes (including adders, the barba amarilla, the bushmaster, the copperhead, the fer-de-lance, moccasins, rattlesnakes and vipers)

INVERTEBRATES
Spiders

Ctenidae of the species of the genus Phoneutria	Wandering spiders
Dipluridae of the species of the genus Atrax	The Sydney funnel-web spider and its close relatives
Lycosidae of the species Lycosa raptoria	The Brazilian wolf spider
Sicariidae of the species of the genus Loxosceles	Brown recluse spiders (otherwise known as violin spiders)
Theridiidae of the species of the genus Latrodectus	The black widow spider (otherwise known as redback spider) and its close relatives

Scorpions

| Buthidae | Buthid scorpions |

Appendix E

DEFINITION OF "ANIMAL" FOR THE PURPOSES OF THE PROTECTION OF ANIMALS ACTS[1]

"**Animal**" means any domestic or captive animal.

"**Domestic animal**" means any horse, ass, mule, bull, sheep, pig, goat, dog, cat or fowl or any other animal of whatsoever kind or species, and whether a quadruped or not, which is tame or which has been or is being sufficiently tamed to serve some purpose for the use of man.

"**Captive animal**" means any animal (not being a domestic animal) of whatsoever kind or species, and whether a quadruped or not, including any bird, fish or reptile, which is in captivity[2] or confinement, or which is maimed, pinioned or subjected to any appliance or contrivance for the purpose of hindering or preventing its escape from captivity or confinement.

"**Bull**" includes any cow, bullock, heifer, calf, steer or ox.

"**Cat**" includes a kitten.

"**Dog**" includes any bitch, sapling[3] or puppy.

"**Fowl**" includes any cock, hen, chicken, capon, turkey, goose, gander, duck, drake, guinea-fowl, peacock, peahen, swan or pigeon.

"**Goat**" includes a kid.

"**Horse**" includes any mare, gelding, pony, foal, colt, filly or stallion.

"**Pig**" includes any boar, hog or sow.

"**Sheep**" includes any lamb, ewe or ram.

---

[1]   Protection of Animals Act 1911, s. 15(a)-(d).

[2]   Mere temporary inability to get away is not a state of captivity: *Rowley v Murphy* [1964] 1 All ER 50. A wild animal which is temporarily unable to escape, or has been restrained with a view to capturing it, is not a "captive" wild animal within the meaning of s. 15, as there has to be some period of time prior to capture during which acts of domination are exercised over it: *Barrington v Colbert* (1997) 162 JP 642. It will be seen that wild animals are not within the definition unless in one of the ways described in the definition of captive animal.

[3]   A sapling is a greyhound in its first year.

279

Appendix F

BIRDS AND ANIMALS PROTECTED BY THE WILDLIFE AND COUNTRYSIDE ACT 1981[1]

The common name or names given in this Appendix are for guidance only. In the event of any dispute, the common name or names will not be taken into account by a court. The reader should refer to the Schedules to the Act.

SCHEDULE 1

Part I – Birds protected by special penalties at all times

Avocet	Gull, Mediterranean
Bee-eater	Gyrfalcon
Bittern	Harriers (all species)
Bittern, Little	Heron, Purple
Bluethroat	Hobby
Brambling	Hoopoe
Bunting, Cirl	Kingfisher
Bunting, Lapland	Kite, Red
Bunting, Snow	Merlin
Buzzard, Honey	Oriole, Golden
Chough	Osprey
Corncrake	Owl, Barn
Crake, Spotted	Owl, Snowy
Crossbill (all species)	Peregrine
Divers (all species)	Petrel, Leach's
Dotterel	Phalarope, Red-necked
Duck, Long-tailed	Plover, Kentish
Eagle, Golden	Plover, Little Ringed
Eagle, White-tailed	Quail, Common
Falcon, Gyr	Redstart, Black
Fieldfare	Redwing
Firecrest	Rosefinch, Scarlet
Garganey	Ruff
Godwit, Black-tailed	Sandpiper, Green
Goshawk	Sandpiper, Purple
Grebe, Black-necked	Sandpiper, Wood
Grebe, Slavonian	Scaup
Greenshank	Scoter, Common
Gull, Little	Scoter, Velvet

---

[1]   As amended by SIs 1982/1217, 1988/288, 1989/906, 1991/367, 1992/2350, 1992/2674, 1992/3010, 1994/1151.

Serin
Shorelark
Shrike, Red-backed
Spoonbill
Stilt, Black-winged
Stint, Temminck's
Stone-curlew
Swan, Bewick's
Swan, Whooper
Tern, Black
Tern, Little

Tern, Roseate
Tit, Bearded
Tit, Crested
Treecreeper, Short-toed
Warbler, Cetti's
Warbler, Dartford
Warbler, Marsh
Warbler, Savi's
Whimbrel
Woodlark
Wryneck

Part II – Birds and their eggs protected by special penalties during the close season, 1 February to 31 August (21 February to 31 August below high water mark) but which may be killed or taken at other times

Goldeneye

Greylag Goose (in Outer Hebrides, Caithness, Sutherland and Wester Ross only)

SCHEDULE 2

Part I – Birds that may be killed or taken outside the close season, 1 February to 31 August[1] except where indicated otherwise

Capercaillie
(close season 1 Feb-30 Sep)
Coot
Duck, Tufted
Gadwall
Goldeneye
Goose, Canada
Goose, Greylag
Goose, Pink-footed
Goose, White-fronted
(fully protected in Scotland)
Mallard

Moorhen
Pintail
Plover, Golden
Pochard
Shoveler
Snipe, Common
(close season 1 Feb-11 Aug)
Teal
Wigeon
Woodcock
(close season 1 Feb-30 Sep, except in Scotland where 1 Feb-31 Aug)

---

[1] The close season for ducks and geese when below high water mark is 21 February to 31 August.

Part II – Birds which may be killed or taken by authorised persons at any time

(This section has been replaced by General Licences with the same effect)

Crow, Carrion	**Magpie**
Dove, Collared	**Pigeon**, Feral
Gull, Great Black-Backed	**Rook**
Gull, Herring	**Sparrow**, House
Gull, Lesser Black-Backed	**Starling**
Jackdaw	**Wood Pigeon**
Jay	

SCHEDULE 3

Part I – Birds which may be sold alive at all times if ringed and bred in captivity[2]

Blackbird	**Linnet**
Brambling	**Magpie**
Bullfinch	**Owl**, Barn
Bunting, Reed	**Redpoll**
Chaffinch	**Siskin**
Dunnock	**Starling**
Goldfinch	**Thrush**, Song
Greenfinch	**Twite**
Jackdaw	**Yellowhammer**
Jay	

Part II – Birds which may be sold dead at all times

Woodpigeon

Part III – Birds which may be sold dead from 1 September to 28 February[3]

Capercaillie	**Pochard**
Coot	**Shoveler**
Duck, Tufted	**Snipe**, Common
Mallard	**Teal**
Pintail	**Wigeon**
Plover, Golden	**Woodcock**

---

[2] Certain birds in Schedule 4 may also be sold under licence provided they are registered with the Department for Environment, Food and Rural Affairs.

[3] It is illegal to offer for sale at any time of the year any wild goose, moorhen, gadwall or goldeneye, although they are legitimate quarry species outside the close season.

SCHEDULE 4

Birds which must be registered and ringed if kept in captivity (including any bird, one of whose parents or other lineal ancestor was a bird of a kind specified in the list below)

Bunting, Cirl	**Honey-Buzzard**, Black
Bunting, Lapland	**Kestrel**, Lesser
Bunting, Snow	**Kestrel**, Mauritius
Buzzard, Honey	**Kite**, Red
Chough	**Merlin**
Crossbills (all species)	**Oriole**, Golden
Eagle, Adalbert's	**Osprey**
Eagle, Golden	**Redstart**, Black
Eagle, Great Phillipine	**Redwing**
Eagle, Imperial	**Sea-Eagle**, Pallas'
Eagle, New Guinea	**Sea-Eagle**, Steller's
Eagle, White-tailed	**Serin**
Falcon, Barbary	**Serpent-Eagle**, Andaman
Falcon, Gyr	**Serpent-Eagle**, Madagascar
Falcon, Peregrine	**Serpent-Eagle**, Mountain
Fieldfare	**Shorelark**
Firecrest	**Shrike**, Red-backed
Fish-Eagle, Madagascar	**Sparrowhawk**, Gundlach's
Forest-Falcon, Plumbeous	**Sparrowhawk**, Imitator
Goshawk	**Sparrowhawk**, New Britain
Harrier, Hen	**Sparrowhawk**, Small
Harrier, Marsh	**Tit**, Bearded
Harrier, Montagu's	**Tit**, Crested
Hawk, Galapagos	**Warbler**, Cetti's
Hawk, Grey-backed	**Warbler**, Dartford
Hawk, Hawaiian	**Warbler**, Marsh
Hawk, Ridgway's	**Warbler**, Svi's
Hawk, White-necked	**Woodlark**
Hawk-Eagle, Wallace's	**Wryneck**
Hobby	

SCHEDULE 5

Protected animals

Common Name	*Scientific Name*	*Application of Wildlife and Countryside Act 1981*
Adder		
Adder	*Vipera berus*	Sections 9(1) "killing & injuring" and 9(5) "sale" only

Anemone
Ivell's Sea   *Edwardsia ivelli*
Starlet Sea   *Nematosella vectensis*

Apus
Tadpole Shrimp   *Triops cancriformis*

Bats
Horseshoe   *Rhinolophidae, all species*
Typical   *Vespertilionidae, all species*

Beetle

Graphoderus zonatus
Hypebaeus flavipes
Paracymus aeneus
Lesser Silver Water   *Hydrochara caraboides*
Mire Pill   *Curimopsis nigrita*   Section 9(4)(a) "dam-
aging etc. a place
used for shelter" only

Rainbow Leaf   *Chrysolina cerealis*
Stag   *Lucanus cervus*   Section 9(5) "sale" only
Violet Click   *Limoniscus violaceus*

Burbot   *Lota lota*

Butterfly
Adonis Blue   *Lysandra bellargus*   Section 9(5) "sale" only
Black Hairsteak   *Strymondia pruni*   Section 9(5) "sale" only
Brown Hairstreak   *Thecla betulae*   Section 9(5) "sale" only
Chalkhill Blue   *Lysandra coridon*
Chequered Skipper   *Carterocephalus palaemon*   Section 9(5) "sale" only
Duke of Burgundy   *Hamearis lucina*   Section 9(5) "sale" only
Glanville Fritillary   *Melitaea cinxia*   Section 9(5) "sale" only
Heath Fritillary   *Mellicta athalia*
High Brown Fritillary *Argynnis adippe*
Large Blue   *Maculinea arion*
Large Copper   *Lycaena dispar*
Large Heath   *Coenonympha tullia*   Section 9(5) "sale" only
Large Tortoiseshell   *Nymphalis polychlorus*   Section 9(5) "sale" only
Lulworth Skipper   *Thymelicus acteon*   Section 9(5) "sale" only
Marsh Fritillary   *Eurodryas aurinia*
Mountain Ringlet   *Erebia epiphron*   Section 9(5) "sale" only
Northern Brown Argus *Aricia artaxerxes*   Section 9(5) "sale" only
Pearl-Bordered   *Boloria euphrosyne*   Section 9(5) "sale" only
Purple Emperor   *Apatura iris*   Section 9(5) "sale" only
Silver Spotted Skipper *Hesperia comma*   Section 9(5) "sale" only
Silver Studded Blue   *Plebejus argus*   Section 9(5) "sale" only
Small Blue   *Cupido minimus*   Section 9(5) "sale" only
Swallowtail   *Papilio machaon*
White Letter Hairstreak *Stymondia w-album*

Wood White	*Leptidea sinapis*	Section 9(5) "sale" only
Cat		
Wild	*Felis silvestris*	
Cicada		
New Forest	*Cicadetta montana*	
Crayfish		
Atlantic Stream	*Austropotamobius pallipes*	Section 9(1) "taking" and 9(5) "sale" only
Cricket		
Field	*Gryllus campestris*	
Mole	*Gryllotalpa gryllotalpa*	
Damselfly		
Southern	*Coenagrion mercuriale*	
Dolphin	*Cetacea*	
Dormouse	*Muscardinus avellanarius*	
Dragonfly		
Norfolk Aeshna	*Aeshna isosceles*	
Frog		
Common	*Rana temporaria*	Section 9(5) "sale" only
Goby		
Couch's	*Gobius couchii*	
Giant	*Gobius cobitis*	
Grasshopper		
Wart-biter	*Decticus verrucivorus*	
Hatchet Shell		
Northern	*Thyasira gouldi*	
Hydroid		
Marine	*Clavopsella navis*	
Lagoon Snail		
	Paludinella littorina	
De Folin's	*Caecum armoricum*	
Lagoon Worm		
Tentacled	*Alkmaria romijni*	
Leech		
Medicinal	*Hirudo medicinalis*	
Lizard		
Sand	*Lacerta agilis*	
Viviparous	*Lacerta vivipara*	Section 9(1) "killing and injuring" and 9(5) "sale" only
Marten		
Pine	*Martes martes*	

Moth

Barberry Carpet	*Pareulype berberata*
Black-veined	*Siona lineata (or Idaea lineata)*
Essex Emerald	*Theitdia smaragdaria*
Fiery Clearwing	*Bembecia chrysidiformis*
Fisher's Estuarine	*Gortyna borelii*
New Forest Burnet	*Zygaena viciae*
Reddish Buff	*Acosmetia caliginosa*
Sussex Emerald	*Thalera fimbrialis*

Mussel

Fan	*Atrina fragilis*	Section 9(1)(2) and (5) "killing and injuring", "possession etc" and "sale" only
Freshwater Pearl	*Margaritifera margaritifera*	

Newt

Great Crested (or Warty)	*Triturus cristatus*	
Palmate	*Triturus helveticus*	
Smooth	*Triturus vulgaris*	Section 9(5) "sale" only

Otter

Common	*Lutra lutra*

Porpoise | *Cetacea* |

Sandworm

Lagoon	*Armandia cirrhosa*

Sea Fan

Pink	*Eunicella verrucosa*	Section 9(1) "killing, injuring and taking", 9(2) "possession" and 9(5) "sale" only

Sea Mat

Trembling	*Victorella pavida*

Sea Slug

Lagoon	*Tenellia adspersa*

Shad

Allis	*Alosa alosa*	Section 9(1) "killing, injuring and taking", 9(4)(a) "damaging etc. a place used for shelter" only
Twaite	*Alosa fallax*	Section 9(4)(a) "damaging etc. a place used for shelter" only

Shark
Basking   *Cetorhinus maximus*

Shrimp
Fairy   *Chirocephalus diaphanus*
Lagoon Sand   *Gammarus insensiblis*

Slow Worm   *Anguis fragilis*   Section 9(1) "killing
                                                       and injuring" and 9(5)
                                                       "sale" only

Snail
Glutinous   *Myxas glutinosa*
Sandbowl   *Catinella arenaria*

Snake
Grass   *Natrix helvetica*   Section 9(1) "killing
                        (otherwise known as   and injuring" and 9(5)
                        Natrix natrix)   "sale" only

Smooth   *Coronella austriaca*

Spider
Fen Raft   *Dolomedes plantarius*
Ladybird   *Eresus niger*

Squirrel
Red   *Sciurus vulgaris*

Sturgeon   *Acipenser sturio*

Toad
Common   *Bufo bufo*   Section 9(5) "sale" only
Natterjack   *Bufo calamita*

Turtles
Marine   *Dermochelyidae and*
                        Cheloniidae all species

Vendace   *Coregonus albula*

Vole
Water   *Arvicola terrestris*   Section 9(4)(a) and
                                                      (b) "damaging etc. a
                                                      place used for
                                                      shelter" and
                                                      "disturbing an animal
                                                      while occupying a
                                                      structure or place of
                                                      shelter" only

Walrus   *Odobenus rosmarus*
Whales   *Cetacea*
Whitefish   *Coregonus lavaretus*

SCHEDULE 6
Animals which may not be killed or taken by certain methods

Badger
Bats, Horshoe (all species)
Bats, Typical (all species)
Cat, Wild
Dolphin, Bottle-nosed
Dormice (all species)
Hedgehog

Marten, Pine
Otter, Common
Polecat
Porpoise, Harbour (otherwise known as Common porpoise)
Shrews (all species)
Squirrel, Red

Schedules 7 and 8 not relevant to this book

SCHEDULE 9
Animals to which section 14 applies (i.e. may not be released into the wild)

Part I – birds and other animals

Bass, Large-mouthed Black
Bass, Rock
Bitterling
Budgerigar
Capercaillie
Coypu
Crayfish, Noble
Crayfish, Signal
Crayfish, Turkish
Deer, Muntjac
Deer, Sika
Dormouse, Fat
Duck, Carolina Wood
Duck, Mandarin
Duck, Ruddy
Eagle, White-tailed
Flatworm, New Zealand
Frog, Edible
Frog, European Tree (otherwise known as Common Tree Frog)
Frog, Marsh
Gerbil, Mongolian
Goose, Canada
Goose, Egyptian
Heron, Night
Lizard, Common Wall
Marmot, Prairie (otherwise known as Prairie dog)

Mink, American
Newt, Alpine
Newt, Italian Crested
Owl, Barn
Parakeet, Ring-necked
Partridge, Chukar
Partridge, Rock
Pheasant, Golden
Pheasant, Lady Amherst's
Pheasant, Reeves'
Pheasant, Silver
Porcupine, Crested
Porcupine, Himalayan
Pumpkinseed (otherwise known as Sun-fish or Pond perch)
Quail, Bobwhite
Rat, Black
Snake, Aescupapian
Squirrel, Grey
Terrapin, European Pond
Toad, African Clawed
Toad, Midwife
Wallaby, Red-necked
Wels (otherwise known as European catfish)
Zander

Part II – not relevant to this book

APPENDIX G

PROHIBITED METHODS OF KILLING OR TAKING WILD ANIMALS[1]

PART I
Methods applicable to all wild animals[2]

1. Setting in position any self-locking snare which is of such a nature and so placed as to be calculated to cause bodily injury to any wild animal coming into contact with it.

2. Using, for the purpose of killing or taking[3] any wild animal, any self-locking snare, whether or not of such a nature or so placed as described in paragraph 1 above, any bow or crossbow or any explosive other than ammunition for a firearm.*[4]

3. Using as a decoy, for the purpose of killing or taking any wild animal, any live mammal or bird whatever.*

PART II
Methods applicable only to the wild animals included in Part III below:[5]

i. Setting in position any of the following articles, being an article which is of such a nature and so placed as to be calculated to cause bodily injury to any wild animal which comes into contact with it:

a. any trap or snare;

b. any electrical device for killing or stunning;

c. any poisonous, poisoned or stupefying substance.

ii. Using, for the purpose of killing or taking a wild animal, any article described in paragraph i above, whether or not of such a nature and so placed as there described, or any net.*

---

[1] For further details, see pp. 187-188. For the meaning of "wild animals", see p. 185.

[2] Wildlife and Countryside Act 1981, s. 11(1).

[3] For an interpretation of "taking", see p. 115.

[4] In proceedings for an offence of using these methods (or any other method indicated by an asterisk), it shall be presumed that the animal in question was a wild animal unless the contrary is shown: Wildlife and Countryside Act 1981, s. 11(5).
For the meaning of "firearm", see note 171 on p. 155.

[5] Wildlife and Countryside Act 1981, s. 11(2).

iii. Using, for the purpose of killing or taking a wild animal:

  a. any automatic or semi-automatic weapon;[6]

  b. any device for illuminating a target or sighting device for night shooting;

  c. any form of artificial light or any mirror or other dazzling device;

  d. any gas or smoke not falling within the descriptions in paragraphs i or ii above.*

iv. Using as a decoy, for the purpose of killing or taking a wild animal, any sound recording.*

v. Using any mechanically propelled vehicle[7] in pursuit of a wild animal for the purpose of driving, killing or taking it.*

PART III

Wild animals protected from the methods described in Part II

See Schedule 6 listed in Appendix F, page 288.

---

6   These weapons do not include any weapon the magazine of which is incapable of holding more than two rounds: Wildlife and Countryside Act 1981, s. 27(1).

7   "Vehicle" includes aircraft, hovercraft and boat: Wildlife and Countryside Act 1981, s. 27(1).

Appendix H

SPRING TRAPS APPROVED BY MINISTERS[1]

TYPE AND MAKE OF TRAP	CONDITIONS
Aldrich Spring Activated Animal Snare manufactured by or under the authority of Mr D Schimetz, PO Box 158, Sekiu, Washington 98381, USA.	The trap shall be used only for the purpose of killing or taking large, non-indigenous, mammalian carnivores.
BMI Magnum 55 manufactured by or under the authority of Butera Manufacturing Industries, 2395 Lynn Drive, Willoughby Hills, Ohio 44092, USA.	The trap shall be used only for the purpose of killing or taking rats, mice and other small ground vermin (except those species listed in Schedules 5 and 6 of the Wildlife and Countryside Act 1981) and set in a natural or artificial tunnel which is, in either case, suitable for the purpose.
BMI Magnum 110 manufactured by or under the authority of Butera Manufacturing Industries, 2395 Lynn Drive, Willoughby Hills, Ohio 44092, USA.	The trap shall be used only for the purpose of killing or taking grey squirrels, stoats, weasels, rats, mice and other small ground vermin (except for those species listed in Schedules 5 and 6 of the Wildlife and Countryside Act 1981) and set in a natural or artificial tunnel which is, in either case, suitable for the purpose.
BMI Magnum 116 manufactured by Butera Manufacturing Industries, 2395 Lynn Drive, Willoughby Hills, Ohio 44092 USA.	The trap shall be used only for the purpose of killing or taking grey squirrels, mink, rabbits, stoats, weasels, rats, mice and other small ground vermin (except for those species listed in Schedules 5 and 6 of the Wildlife and Countryside Act 1981) and set in a natural or artificial tunnel which is, in either case, suitable for the purpose.

[1] Spring Traps Approval Order 1995, SI 1995/2427. See further pp. 144-146.

291

Fenn Vermin Trap Mark I, Vermin Trap Mark II, Vermin Trap Mark III and Vermin Trap Mark IV (Heavy Duty) manufactured by or under the authority of Mr A A Fenn of FHT Works, High Street, Astwood Bank, Redditch, Worcestershire and specified in British Patent Specification No 763,891 and as illustrated in figures 1 to 3 of that Specification, and Springer No 4 Multi-purpose (Heavy Duty) manufactured by or under the authority of AB County Products Ltd, Troy Industrial Estate, Jill Lane, Sambourne, Near Ashwood Bank, Redditch, Worcestershire.

The traps shall be used only for the purpose of killing or taking grey squirrels, stoats, weasels, rats, mice and other small ground vermin (except for those species listed in Schedules 5 and 6 of the Wildlife and Countryside Act 1981) and set in natural or artificial tunnels, which are, in either case, suitable for the purpose.

Fenn Vermin Trap Mark VI (Dual Purpose) manufactured by or under the authority of Mr A A Fenn of FHT Works, Hoopers Lane, Astwood Bank, Redditch, Worcestershire and specified in British Patent Specification No 763,891, and Springer No 6 Multi-purpose manufactured by or under the authority of AB Country Products Ltd, Troy Industrial Estate, Jill Lane, Sambourne, Near Ashwood Bank, Redditch, Worcestershire.

The traps shall be used only for the purpose of killing or taking grey squirrels, mink, rabbits, stoats, weasels, rats, mice and other small ground vermin (except for those species listed in Schedules 5 and 6 of the Wildlife and Countryside Act 1981) and set in natural or artificial tunnels which are, in either case, suitable for the purpose.

Fenn Rabbit Trap Mark I manufactured by or under the authority of Mr A A Fenn of FHT Works, High Street, Astwood Bank, Redditch, Worcestershire.

The trap shall be used only for the killing or taking of rabbits and set in a natural or artificial tunnel which is, in either case, suitable for the purpose.

Fuller Trap manufactured by or under the authority of Fuller Industries, Three Trees, Loxwood Road, Bucks Green, Rudgwick, Sussex.

The trap shall be used only for the purpose of killing or taking grey squirrels and fitted with an artificial tunnel which is suitable for the purpose.

Imbra Trap Mark I and Mark II, both manufactured by or under the authority of James S Low and Sons Ltd, Atholl Smithy, Atholl Street,

The traps shall be used only for the purpose of killing or taking grey squirrels, rabbits, stoats, weasels, rats, mice and other small ground

Blairgowrie, Perthshire and specified in British Patent Specification No 682,427 and as illustrated in figures 1 to 4 of that Specification.

Juby Trap manufactured under the authority of the Department for Environment, Food and Rural Affairs, Whitehall Place, London SW1 and specified in British Patent Specification No 813,066 and as illustrated in figures 1 to 3 of that Specification.

Kania Trap 2000 manufactured by or under the authority of the C E Kania Corporation, 124–21, 10405, Jasper Avenue, Edmonton, Alberta, Canada.

Lloyd Trap manufactured under the authority of the National Research Corporation, and specified in British Patent Specification No 987,113 and as illustrated in figures 1 to 3 of that Specification.

Sawyer Trap manufactured by or under the authority of James S Low and Sons Ltd, Atholl Smithy, Atholl Street, Blairgowrie, Perthshire.

vermin (except for those species listed in Schedules 5 and 6 of the Wildlife and Countryside Act 1981) and set in natural or artificial tunnels which are, in either case, suitable for the purpose.

The trap shall be used only for the purpose of killing or taking grey squirrels, rabbits, stoats, weasels, rats, mice and other small ground vermin (except for those species listed in Schedules 5 and 6 of the Wildlife and Countryside Act 1981) and set in a natural or artificial tunnel which is, in either case, suitable for the purpose.

The trap shall be used only for the purpose of killing or taking grey squirrels, mink, stoats, weasels, rats, mice and other small ground vermin (except for those species listed in Schedules 5 and 6 of the Wildlife and Countryside Act 1981) and fitted with an artificial tunnel which is suitable for the purpose.

The trap shall be used only for the purpose of killing or taking grey squirrels, stoats, weasels, rats, mice and other small ground vermin (except for those species listed in Schedules 5 and 6 of the Wildlife and Countryside Act 1981) and set in a natural or artificial tunnel which is, in either case, suitable for the purpose.

The trap shall be used only for the purpose of killing or taking grey squirrels, stoats, weasels, rats, mice and other small ground vermin (except for those species listed in Schedules 5 and 6 of the Wildlife and Countryside Act 1981) and set in a natural or artificial tunnel which is, in either case, suitable for the purpose.

Appendix I

SPECIAL GROUNDS OF APPEAL AGAINST A NOTICE REQUIRING STRUCTURAL WORKS UNDER SECTION 4 OF THE PREVENTION OF DAMAGE BY PESTS ACT 1949

"(3) A person served with such a notice as aforesaid[1] may appeal to a court of summary jurisdiction on any of the following grounds which are appropriate in the circumstances of the particular case:

(a) that the notice or requirement is not justified by the terms of the section under which it purports to have been given or made;

(b) that there has been some defect, informality or error in, or in connection with, the notice;

(c) that the authority have refused unreasonably to approve the execution of alternative works, or that the works required by the notice to be executed are otherwise unreasonable in character or extent, or are unnecessary;

(d) that the time within which the works are to be executed is not reasonably sufficient for the purpose;

(e) that the notice might lawfully have been served on the occupier of the premises in question instead of on the owner, or on the owner instead of on the occupier, and that it would have been equitable for it to have been so served;

(f) where the work is work for the common benefits of the premises in question and other premises, that some other person, being the owner or occupier of premises to be benefited, ought to contribute towards the expenses of executing any works required.

(4) If and so far as an appeal under this section is based on the ground of some informality, defect or error in or in connection with the notice, the court shall dismiss the appeal, if it is satisfied that the informality, defect or error was not a material one.

(5) Where the grounds upon which an appeal under this section is brought include a ground specified in paragraph (e) or paragraph (f) of subsection (3) of this section, the appellant shall serve a copy of his notice of appeal on each other person referred to, and in the case of any appeal under this section may serve a copy of his notice of appeal on any other person

---

[1] See pp. 230-231.

294

having an estate or interest in the premises in question, and on the hearing of the appeal the court may make such order as it thinks fit with respect to the person by whom any work is to be executed and the contribution to be made by any other person towards the cost of the work, or as to the proportions in which any expenses which may become recoverable by the local authority are to be borne by the appellant and such other person.

In exercising its powers under this subsection, the court shall have regard:

(a) as between an owner and an occupier, to the terms and conditions, whether contractual or statutory, of the tenancy and to the nature of the works required; and

(b) in any case, to the degree of benefit to be derived by the different persons concerned."

Appendix J

ANIMALS (SCIENTIFIC PROCEDURES) ACT 1986, SCHEDULE 2A[1]

ARTICLE 8 OF COUNCIL DIRECTIVE NO. 86/609/EEC

1. All experiments shall be carried out under general or local anaesthesia.

2. Paragraph 1 above does not apply when:

    a. anaesthesia is judged to be more traumatic to the animal than the experiment itself;

    b. anaesthesia is incompatible with the object of the experiment. In such cases appropriate legislative and/or administrative measures shall be taken to ensure that no such experiment is carried out unnecessarily.

    Anaesthesia should be used in the case of serious injuries which may cause severe pain.

3. If anaesthesia is not possible, analgesics or other appropriate methods should be used in order to ensure as far as possible that pain, suffering, distress or harm are limited and that in any event the animal is not subject to severe pain, distress or suffering.

4. Provided such action is compatible with the object of the experiment, an anaesthetised animal, which suffers considerable pain once anaesthesia has worn off, shall be treated in good time with pain-relieving means or, if this is not possible, shall be immediately killed by a humane method.

---

[1] Inserted by Animals (Scientific Procedures) Act 1986 (Amendment) Regulations 1998, SI 1998/1974.

INDEX

A

F

G

I

J

S